THE PUBLIC AT PLAY

Gender and the Politics of Recreation in Post-War Ontario

In Ontario in the 1950s play was a serious business. *The Public at Play* brings to light a forgotten moment of failed political idealism, when leisure meant much more than fun. Between 1945 and 1961 the government funded the hiring of a cadre of recreation directors in the villages, towns, and cities of Ontario. Liberal thinkers saw this funding as a way to foster a democratic and participatory society; working with these directors, municipalities could start grass-roots community activities, in the process conditioning mind and body for active citizenship. The ideals were high: women and men would play equal roles; volunteers would be integral to the shape local recreation would take; and the whole effort would be guided by and instilled with the democratic spirit of the emerging welfare state.

From this high ground, the movement went rapidly into a tailspin. Volunteers fell into petty roles or simply slid into consumerism, leaving power in a few familiar hands. Women and girls were pushed out of the process.

As Tillotson examines just what went wrong, the intrinsic connection between the sidelining of women's leadership and the calcification of regional recreation schemes into bureaucracies becomes all too apparent. Yet while Tillotson fully develops the central motif of gender, she is never reductive. Scholars and policy makers will value her sophisticated examination of the many lines of force involved when high politics meets the entrenched value systems of communities.

(Studies in Gender and History)

SHIRLEY TILLOTSON is an associate professor in the Dalhousie University History Department.

STUDIES IN GENDER AND HISTORY

General editors: Franca Iacovetta and Karen Dubinsky

The Public at Play

Gender and the
Politics of Recreation
in Post-War Ontario

Shirley Tillotson

UNIVERSITY OF TORONTO PRESS
Toronto Buffalo London

ISBN 0-8020-4730-0 (cloth)
ISBN 0-8020-8296-3 (paper)

Printed on acid-free paper

Canadian Cataloguing in Publication Data

Tillotson, Shirley Maye, 1956–
The public at play : gender and the politics of recreation in post-war Ontario

(Studies in gender and history series)
Includes bibliographical references.
ISBN 0-8020-4730-0 (bound)   ISBN 0-8020-8296-3 (pbk.)

1. Recreation and state – Ontario.   2. Recreation – Social aspects – Ontario.
3. Recreation – Political aspects – Ontario.   4. Sexism – Ontario.
I. Title.   II. Series.

GV56.O5T54 2000   790'.09713   C99-932732-1

The author thanks the University of Toronto Press for permission to reprint
parts of Chapter 5 from a previously published article:
'Citizen Participation in the Welfare State: An Experiment, 1945–57,'
Canadian Historical Review 75, no. 4 (1994): 511–42.

University of Toronto Press acknowledges the financial assistance to its
publishing program of the Canada Council for the Arts and the
Ontario Arts Council

This book has been published with the help of a grant from the Humanities and
Social Sciences Federation of Canada, using funds provided by the Social
Sciences and Humanities Research Council of Canada.

University of Toronto Press acknowledges the financial support for its
publishing activities of the Government of Canada through the Book Publishing
Industry Development Program (BPIDP).

Contents

Acknowledgments

My passion for the subject of this book has its taproot in feelings about the generational conflict that shaped the political world I have known since the 1970s. Born at the height (though not at the leading edge) of the baby boom, in a small university town, I saw the fractious rupture between the apparently sleepy, black-and-white fifties and the multi-hued, indisputably political sixties (which spilled over into the early seventies). The sea change of the 1960s is part of my own past. But the generational aspects of this era have always puzzled me. I was raised by two people who seem not to have had a reactionary bone in their bodies, who welcomed at least some of the signs of the new times, and whose view of 'the Establishment' was quietly sceptical and sometimes actively oppositional. My parents, Glen and Doreen Tillotson, could not be made over, even by my adolescent imagination, into tyrannical agents of generational oppression. Curiosity about the part of the 1950s political culture that had produced them, and those like them, started me out on this project and helped me stay with it over the long haul.

Joy Parr supervised the thesis that is at the origin of this book with a light hand and a busy editorial pencil, improving the thesis while allowing me to make it my own. Most important, she encouraged me to pay close attention to Joan Scott's theoretical work, especially in some of its earliest appearances. The thesis research took me around rural Ontario, where I enjoyed the hospitality of people with roots in the culture I was studying. I especially appreciated the generosity of Alice and Pat Forestell and of Alma and Walter Cooke, Sr. In Toronto, the temporary home Lynne Marks gave me was only the first of many much-appreciated expressions of interest she showed in this project. At the Archives of Ontario, I benefited from the special efforts of Don McLeod and Hazel

Blyth, who helped me deal with the difficulties of the Freedom of Information and Protection of Privacy Act. Friendly fellow researchers there and at the National Archives of Canada provided some of the most valuable comments on the work in progress, as we talked in the special typing rooms those institutions then provided. At Queen's University, the social history seminar that Ian McKay organized in 1990–1 gave me an early forum to present my work and my first occasion to defend its importance. McKay contributed again as a member of my defence committee. Both he and the external examiner, James Struthers, provided immensely valuable, detailed comment that helped to direct the revision of the thesis into its present form. I also owe debts of gratitude to Suzanne Morton and John Zucchi, both of whom read the thesis soon after it was completed and offered important encouragement.

In the final stages of my revising the thesis to make it a book, colleagues at Dalhousie and other Halifax-area universities provided essential challenges and support. Margaret Conrad, Michael Cross, Frances Early, Judith Fingard, Janet Guildford, Jane Parpart, and Philip Zachernuk were among the last of my collaborators in the long process of making an idea into a book. They helped me get the manuscript ready to show to the editors of the Gender and History series, Karen Dubinsky and Franca Iacovetta. This series has made a significant contribution to Canadian historical scholarship, and I am very glad of the opportunity they gave me to add my book to the list. At the University of Toronto Press, Gerry Hallowell's practised skill in managing the process of the manuscript's assessment made relatively painless what might have been much more nerve-wracking. The careful reading of the manuscript by peer reviewers provided a very satisfying response to the long labour this book represents. As I send the book out to a larger audience, I acknowledge everything I owe to its various readers so far, but I accept that its remaining shortcomings are my own.

For computer help and many other kinds of support, going back even before the beginning of this project, I want to thank Walter Cooke. He was, among everything else, a very good friend.

The newspaper of the Communist Party of Canada photographed this 1950 demonstration by some of the constituents of the public recreation movement in Ottawa. The trumpet being brandished on the right illustrates recreation's non-sport side, and the trumpet player's cigarette indicates that leisure reformers in the post-war period were willing to accept without moral judgment some pleasures that had once been considered delinquencies. The idea of a universal right to enjoyment, akin to the universalist language used in other aspects of post-war social policy, underpins the complaint of 'unfairness' that these protesters were making. The sign summoning the bogey of 'juvinile' delinquency reaches backwards to older justifications for recreation services as therapies aimed at particular deviant groups, rather than as universal citizen entitlements. The genial male recreation director, dressed in respectable attire, is public recreation's persona.

ART
GAMES
DISCUSSION
CRAFTS
LEADERSHIP
DRAMATICS
SPORTS
MUSIC
PLAYGROUNDS
DANCING

To promote the notion that 'recreation' was for everyone, public recreation's leaders relentlessly 'interpreted' it. Images such as this were designed to fill an old concept with new content.

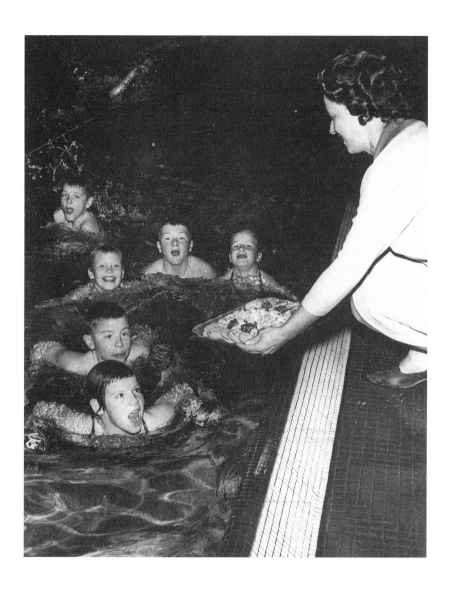

A tray of neatly arranged cookies, offered by a well-groomed woman to this school of recreational swimmers using a new municipal pool in Etobicoke: this is just one image of the domestic work that the new publicly funded recreation programs asked of mothers in post-war Ontario.

Public recreation facilities offered some new opportunities for enjoyable leisure pursuits to women, and not just to their families. Where centres managed to organize 'babysitting services' to go with their 'keep-fit' classes for women, the promise that recreation was every citizen's right was more likely to be fulfilled for the busy younger mother.

To make recreation accessible to the broadest possible social range, the provincial recreation service tried to encourage municipalities to serve people other than potentially delinquent boys and girls. Archery was enthusiastically promoted as suitable to all ages and both sexes, and was often included in a municipality's program of physical recreation to counterbalance the abundant sports programming that was for boys only.

In the early years of the post-war period, some public recreation leaders held that an emphasis on raising funds for and then managing new centres took valuable energies away from the real business of the movement: organizing people so that they could set up and sustain their own community's recreation programming. For rural Ontario governments, such as that of Simcoe County, the expense of new facilities was often happily avoided. In prospering suburbs like Leaside, however, Community Councils became enthusiastically involved in designing and building their first municipal recreation centres. The gender composition of the group shown above reflects the typical absence of 'the mothers of the community' from this aspect of recreation work.

THE PUBLIC AT PLAY

*Gender and the Politics of Recreation
in Post-War Ontario*

Introduction

Politics and Playgrounds

This book was conceived in 1988, the year before the end of the cold war. It was supposed to be about gender, leisure, and the welfare state, and it is. But it has also turned into a book about democracy and, in particular, liberal democracy. The book's subject is Ontario's government-funded recreation program from 1945 to 1961. This program helped provide many towns and villages with their first recreation director or municipal playground or Little League teams. In addition, its regulations fostered a province-wide network of municipal recreation committees. The political meanings that were attached to these committees, and to their eventual atrophy, were what turned my attention to the gendered links between liberalism, democracy, and leisure in the welfare state. Public recreation committees were supposed to help develop a liberal democratic culture. That culture was meant, among other purposes, to advance girls' and women's chances for social equality. But the liberal element in that cultural project also helped mould Ontario's new public services for leisure in patterns of gender hierarchy.

I would not have been as likely to see these links had I not been influenced by socialist feminism. This kind of feminism directs attention to the ways people make and use the categories of social power in daily life, as they go about the business of raising children, having a good time, earning a living, forming friendships, falling in love, and fighting for what they need and what they want. Socialist feminism is also a critique of liberalism, one of democratic theory's most influential tributaries. In the years after 1989, as the political world watched the consequences of capitalism's (and democracy's) apparent triumph, and I read archival documents, I saw in those documents connections between the abstract language of political philosophy and the ordinary struggles of people arranging for playground supervisors and figure-skating classes. In documents about public recreation, I heard resonances of democracy's grand themes: the rights and freedoms of citizens, political legitimacy, and the public interest. It became clear to me that public recreation was intended to be an instrument for making the welfare state democratic in a distinctively liberal form. The idea behind public recreation was an attempt, in philosopher Benedetto Croce's words, to 'insinuate' a commitment to liberal values 'in the most acceptable way, in the guise of common sense, into the many minds which are little or not at all disposed or trained to speculation.'[1] 'Liberal values' included a commitment to transcend prejudices, among them (supposedly) presuppositions about the lot of women in life.

It might seem incongruous that these grand themes should have appeared in the mundane matters of providing for craft instructors or rink time. But in the 1940s some political theorists thought there were important connections between the small concerns of municipal politics and the big ideas of democracy. The language of democracy one finds everywhere in the period was 'shapeless' in some hands,[2] but it was also the object of more precise definition in others. In the inter-war years and later, the rise internationally of authoritarian regimes and the emergence of new nations out of former colonies had fixed the attention of intellectuals on defining exactly what democracy was. They also talked and wrote about liberty (a different, if related, subject). They argued that if the electorate was ill-equipped to understand and to value the mechanisms that protected liberty (the rule of law, religious toleration, and the preference for reason over force), then popular rule (democracy) could be illiberal and support authoritarian government.[3] But liberalism would not necessarily generate democracy. A purely formal liberalism, informed by a narrow understanding of freedoms, could be undemocratic. It might fail to serve all the people. Liberal governments, to be democratic, required an electorate whose organizational and community bonds were sufficiently well developed to enable 'public opinion' to represent broadly and inclusively the interests of 'the people.'[4] Only then would freedom ensure equity.

Both democracy and liberalism could be subverted by what one recreation leader in 1955 called 'the wolf Bureaucracy.'[5] The large discretionary and coercive powers wielded by unelected officials in welfare departments such as public health were suspiciously arbitrary and uncontestable. That bureaucracy was a part of authoritarian government seemed strongly to have been suggested by the recent record of European dictatorships. The expansion of government functions through the creation of social programs posed the threat that bureaucracy would expand, and therefore that both popular rule and civil freedoms would be compromised.[6]

With these concerns clearly in mind, some political theorists and activists nonetheless hoped that the welfare state could be made both liberal and democratic. In 1946, leading Canadian political scientist (and, later, federal policy adviser) J.A. Corry argued that 'democracy, like charity, begins at home,' in local government. More than just schools for aspiring politicians, municipal councils and agencies (such as recreation services) gave all citizens an opportunity to judge the competence of those they elected. Without mystifying distances of place or of expertise separating the leaders and the led, voters were more likely and more able to scrutinize rationally the doings of local politicians. In local government, there might be a rule of reason that was also rule by the people. Other orders of government might be formally democratic, but the larger the jurisdiction, the more likely it was that non-rational (and hence illiberal) elements would enter the political process.[7]

The year 1946 saw another, more widely heard, call to centre democracy in local government, when Saul Alinsky published *Reveille for Radicals*, a manifesto for social transformation. Alinsky advised activists to start with neighbourhood political issues, often about recreation. Famous in the 1960s for his influence on urban grass-roots politics, community organizer Alinsky was already arguing in the 1940s that democratic government began with citizen participation in local affairs, where popular organization could effectively counter the strength of the local state.[8] The public recreation movement represented a serious attempt, in light of the political theory of its day, to put into practice an ideal of a liberal participatory democracy. The small scale of the attempt was intrinsic to its purpose.

The limits of 1950s liberal democratic ideas are apparent in the ways in which the movement for public recreation both succeeded and failed. To its credit was the creation of numerous recreation departments in municipal governments throughout Ontario. Recreation services became an accepted and popular state function. On the debit side, by the 1960s volunteer leadership in policy making had given way to professional administration. The network of municipal recreation committees had shrivelled in size and influence. The number and functions of professional recreation directors had expanded. This phenomenon, professionalization, appears to have resulted in more consistent standards of service, but, according to the movement's democratic ideals, the professionalization of the movement's leadership represented failure. Rule by 'the people' had been supplanted by the leadership of experts. Even in municipal politics – politics on a human scale – new welfare programs produced bureaucracy. Recreation had declined from a social movement to a public service.

It is my contention in this book that the decline of recreation from a movement to a service tells us something that is important about an ill-understood era in Ontario's (and possibly Canada's) political culture. Through the story of recreation, we can see the character of the liberal democratic idealism bequeathed by the 1930s and the war. The crises of those years had helped generate a vision of participatory democracy and social liberalism. We can also see how the people whose social activism grew out of this vision found themselves presiding, in the end, over a program that had lost or had failed to develop any substantively democratic features. What was left was liberal in mainly formal ways. As a story of political atrophy, the recreation movement's experience, I would suggest, may well have been a common one among social movements.[9] Recreation leaders and activists were part of these, and shared many of their aspirations. As well, some of the pressures that reshaped the recreation experiment seem likely also to have militated against other attempts to further social democracy. The popular apathy and social disengagement that sociologist John Porter took as an inescapable fact of political life in 1965 may not have been simply the inevitable adjunct of 'mass society.' I would suggest that we can see it instead as having been produced by multiple experiences of bureaucratization, one of which was the recreation movement's.[10]

I would also like to suggest that in order to comprehend the bureaucratization represented by the recreation movement's history we need to understand the part played in the formation of liberal democratic welfare states by gender relations and gender discourse.[11] Gender was inextricably involved in phenomena of the emerging welfare state: the relations of power among professionals, civil servants, citizens, and clients. A gender analysis is not, therefore, just an inquiry into the welfare state's effects on women, although it does include that. Rather, a gender analysis, as I practise it in this book, examines an aspect of state formation and explores the part played in that process by gender relations and gender discourse. If the formation of bureaucracy is a gendered process and if bureaucratization is a failure of democracy or a compromise of liberalism, then the failure and the compromise must be gendered. A similar logic connects gender to citizenship through public recreation services. If citizenship practices can be shaped through recreation services, and if these (like private leisure pursuits) are structured on gendered lines, then citizenship cannot escape being marked by gender.[12]

The context necessary for this kind of gender analysis of welfare policies in general and the recreation story in particular is an understanding of the links between liberalism, democracy, and gender. In recent years, these have been explored in a variety of ways by feminist politics scholars and historians. All have influenced in some fashion, whether as target or model, the analysis offered in this book. Some culturalist feminists have argued that democracy is compromised by masculine values about authority and knowledge, values that drive bureaucratization. In this view, liberalism is implicated in democracy's decline because its narrow conception of rights provides no defence against the tyranny of bureaucratic control.[13] This perspective is part of the left-libertarian critique of the state, and it extends it by asking us to accept that there are gender cultures more or less prone to producing bureaucratic means of governance.[14] In response to the gender essentialism implicit in this view, I argue that historically specific *representations* of sets of values as masculine or feminine played a part in the bureaucratization of Ontario's public recreation movement. In other words, it did matter that the actors in this story typed roles and responsibilities and intellectual capacities in gendered terms, even if in their own lives they were themselves not, as individuals, reducible to one or the other gender type. In a gender analysis of the welfare state, then, culturalist feminism may mislead us by treating gender categories as descriptive of the real traits of individuals. But this mistake should not lead us to ignore the effects of gender categories, which have been themselves contributors to the process of bureaucratization.

The analysis by socialist feminists of the welfare state links feminism, liberalism, and democracy primarily through a critique of social policies as undemocratic. They have pointed to the failure of welfare states to serve equally the needs and interests of all their citizens, and particularly those of women as reproductive workers.[15] This line of analysis centres not on politics per se, but on the exploitation in social programs of women's work (paid and unpaid), and thus on the welfare state's contribution to women's economic vulnerability. These concerns are very much a part of the story this book tells about public recreation. To what extent did Ontario's public recreation program usefully address women's needs as mothers? How did public recreation pro-

grams treat the women who were employed in them? Did these programs support or exploit women's unpaid domestic labour? Were men
and women equally likely to get from these programs the services they
wanted and needed? Did the programs benefit (or harm) working-class
and middle-class women in the same ways?

The answers to these questions illuminate the material conditions that
formed barriers to the participation of women as citizens and to their
enjoyment of equal benefits as clients of public programs such as recreation. But to be served by these programs and to be included in their
administration were not unambiguous goods. Recent work by socialist
feminists working with moral regulation theory reminds us that some
freedoms usher in new forms of constraints. For example, to celebrate
diminishing sexual repression in the 1950s is to overlook how expressions
of sexual liberalism such as *Playboy* and proposals for sex education
classes helped to define as deviant both celibacy and homosexuality.[16] We
need, then, to be concerned both with the material conditions and interests that excluded women and girls and with the terms on which they
were included as consumers and as leaders. To understand these terms,
and their mixed consequences, we have to look at the complexities and
tensions within liberal ideology. It was in liberal terms that recreation
movement leaders encouraged the involvement of women, and in the
period from 1945 to 1955 many women and girls leapt into action in
response. But over the period of the mid-to-late 1950s, the role of women
in directing recreation and the benefits they received as participants stag-
nated or contracted, in spite of the equality they had been promised. On
the same rhythm, the movement mutated into a department of government. This bureaucratization, like the pattern of women's involvement,
ensued apparently in spite of the liberal values in terms of which the
movement was originally conceived. For both developments, an important part of the explanation for change lies in the specific ways liberalism
situates women as a kind of political agent.

Carole Pateman's work on political theory provides the crucial connection between liberalism and gender through which we can understand the role of political culture in these changes. The chief elements
of 1950s political culture were specifically liberal notions of citizenship,
freedom, and the boundaries that separate government from the private world of family, commerce, and voluntary association. Pateman
argues that liberalism's concern to protect private pursuits and private
loyalties from public control consigns women to non-citizenship. Insofar as women appear to the state as mothers or as potential mothers,

they are not part of the public world of contract, civil liberties, and social rights, but belong instead to the private realm of familial ties, moral obligations, and personal needs.[17] Women are defined by supposedly traditional social practices, sealed off from the innovations of the modernizing polity. By contrast, men appear to the state as long-term participants in the labour market or as potential members of the national defence force. These are the services that come to create citizenship, incrementally, for men in the emerging liberal states of modern Western societies. As citizens, men enjoy both public entitlements and rights to privacy. Women, seen as marginal, secondary workers and non-combatants, derive their entitlements as citizens indirectly, as dependents of men, and are offered no protections for their freedoms. On this logic, nineteenth-century Euro-Canadian women were seen as having representation in political life primarily through their male kin. In polities shaped by liberalism, women as a group have been assigned a derivative citizenship and have been associated with a distinctively separate private world of familial welfare. In Pateman's view, liberalism's protection of private freedoms is reserved for men and confers on women a political status that contradicts another liberal value: that individual merit, not caste or tradition, should determine social and political relations.

In the debate about the shape of the state in post-war Canada, it is readily apparent that Canadian political culture was shaped by liberal values. Canadians expressed the characteristically liberal concern that a welfare state must fulfil public entitlements without interfering with the ways needs are met in private life. Some welfare services, such as those relating to adoption, had to remain private (non-governmental) because they intervened too profoundly in private (familial) life.[18] The context of this debate was, of course, very different from the one that surrounds its late 1990s equivalent, when Canadians are arguing about whether public programs should be fewer and smaller. In the 1940s the country was considering more and larger state services. Canadians were used to a state that provided little for the needy or for social development.[19] The main social programs available in most parts of Canada before the 1940s were workers' compensation, municipal relief (and the related poor houses), allowances for some single mothers, and pensions for the poorest of the old, for the blind, and for disabled veterans. Wholly funded by tax dollars, some of these programs used private resources, especially volunteer social workers, to assist in administration.[20] By contrast with public programs, private agencies and the services they provided were numerous. Even an incomplete but representative list is long: nursing services, adoption agencies, sailors' homes, orphanages, children's aid societies, birth control counselling, day nurseries for children of single wage-earning mothers, literacy training, cooking classes, hostels for homeless men, immigrant aid societies, and clinics and dispensaries for maternal and infant health services. Many of these services benefited from some public subsidy, but their management remained in private hands.[21] Recreation services were among the most common supplied by private welfare agencies, and they included a vast array of clubs, camps, and associations that provided for and controlled the use of leisure, mainly (but not exclusively) by children.

Definitions of the state's responsibilities in this context could not simply refer to actual distinctions that were consistently put into practice. 'Public' and 'private' welfare sectors were in reality intermingled. Throughout the 1930s, 1940s, and 1950s, attempts to frame principles for moving programs from private to public aegis show the continuing power of liberal concerns about limiting public authority and protecting the private sphere, in both its familial and its market dimensions. In 1934, prominent social worker Charlotte Whitton expressed the most common social work guideline in her appeal for donations to the community chests of Canada. Public welfare programs supplied the material means of existence, she said, while private agencies assumed the responsibilities of care and encouraged the expression of fellow feeling. The same supposed principles appeared in other speeches for the appeal by Prime Minister R.B. Bennett and labour leader Tom Moore.[22] According to a Vancouver charity leader, American president Franklin Roosevelt had also expressed the same distinction: public welfare programs were to make life possible, private services to make it worth living.[23] For social policy adviser Leonard Marsh, writing in 1943, the best public programs were those that respected 'individuality,' by which he meant family privacy.[24] Concerns about privacy also played a part in the views of Deputy Minister of Health and Welfare George Davidson when he explained in 1944 to family allowance supervisors that public opinion had increasingly become opposed to discretionary assessments of income assistance needs.[25] Even in the mid 1960s, political scientist C.B. Macpherson, arguing for increased government involvement in meeting social needs, had to justify state expansion as a means of protecting private property ownership against more revolutionary projects of state expansion.[26] Thus, beginning in the 1930s and continuing into the 1940s and 1950s, promoters of increased provision for public welfare responded to the power of liberal concerns about limiting public authority and protecting the private sphere, in both its familial and its market dimensions.

The debates in the post-war period about the appropriate boundaries of the state were coloured by one of the legacies of the 1930s. The unemployment relief crisis had left a widespread conviction that a *liberal* welfare state should provide people with assistance without taking control of their private, moral, or simply personal decisions. Popular feeling in support of this conviction came from the common experience in the 1930s of both the tyranny of poverty and the authoritarian power of relief officers and social workers. The politics of the cold war added to the protectiveness about the private sphere, with rumours of totalitarian excesses giving credence to sermonizing about freedom and democracy. Even day care for children could be depicted as a threat to freedom and a source of Communist influence, as Susan Prentice has shown.[27] In general, promoters of welfare programs had to respond to concerns that authoritarian regimes, whether Communist or Fascist, had tended to expand the services provided by the state and to generate bureaucracies. In this vein, apparently innocuous proposals made by public recreation enthusiasts were met with reminders that the Nazi Youth movement had been a state-sponsored program of recreation and informal education. Speaking in the same political language, recreationists replied that democracy was a matter of everyday culture, and that only in leisure were people truly at liberty to practise living as citizens of a free society.[28] Because public recreation was proposed as something to serve 'all the people,' not just the poor, it generated discussion on key political questions of the welfare state's formative years: Did welfare programs threaten freedom by extending the arm of the state too far? Was the creation of new cadres of state experts, such as the professional public recreation directors, a recipe for the infiltration of personal life by agents of the state?

As Pateman's analysis of liberalism would lead us to expect, a familiar pair of gender terms, male breadwinner and female homemaker, was deeply implicated in discussions of the public–private boundary in welfare.[29] Historians Linda Gordon and James Cronin have suggested that this gendered metaphor for normal society played an important part in welfare thinking in the formative years of the British and American welfare states.[30] Some kinds of welfare were typed as feminine caregiving, and others as masculine providing. This line of analysis also serves well in the Canadian case. Comparing the public and private welfare programs of the pre-war period confirms that many private agencies did welfare work normatively associated with women. Private agencies, like mothers, trained and socialized the youngest children in basic life skills. Also like mothers, but like wives, sisters, and daughters too, they nursed the ill and safeguarded health, aided kin in life's crises and difficult transitions, and helped relieve the burden on the wages of the bread-winners. Correspondingly, public welfare operated in masculine areas, supplying, through income assistance to the needy, the main means of family subsistence, just as the male breadwinner did. In actual families, of course, the provision of bread and care was not always so sharply divided on gender lines. And both in norm and in practice, a father's responsibilities included socialization of his older sons. But because the normative gender division of labour in families generally assigned to women the responsibility of care and to men that of providing the means of subsistence, the parallels in the public–private division of wel-fare had marked gender associations.[31]

In the post-war years, these associations were still culturally available. But new programs were challenging the separation of care and income. Chief among these programs was the federal family allowance, which disbursed its payments to mothers, not fathers, and which also advised mothers on how to care for their children. To a certain degree, this advice was backed with coercive measures. The distress of conservatives at these arrangements, and particularly at the compromise of paternal control over income, reflected the persistence of the normative gender division of family welfare responsibilities. At the same time, the fact of the family allowances' novel arrangements and the ingenious terms by which they were defended as liberal democratic measures were signals that old categories and meanings were being shaken.[32]

Similarly, public recreation disrupted liberalism's notional separations of public and private responsibilities and of masculine and feminine wel-fare duties. The categorizing of recreation services by gender or by sec-tor was not simple. Recreation's place in the public–private division of welfare might seem quite clearly to have been in the feminine, private realm of care. No one would have claimed that recreation services were as necessary as food and shelter. Provided mainly for children, they were a kind of socialized mothering and, in their sports dimensions, social fathering. But in spite of the state's supposed lack of obligation in these areas, there had actually been some public recreation services before the late 1940s. A few of Canada's largest cities had programs for publicly funded playgrounds since the 1910s. And, in the late 1930s and 1940s, several Canadian jurisdictions initiated more comprehensive state recre-ation programs, including services to adults. British Columbia's Pro-Rec

(1934) was the first and most inclusive provincial program. In 1937 the Dominion government briefly involved itself in sports and fitness when it subsidized such activities through a cost-shared Unemployment and Agricultural Assistance Act. In the war years, discussions of a national health insurance plan led to a National Physical Fitness Act (1943), intended to fund certain leisure pursuits as preventive health measures. The Ontario municipal-provincial program examined in this book was one of a series initiated across the country in response to that legislation. It is clear that recreation was capable of being described as a public welfare responsibility, even though, historically, it most often had been privately funded, like other services of care.[33]

Neither definitively mother's work nor unambiguously that of the father, recreation was able to move across, and even to reposition the gendered public–private boundary. Recreation's place in both maternal and paternal work is part of what makes recreation services useful as a means of studying the gendering of the welfare state. Recreation's uncertain standing, at the edge of a state whose shape itself was changing, elicited from public recreation's proponents intensive ideological work to justify their claim on government money against liberal concerns that the work they did was more appropriately private, like family care. If the public purse was seen as responsible only for supplying a social wage when the breadwinner's market wage failed, then recreationists had to find other principles on which to claim that tax dollars should be spent to provide equivalents to women's private, unpaid work of supervising children's play or arranging family entertainment. What sorts of rationales had to be offered to reconcile the fact of agents of the state performing works of personal care with the liberal heritage (however weakened) of protecting family privacy from state intrusion? Insofar as recreation services were intended as means to 'build character,' they were psychological interventions, like family casework. What sort of universal right might be offered as a warrant for government involvement in such apparently private matters of personal development?[34]

Public recreationists answered these challenges by drawing on the mixed legacy of early twentieth-century private recreation services. One element of that tradition was both illiberal and elitist, with little real interest in substantive, social democracy.[35] This tendency led clearly to rule by experts. The other element (less studied by historians) made democracy its central concern and displayed liberal concerns about constraining governments, at the same time that it was fundamentally communitarian, even socialist, rather than purely liberal.

The illiberal tendency defined recreation services as a means by which wise and well-washed folk could correct or prevent moral decay among the weak. As Sara Burke has shown, the British model of the settlement house – a leading agent of urban leisure reform – brought to Ontario's private recreation organizations the notion that personal contact among the classes could attract the poor to supposedly middle-class moral standards.[36] In the inter-war years, this notion's appeal was undermined by developments in the social sciences, in particular the Chicago social ecology school.[37] But, in spite of attacks on moral uplift, many of the private recreation providers – the Ys and the Boy Scouts, for example – never entirely gave up their belief that recreation was fundamentally a means of therapy. Not surprisingly, then, during the 1930s they once again presented recreation as a means of healing for a morally endangered group, the unemployed and their families. Leisure services, with programs of constructive activities, were to complement the material relief offered by the dole and by make-work projects.[38] Like relief policies, these forms of recreation were meant to prevent 'demoralization.'

But recreation services could also claim a social-liberal, participatory-democracy tradition, committed to creating in the associational life of civil society the real means to popular power. In this vein, recreation services enabled the less powerful to find their strength as citizens through social action. The settlement house movement included American as well as British influences. Although the movement in the United States had some deeply conservative elements, especially in small urban centres, its moral vocabulary included democracy as a positive good.[39] In this vocabulary, recreation offered an informal education in the ways of community life. But only if recreation was self-directed – an expression of popular tastes – would it empower and unite the fragmented neighbourhoods of the poor and the socially marginal. As John Dewey, a philosopher influential in adult education and settlement house circles, wrote, community services such as recreation could be the means by which 'a scattered, mobile and manifold public may so recognize itself as to define and express its interests.'[40] Recreation could help to construct a public capable of acting as 'the people,' as required by a liberal democratic state.

Reformers working in this tradition focused not on private personalities but on public subjectivities. They saw individuals in relation to groups and to the social structures of communities.[41] They tended to conceive of their 'clients' as healthy and normal, and claimed that their intervention in social groups was to help produce effective citizens, not to cure personal maladjustments. Recreationists, like adult educators, were social workers, but they were not caseworkers. And by the late 1930s this distinction was marked by a specific name for these people: 'group workers.' The social work specialty to which this referred was 'social work with groups,' or simply 'social group work.' It was through recreation's association with this group work tradition that the links between cold war democratic ideals, liberalism, and public provision for leisure would be forged. As Ontario premier George Drew said in 1948, government subsidized the recreation movement because it was an example of 'how free people live together.'[42]

In other words, public recreation programs were meant to regulate popular values, but to do so in ways that were consistent with liberal conceptions of freedom. The purpose of state-funded recreation, like that of public education, was to mould a certain citizen personality.[43] This personality, or subjectivity, was to have some of the qualities that private recreation programs had always sought to promote: self-discipline, religious faith, patriotism, and commitment to the heterosexual family.[44] But more novel was the attempt to develop a subjectivity that encompassed both a submission to the constraints required of a liberal citizen (tolerance, avoiding violence) and also a passion for participation in community life. Public recreation's advocates wanted Ontarians to *want* to be involved in public affairs, to really *care* about their 'democratic right ... to have a voice in decision making.'[45] The citizen they imagined was not only an individual (who was defined by personal uniqueness, not group identity, and the bearer as such of rights and freedoms), but also a social being who would long for and work towards a rich network of connectedness to others in the community. They thought recreation programs could bring people to conceive of themselves as this sort of subject.

In 1945 the recreation movement's approach to making citizens seemed opportune to both Ontario and federal politicians. Like economic welfare programs, cultural programs such as recreation promised to contribute to a sense of belonging among the 'new Canadians' of the post-war immigration and others dislocated by wartime work and service. Recreation could help to foster social integration and even to forge a national identity.[46] Concerns about war-related juvenile delinquency added to the attraction of programs that had long been seen as remedying or preventing youth crime.[47] But in spite of recreation's allure as a means of addressing public policy goals, politicians were aware that establishing such programs of cultural direction risked opening them to charges of totalitarian ambitions and of seeking to exercise bureaucratic domination. The characteristically liberal solution politicians and civil servants adopted was for new recreation programs to have policy leaders and even administrators who were volunteers instead of employees of the state. In this approach, they continued the tradition of the 'mixed social economy' that had begun in nineteenth-century philanthropic institutions and then developed in the children's aid societies, mothers' allowances commissions, and old-age pension boards of the twentieth century.[48] In the rhetoric of the 1940s, they affirmed that 'the people,' not 'government,' were to be public recreation's guiding force. In this way, the private world could be saved from state domination.

This liberal solution was, however, an unstable one. It would remain so for most of the 1950s, and would finally give way to bureaucratization by the 1960s. The explanation of this failure of the movement's democratic aspirations lies in understanding two contradictions in the public–private relationship. The first is that welfare services that were public brought with them an implied universality: enjoyment of public services was the right of all citizens. By contrast, private provision for leisure, whether by charities or by business, was always particularistic, inescapably structured by social divisions. Collegiate high schools held respectable dances for middle-class students, while wage-earning teenagers attended rowdier affairs in commercial halls. Racial, religious, and ethnic groups had their own exclusive community centres. Many leisure pursuits were organized by gender: sports, clubs, service groups, radio and TV programming, even movies, were attended or consumed by, and often explicitly designed for, either men or women, boys or girls. Part of liberalism's rationale for limits on the state is precisely to protect as a realm of personal freedom the sorts of leisure pursuits in which people express such personal tastes and private loyalties.[49] To make recreation *public* entailed policy goals that were difficult to reconcile with particularism. One of these goals, social integration, was in fact meant to break down the very sub-cultures, gendered or otherwise, that private leisure pursuits helped to maintain. In effect, the attempt to foster a general citizenship through public recreation intruded on private preferences.

A second contradiction implied in public recreation lay between volunteer leadership and respect for liberal democratic values. The strategy of involving 'the public' in organizing public recreation was meant to avoid authoritarian state control, but the people attracted to volunteer leadership in the new public programs often brought with them their own regulatory instincts. These impulses were inimical to the kind of democratic self-organization that liberal group workers envisaged for public recreation programs. 'Democratic' recreation programs were not supposed to prescribe 'constructive' programs to the public, but were meant to assist in the realization of popular initiatives.[50] Decision making in these programs was intended to be an exercise in participatory democracy, but the volunteers and professionals with private agency experience often came to their new roles in public recreation with illiberal social work values. These experienced leaders saw their role as 'doing good' for the dependent members of the community and protecting it from delinquency or dangerous immigrant cultures. In this view, recreation was administered by elite groups and consumed by the 'less fortunate.' In addition to these class and ethnic prejudices, they also brought with them gendered expectations about who would do the different kinds of work that organized leisure entailed. The new public recreation director's profession was as vulnerable as other occupations to the forces that assigned unequal roles to women and men. So, too, was the process by which volunteer leadership was constituted. In short, non-state traditions of social work meant that the voice of 'the people' in expressing recreation needs was rarely gender-neutral or gender-balanced. Public recreationists with a liberal vision of egalitarian participatory democracy thus had to struggle to establish new organizational methods, while working with leaders committed to existing, contradictory conventions of social power. In imagining that public recreation might be made both democratic and liberal by having 'private' people as its leaders, its designers built into it such contradictory features that its decline from movement to service was virtually guaranteed.

In what follows, I tell the story of the actors, events, and circumstances by means of which the initial contradictory design of public recreation evolved into its final, more stable, and more bureaucratic form. I begin in Chapter 1 by explaining the liberal democratic definitions of recreation that emerged in the 1940s and 1950s and the ways this vocabulary was linked to gender discourse and gender relations. What was new was the rejection of the explicitly therapeutic goals of earlier leisure reformers. The alternative that was offered, a kind of hedonist individualism, treated the subject of 'leisure need' as a masculine figure, the leisure consumer, but also opened up possibilities for women to claim leisure services as individuals and not just as mothers. These innovative ideas about leisure entitlements competed with older ones that emphasized the cultivation of 'better' tastes. In Chapter 2, I show how this competition shaped a new agency within Ontario's education bureaucracy, the Community Programmes Branch (CPB). What this new agency would offer to women as citizens depended both on which vision of leisure dominated within the branch and on what emerged as the particular liberal and democratic means by which the branch would contribute to leisure reform.

In the middle chapters of the book, I examine how the designs of the CPB intersected with the forces of circumstance. One of these forces was the threat that recreation would be expelled from the realm of 'public' services. The other lay in the challenges posed to a liberal democratic dream by particular community politics. In Hamilton, Gravenhurst, Brantford, Kenora, Chatham, Dunnville, Barrie, and Cornwall, among dozens of other towns and cities, recreationists encountered the 'molecular networks of power relations' that were the living, breathing, and often profoundly undemocratic and illiberal realities of community life in post-war Ontario.[51] Chapters 3 and 4 speak most directly of the fate of the recreationists' ideal of leadership when it encountered these forces. Chapter 3 explains how a specifically liberal method of public administration, faced with the prejudices and conventions of community life in post-war Ontario, led to the creation of a predominantly male cadre of recreation directors, in spite of the fact that the occupation was supposedly, in good liberal terms, open to merit regardless of gender. Chapter 4 explores the forces, including gender discourse, that pushed the men recreation directors into adopting a bureaucratic form of practice, in spite of an occupational culture that stressed volunteer leadership.

Having explained the parts that liberal ideology and gender played in the process by which the recreation directors helped produce bureaucratization, I turn in Chapters 5 and 6 to consider how 'the people' fared and factored in the slide towards bureaucracy. In a close study of the recreation movement in Brantford, I argue that social hierarchies (both of gender and class), and not just the will to power of professionals, helped stifle the experiment in citizen participation. Chapter 6 in particular examines the consequences of public recreation's claim to empower women citizens. In spite of some spirited attempts to retain control of their own 'sphere' and even to advance beyond maternalism, women in public recreation found themselves performing variants of domestic labour, even while having supposedly enlarged their lives beyond home and hearth. In Chapter 7, I return to the provincial civil servants when they attempted, in adverse circumstances in the final years of the 1950s, to revitalize the project of leadership 'by the people' that they and others had imagined in the climate of post-war idealism. The consumerist solution that the CPB devised in 1958 speaks sadly of populist liberalism's limits. Its shortcomings also help explain why public recreation's liberal values were so often rejected by those who practised more radical democratic organizing in the 1960s. The concern for freedom that lay behind the recreationists' respect for the will of 'the people' ended up reproducing in new ways, rather than challenging, the limits on opportunities for women and girls. To use play as a means to form a new public for the democratic welfare state served only to carry into the state the gendered organization of leisure.

Both in researching and writing, I have remained fundamentally ambivalent about the people in this movement.[52] While I can certainly interpret the meaning of their project as a whole, the individuals involved were a mixed bag – appallingly innocent, contemptibly complacent, bracingly pragmatic, and deeply idealistic – and thus impossible to characterize collectively. It was clear to me that the municipal stage attracted more than a few scoundrels and fools. But in that respect, the smaller stage is surely no different from many larger ones, and its dramas do not, on these grounds, lose their claim on our interest. Perhaps because I was raised by parents who lived out their political lives in various battles for community services and workplace democracy, I have no difficulty taking seriously the recreation movement's concerns, even while recognizing the limits of some of its agents.

In their attempt to make a liberal democratic welfare program, the public and private leaders of the recreation movement encountered the problem of how it is difficult simultaneously to foster community and further freedom. Of the many things we can learn from their efforts, one is an idea of how gender shaped the response to this challenge, which is endemic to the welfare state. In public recreation, and perhaps in other programs of the welfare state, gender differences (or at least perceptions of them) were among the social divisions public policy makers sought to overcome. At the same time, respecting freedom of choice in recreation seemed to endorse some kinds of gender segregation or to require affirmative action, rather than just response to demands of 'the people.' Private leadership afforded protection against bureaucratic state domination, but private leadership might itself preserve the inequalities of social politics, including gender. Gender hierarchy was part of the structural and discursive context in which were formed the 'solutions' to the dilemmas of a liberal democratic welfare service. Therefore, the task of explaining the decline of public recreation from a movement to a service takes us deeply into the connections between liberalism, democracy, and gender in the welfare state of the 1950s.

1

Defining Recreation and
Expressing Needs in a 'Free Society'

In 1953, Brantford's Bellview community recreation committee invited
the general public to watch the coronation of Queen Elizabeth II on a
television set at their community centre.[1] Probably some people came
out to this communal viewing because they did not own a TV. Not everyone could afford one. Some of those who did have the necessary dollars
very likely had doubts about whether the 'idiot box' belonged in a cul-
tured home. But a coronation was a significant public ceremony. Viewing it on TV with a group might have seemed a bit like joining the crowd
along the new queen's processional route, which was not below the dig-
nity of any loyal subject. The new entertainment technology was not yet
essential for cultural belonging, but the communal viewing of that
broadcast prefigured television's role as the collective hearth. To watch
the coronation on television was both a pleasure and a duty, and by
making it available in a public space, the Bellview committee was serving
what they understood to be a community recreation need.

The event organized by the Bellview committee, like much else in the
1940s and the early 1950s, is in some ways reminiscent of the 1930s and,
in other ways, foreshadows the 1960s. Edward VIII's 1936 abdication
announcement, which had been broadcast on radio, and George VI's
royal visit in 1939 were both still vivid memories for many Canadians.
The broadcast of Elizabeth's face and figure in 1953, while a similar
event, provided as well a taste of the technology that, in the decades to
come, would draw Canadians away from public spaces and yet join them
in a multinational common culture. A similar blend of past influences
and signs of change can be found in the theories of recreation and in
the expressions of recreational need that informed Ontario's public recreation program. The ideas of the 1930s loomed as an image of bad, old,

undemocratic ways, whose compelling influence had consciously to be resisted. Modern ways of defining recreation need anticipated both the individualist hedonism of the 'do your own thing' language of the 1960s and the New Left's redescription of needs as the basis of rights. In Ontario's cities, towns, and villages in the late 1940s and the 1950s, men and women used both old and new languages of need to make claims on the recreation agencies of both local and provincial governments. In the vocabulary they chose and the associations they drew, people who spoke about skating rinks and singalongs showed that they were at the same time talking about rights and power. In short, politics.

Defining 'Recreation'

In the post-war years, recreationists, in their attempts to define recreation, responded to the intellectual legacy of the 1930s, when recreation theorists had promoted its social utility and had distinguished without hesitation the harmful from the wholesome pleasures. Recreation served an essential social purpose: the formation of the moral aspects of the personality, in the broad sense of 'character-building.'[2] Charlotte Whitton pointed to recreation's social usefulness in 1931 when, as head of Canada's leading welfare agency, she wrote that 'the very conditions of depression and unemployment prevailing at the present time indicate as rarely before, the urgent social necessity from the angle of character conservation of the better organization for constructive activities to employ the idle time of our population – juvenile, adolescent or adult.'[3]

Not only the goals of recreation but also its most basic terminology reflected Depression-era concerns. This effect is evident in the 1936 undergraduate textbook by Martin H. Neumeyer and Esther S. Neumeyer, *Leisure and Recreation*.[4] They distinguished between idleness and leisure and between leisure and recreation. Idleness was a source of danger: large numbers of unemployed men gave new relevance to the view that spare time could be a social problem.[5] To the Neumeyers, unemployment was not 'true leisure,' because its attendant worries and deprivations constrained creativity and choice. Spare time spent in idleness was not leisure, because leisure was more than just time off from work. 'Free' time only counted as leisure when it was used to do something creative, in a relaxed fashion. Leisure was thus distinguished from idleness, but leisure nevertheless shared with idleness the reference to non-work time. Its evaluative connotations aside, the term leisure meant: the time surplus remaining after the practical necessities of life have been attended to. By contrast, the term recreation referred to activity rather than to time. In addition to this distinction, recreation was differentiated from leisure-time pursuits generally, as well as from work, by its consequences. The Neumeyers described both work and some leisure activities as exhausting and enfeebling, whereas recreational activities 're-created' or restored physical and mental well-being.[6]

Depression-era recreation theory perpetuated the moral reformers' view that 're-creation' was not accomplished equally by all forms of enjoyment. For the Neumeyers, recreation was the right use of leisure, a necessary corrective to 'the misuses of leisure.' These misuses consisted mainly of commercial amusements – entertainment that could be paid for – that required 'only a minimum amount of physical and mental exertion' and thus provided no recreative effect. Moreover, commercial amusements were not considered recreational because leisure entrepreneurs, who were animated by the profit motive, frequently 'catered to human weakness,' offering pleasures that were, in the recreationists' view, degrading to mental and physical health. Like the Neumeyers, Canadian leisure reformers called for efforts, among 'laymen' and professionals alike, 'to control the strength of commercialized activities.'[7]

In this judgmental vein, William Cook of Canada's YMCA National Council stressed that 'active participation' distinguished 'recreative spare time occupations' from other forms of enjoyment. He added a list of experiences that leisure should include if it was to be truly recreational: '[Recreation] is more than sport. The occupation of leisure should include opportunities for the pursuit of knowledge, the appreciation and enjoyment of beauty in art, music, drama, literature, and nature, and the expression of creative powers through co-operative activities and individual hobbies.'[8] Like the Neumeyers, Cook saw leisure-time pursuits as potentially conducive to social welfare, providing they required effort, did not threaten health, and developed what the recreation theorists deemed to be desirable intellectual and moral qualities. The key expressions in this understanding of recreation were 'the joy of effort,' 'wholesome,' and 'constructive.'

In Depression-era recreation theory, recreation was defined as both an alternative to work and its complement. As a second-best alternative to work for the jobless, recreation was said to offer, through physical and mental activity, a means of maintaining in working order the faculties and capacities of the unemployed. In this spirit, the British Columbia provincial recreation program of the inter-war years offered men industrial weight-lifting exercises, and the 1937 Dominion-Provincial Youth Training Act included 'physical training to promote fitness and to raise morale' as part of the preparation for employment offered to men and women from age sixteen to thirty. Another recreation program, community gardening, in addition to providing food, was said to contribute to 'the courage, contentment and welfare of the jobless worker.'[9] 'Constructive' recreation was like work, because it required effort and produced results, whether in knowledge, physical performance, or, more intangibly, character. The view of recreation as a complement to work is captured in one recreationist's comment on New Zealand's 1937 Physical Welfare and Recreation Act, which she called 'a policy that would rescue, during the moments of leisure, the personal initiative and ability that is gradually and surely being swallowed up by the mechanization of industry.' In this view, work does not permit self-expression, creativity, or pleasure in achievement; certain non-work activities are defined as recreation because they offer these experiences and thus fill a gap left by work.[10]

Both as alternative and complement, the definition of recreation with reference to work implied that recreation was for the working class, and most often, the industrial worker. The professionals who offered these definitions had not given up on their own work's potential for self-expression; they were thinking of the modern factory worker when they counselled recreation as a complement. In advocating the use of recreation as an alternative to work, they argued that unemployment resulting from technological changes might perpetuate the unemployment rates of the 1930s, and that recreation would therefore be increasingly necessary. Again, the manual labourer, rather than the professional, was the object of this analysis. While industrial workers were, in reality, sometimes female, in recreation theory, wage-earning women's leisure was treated more as masculine than feminine. To have non-work time was to be in a quasi-masculine social position, separate from and prior to the specifically feminine positions of wife and mother, which imposed their own kinds of time discipline and which offered distinctive kinds of leisure. The leisure needs of women as mothers were addressed in 1930s recreation theory by 'the age-old prescription: "Play with the children."'[11] In this view, nature provided women, in their role as mothers, with a ready-made form of wholesome recreation. The threat of the 'empty nest' endangered only individual happiness, and even this might be preserved by the appearance of grandchildren. Only the leisure of waged workers presented a social problem, and for lifelong earners, who were assumed not to be mothers, work remained a continuing cause of recreation 'need.'

The links between work and recreation were both clear and plainly organized by gender in the first 'made-in-Canada' recreation theory, which was set out in a series of pamphlets by Eric Muncaster published in 1934 by the Leisure Time Activities Division of the Canadian Council for Child and Family Welfare. Of these pamphlets, two were focused specifically on gender. One outlined *The Special Needs of Men and Boys*, and another described appropriate *Recreation Services for Women and Girls*. The first included a summary of 'boys' work' that is, the work done to provide for boys an array of organized sports and club activities. These activities were educational, tied to labour and to citizenship, and not just for fun. Muncaster recommended holding 'Kangaroo Courts' as a means of securing discipline in boys' camps, and suggested classes in 'practical subjects' (that is, employment-related ones). The pamphlet urgently warned that a failure in recreation for men and boys might bring 'untold possibilities of danger both to the individual and to the state.'[12]

The pamphlet on women and girls also promoted girls' work, but for different reasons. Absent was any hint that recreation should teach work skills or offer safe channels for aggressiveness. Rather, in the interests of protecting girls' supposedly sensitive and delicate systems, Muncaster warned recreation leaders not to expect girls to play 'keenly competitive games' and not to have girls perform 'violent' exercise. Nowhere did the pamphlet suggest that recreation was needed to help protect society from dangers posed by idle girls. Instead, Muncaster closed on a sunny tone, urging society to provide women and girls with opportunities to achieve personal happiness.[13]

While Muncaster enthusiastically advocated recreation for girls, he felt no need to support his case with warnings about the risk girls presented to the foundations of social order. Even on sexual matters, the central concern of moral reformers in discussions of working women's leisure, Muncaster was apparently hesitant to sound an alarm. Sexual discipline had not ceased to be a concern in general culture, of course,[14] but in this authoritative expression in 1934 of the views of mainstream Canadian social workers, there is not the slightest hint of anxiety about the sexual morality of women or girls. Muncaster offers no advice on how to arrange mixed-sex leisure pursuits for young women. Nor is the contribution of women's leisure to a happy heterosexual family life a theme he takes up. He wants to see the health of girls and women improved by more physical exercise, and he wants them to have more opportunities to join women's hobby and adult education groups. There is, perhaps, a subtle hint that recreation services must teach women not to depend on commercial amusements. But this small concern that women may feel dissatisfied when too poor to shop or to attend a show pales by contrast with the importance of the social issues he links to recreation for boys and men. Muncaster made much of the work habits and political discipline inculcated by boys' work, deeming them essential measures to regulate morality and to preserve the integrity of the state. The understandable obsession of social workers with the unemployment crisis apparently privileged recreation's links to paid work.

By linking work and recreation in these ways, the recreation theorists of the 1930s perpetuated the most conservative moral and social reform traditions of the playgrounds movements, youth agencies, and settlement houses. Like other, more democratic social group workers, they saw recreation as a means of incorporating into full citizenship people marginalized by poverty. But the pressures of the Depression had given renewed weight to the therapeutic emphasis in recreation theory. In the same way that, in the 1950s, 'youth' would become the focus of a moral panic, in the 1930s, social anxieties centred on the industrial worker, who became paradigmatically the person in need of recreation.[15] Vulnerable to unemployment, he was therefore dangerously at risk of moral decay. Recreation was a remedy, like social insurance, for the particular perils of wage-earning. When recreation services were lauded as a response to unemployment, they were linked more strongly than ever to welfare as moral regulation, with a particular emphasis on the moral dangers that threatened men and boys.

During the Second World War, events prompted a shift away from the view of recreation as a therapy for the economically disadvantaged. In the early 1940s, unprecedented numbers of adult Canadians experienced publicly provided recreation. War-time Housing Ltd provided recreation services in the sixty or seventy Canadian municipalities that housed more than fifty new war-time houses. The armed forces employed sports officers and organized tournaments, craft classes, movies, and dances for enlisted men and women. In addition, private agencies like the YMCA and the Salvation Army ran the 'special services,' providing recreation facilities such as canteens both for war-workers in cities like Hamilton and for men and women in the service.[16]

On one hand, the purposes served by these programs were identical to the most instrumental of settlement house services. By virtue of their displacement, war-workers and enlisted people were as much 'deviant' populations in 'need' of moral regulation as any of recreationists' earlier targets. That the publicly provided recreation services were intended to steer service people and war industry staff clear of sex and drink towards more unequivocally wholesome activities did not go unnoticed. But, on the other hand, years later recreationists would remember the war services as having been popular. One former soldier approvingly described armed forces sports as highly organized and competitive. War services dances were also bigger and better than many workers or soldiers (especially those from small towns and rural areas) had ever seen in peacetime. The recreation services could be viewed not as therapy, but as amenities like the other 'comforts' sent from home.[17] They were supplied, not as charity, but as the due entitlements of soldiers and war-workers – the very least society could do for citizens performing their national duty.

Young, single men and women were those most likely to have enjoyed the social and recreational opportunities of war time. Its intense combination of danger and excitement, trauma and pleasure, must have left many unable to accept unquestioningly conventional norms. Like veterans of the First World War, this group was aware of the most visceral emotions, and contemptuous of hypocritical Victorians like Prime Minister Mackenzie King. Many of this generation would take enthusiastically to popular Freudianism, with its horror of neuroses generated through the repression of desire.[18] Their battle for political liberties meshed readily with ideas in favour of an expansion of personal freedoms. Even in the din of moral panics in the post-war era about pulp fiction and juvenile delinquency, there can be heard a new liberalism, contending with the Victorian leftovers who populated such forums as the Senate Committee on Salacious and Indecent Literature.[19] For the generation of veterans of the Second World War, this committee's concerns seem less representative than the frankness of the Kinsey Report. In recreation theory, the affirmation of free choice and the acceptance of popular tastes similarly captured and reproduced the distinctive culture of this generation of young adults.

The work of G. Ott Romney, an American physical education professor, represents this new liberalism in recreation theory; it is freeing, and yet in its own way regulatory. Romney was a significant source of ideas for Ontario's nascent public recreation movement. He was the keynote speaker at the 1948 Ontario Recreation Conference, and in the late

1940s his book, *Off the Job Living*, was the only 'philosophy of recreation' title in the provincial recreation agency's circulating library.[20] Although public recreation activists heard many 'philosophies of recreation,' Romney's ideas were important because they represented the increasingly liberal tendencies in recreation theory. Critical of any recreation theory based in welfare work, Romney prescribed a 'Modern Concept of Recreation' for 'the Postwar World.'[21]

Rejecting the moral reformers' instrumental view of recreation, Romney contended that pleasure must be its own purpose. He deplored 'negative' definitions of recreation for making it merely 'an antidote for juvenile delinquency or a take-the-children-off-the-street movement or an anesthetic to relieve the pain of [an] empty house.'[22] Seeking to sever recreation's links with moral prescription, he scorned fixed lists of recreational activities. To promote recreation as a set of wholesome or constructive activities was, according to Romney, irrational, akin to 'cult' worship. The 'true meaning of recreation' was obscured by such unthinking loyalty to a 'charmed circle.' Disdaining priestly authority, Romney instead sported science's mantle of rationality. He defined recreation with a metaphor drawn from physiology. Recreation offered 'balanced living,' necessary as 'a chance to meet the demands of [the individual's] body chemistry.' For the sake of the 'balance' required by the body, the individual 'must be granted a chance to live as a total human being, exercising, on his own time, the muscles, the emotions and the mental processes which find no nourishment in the usual work routines in an age of machines and high specialization.' In this way, Romney retained the notion of recreation as a complement to the industrial worker's job, even though he rejected the notion of recreation as 'a sop for the poor or unemployed.'

In Romney's view, to offer recreation as a welfare service to the unemployed was to reduce recreation to a second-best option and so to distort the meaning of recreation. According to Romney, recreation was by definition something desirable, something freely chosen; it was essentially 'any experience indulged in by choice for its own sake, paying off in the gratification of the doing.' It served society only incidentally. If government was to fund recreation programs, its reason for doing so should be to maximize leisure options for individuals. 'Since so few people can afford their own swimming pools and golf courses, their own craft shops and stages, their own picnic grounds and sports fields; and since leadership is so essential, it becomes necessary for people to pool their resources to provide adequate opportunities.' Government was proposed

as the best channel for this cooperative effort. Recreation belonged with
social policy, not as a means to 'character conservation,' but because
enjoyment itself was a social right. Like the services provided for the
forces during the war, recreation was a citizen's entitlement. Echoing this
view, a Canadian government film promoting public recreation services
in 1948 announced that: 'In their new wisdom, people are realizing that
recreation is an indispensable human right, as important to a community
as health or welfare or education.'[23]

Recreation theory such as Romney's made possible a new emphasis in
the justifications that would be made for the state role in recreation. No
longer did recreation need to rely on 'the delinquency threat, group
work or rehabilitation' for social support, theorist Charles Brightbill
told a conference of Ontario recreation enthusiasts. He urged his audience to spread the word that recreation represented an 'opportunity for
wholesome and abundant living ... [that was] indispensable in the lives
of all people.' Later, Brightbill avoided even the adjective wholesome,
using instead the less morally judgmental term 'full.'[24] While the concern for health and the promotion of effort were still part of recreation,
post-war theorists sought strenuously to shake the tradition of moral
therapy.

For them, popular tastes were no longer suspect. Quite the contrary.
In Romney's physiological metaphor, the demands of body chemistry
would ensure that individuals, given abundant opportunities, would naturally seek 'balanced living.' The provision of public recreation could
therefore best be guided, not by social utility (a welfare concept), but by
'popular demand.' This consumerist vocabulary allowed public recreation to distinguish itself from the social welfare-oriented private recreation agencies. While the Ys, Scouts, Guides, settlement houses, and
churches might continue to organize recreation along certain predetermined, constructive lines, public recreationists could offer services in
response to popular demand. At the same time, the notion that individuals were possessed of a right to enjoyment formed recreation's basis to
a claim on public funds.

Defining public recreation in contrast to private recreation was not
simply a matter of rejecting the link to charity. In addition to the
'public/charitable' contrast, public recreationists also defined their programs in relation to another meaning of 'private' recreation. In this second dualism, the term 'private' meant 'nobody's business but my own.'
Small-l liberal critics of public recreation drew on this meaning of privacy to question whether the state had any place at all in organizing

leisure-time pursuits. In response, public recreationists depicted these opponents as reactionary, vaguely comic curmudgeons, who grumpily asserted that recreation services were never needed 'when I was a boy' and that in their youth they had amused themselves on their own and kept themselves out of trouble.[25] For these people, if leisure was to be organized at all, it should be through the mechanisms of the market place. Leisure was private in a commercial sense, rather than in a charity sense. Some public recreation promoters, mainly professional recreationists, tried to minimize the difference between public and commercial recreation, claiming, as did Romney, that the term recreation included all enjoyable leisure-time pursuits.

The new theoretical tendency thus defined public recreation in relation to two different meanings of private. As Mariana Valverde and Lorna Weir have observed, 'there is no single paradigmatic instance of privacy, but rather co-existing and shifting boundaries between public and private.' Nor is 'the private' necessarily always feminine terrain.[26] In the case of public recreation, the gender associated with 'the private' varies. Public recreation's claims to be different from its social work past in private recreation were attempts to make the image of their programs into a masculine one. In this strategy, public was masculine and private feminine, with public recreation's meaning being derived from a contrast with private. But when public recreationists conceived of their programs as analogous to commercial leisure provision, they were attempting to describe something public as similar to something private, rather than contrasting the two spheres, and the gender of the private sphere was masculine, as was the public.

Why was private in the commercial sense a masculine category? Choices among commercial recreations, however limited the options, were seen as individual, in the sense of being free from determination by government or employer. This individual freedom (such as it was) was more likely to be enjoyed by men than by women, probably because men of any given age, class, or ethnic group were likely to control more disposable income than their female counterparts.[27] Data from the mid-1950s show that, in a random representative sample of 1,741 Ohio residents, the use of 'commercial amusements' by males was about 44 per cent greater than by females. In all but one social class (using a four-strata analysis), men and boys were more likely than women to spend money for leisure pursuits.[28] The exception was the upper middle class, the highest social stratum studied; here men and boys were slightly less likely than women and girls to use commercial amusements. But, even though a corporation lawyer's wife or daughter was apparently more likely to go to a show than he was, she was still less often in the market for commercial entertainments than were most men and boys. The male clerk or tradesman or labourer, or his sons, purchased their entertainment 10 per cent more often than did even the most well-to-do leisured women and girls. Although there were some women-only commercial leisure establishments, such as urban tearooms, and many venues for mixed-gender entertainment, such as movies, large sections of the market in leisure, such as bar rooms and pool rooms, were for male customers only, or for women plying the prostitute's trade.[29] In mixed-gender venues that were patronized by dating couples, the man's obligation to treat made him effectively the customer. Both men and women used commercial amusements, then, but most often the consumer of leisure services was male.

Public recreationists wanted to respond to popular demand as providers of commercial amusements did. They claimed that they shared the commercial providers' respect for freedom of individual choice. They accepted the notion that the individual choices represented by 'demand' were private, in the sense of not appropriately being subject to direction by government in a free society. Because it was more often males who were accustomed to exercising such 'free' private choices in leisure, the concerns of public recreationists about respecting choice responded primarily to men's and boys' experiences. When recreationists assumed that all of the 'public,' like adult men, chose leisure-time pursuits simply according to individual preferences, their notion of private choice was infused with a masculine bias.

Most women and girls experienced leisure as something less individual, less market-based, and less purely idle. While adult men enjoyed much of their leisure as independent consumers, women's leisure, and especially married mothers' leisure, was more likely to be family-centred.[30] Such familial leisure was intrinsically relational, rather than individual, and it included both work and non-work. For women with domestic responsibilities, daughters as well as mothers, the private sphere was not a realm of leisure, but of labour, with necessities often crowding out choice. While single men relied on female kin or commercial providers for their cooking and cleaning, independent women (unless well-to-do) did these for themselves in their 'leisure' time. For mothers of infants and small children, time was rarely free of obligations; leisure in the individualist sense of one's own free time hardly existed. Instead, even for childless wives or helping daughters, leisure

for families frequently meant women's work: amusing children, entertaining guests, or making holidays and birthdays delightful occasions
with decorations and special food.[31] Enjoyment was tied to family and
conjugal pleasures. The free time and individual choice in leisure pursuits of adult women undoubtedly varied among families. But a 1948
radio play made by recreationists suggested that the leisure needs of the
'normal' adult woman, that is, the mother, were represented in recreation discourse as distinctively familial, not individual. In *The Juniper
Family's Spare Time*, each family member expresses a leisure need. The
mother has two needs. One is for 'something we could all do together'
(mother as the dramaturge of family togetherness). The other is related
to maternal work: she wants leisure alternatives for her youngest son, to
replace the horror movies he watches. Why? Because she is the one who
has to sit up with him when the scary movies make him sleepless.[32] In
such an interpretive framework, recreation for women appeared as private in more a familial than an individualist sense. And the leisure time
of family members was an occasion for women's labour.

In Depression-era recreation theory, the connections between
women's leisure and their family labour had been clearly acknowledged.
Like the leisure of wage-earners (perceived as masculine), the leisure
women enjoyed was defined in relation to their work. For women, the
relevant work was the paradigmatically feminine labour of serving their
children and husband. Recreation helped people to do their work better and in so doing to fulfil their social obligations. This older recreation theory was rooted in what Rooke and Schnell have labelled a
'solidarist' conception of enjoyment and its social function. Akin to the
philosophical idealism that shaped the University of Toronto's School
of Social Work in the early part of the century, solidarism viewed society
as 'a moral organism' that was ordered by the observance of mutual
rights and duties.[33] In this view, recreation was a means for individuals
to orient themselves in collective life – a method for learning beneficent
social relations. This conception of recreation was basic to recreation
programs that were designed to help socialize children – the 'playgrounds, not prisons,' orientation. As well, it was the basis for therapeutic recreation programs in prisons, psychiatric wards, and church
missions. In these programs, recreation was meant to help participants
'to relate themselves more effectively to each other and to experience
growth opportunities in the process. This growth is in the direction of
socially-desirable goals ...'[34] In its focus on nurturing and educative relationships, recreation in the solidarist tradition was modelled on a family

ideal. Viewed in this way, private recreation resembles representations of mothers' work as socializers of children and orchestrators of family relationships.

The shift in recreation theory away from its moral reform and social welfare origins towards a 'modern' liberalism arranged the elements of recreation theory according to the model of the market place. The subject of recreation theory became the individual consumer. The definitions of need had to do with personal pleasure. Recreation was redescribed so as to resemble commercial entertainment, minus the customer's ticket price. In imitation of owners of taverns and dance halls, the community was to provide facilities that differed from commercial ones mainly in that access was not through individual purchase or membership. The consumption of recreation services was by individuals, making private choices. The community role was to serve responsively, not to exert collective direction or control. Although this view of recreation services left the community a role as a provider, it represented an increased individualism in recreation theory.

The shift from solidarism to individualism was a shift in recreation theory towards masculinity. This is not to say that no women were individualist or that no men were solidarist. Neither is it to say that women were never consumers of leisure or that married men never joined their families at play. Rather, it is to recognize that, in the early 1950s, individualism in its fullest extent was still reserved normatively for the male social role. This is evident in the sex roles constructed by Parsonian sociologists in the early 1950s. The positively rated 'male' role traits were tenacity, aggressiveness, curiosity, ambition, 'planfulness,' responsibleness, originality, competitiveness, and self-confidence. The positive 'female' traits in this scheme were affectionateness, obedience, responsiveness to sympathy and approval from adults, speedy recovery from emotional disturbance, cheerfulness, kindness, and friendliness. These are not true essences of maleness and femaleness, but rather, as Kate Millett argues in *Sexual Politics*, indicators of cultural values and 'the approved relationship between the sexes.'[35] However grotesquely these sex roles may have misrepresented the range and variety of human possibility, they indicated a typology of gender that was common in the white, middle-class social milieu of academic recreation theorists in the 1950s.[36]

The masculine traits in this list, with the exception of 'responsibleness,' are self-serving; the feminine ones, possibly excepting emotional resilience, indicate dependence on and service to others. The inclusion of responsibleness saves this view of masculinity from being radically individualist. From masculine responsibleness can be read the role of breadwinner, so central to the definition of fatherhood. But even this familial role carried with it a sense of entitlement to leisure, as Robert Rutherdale has shown. Being a breadwinner earned a father a right to his free time, a space for personally chosen pleasures.[37] On balance, then, and compared with the female list of traits, the male role in the predominant language of social description of the 1950s was more oriented to self than was the female role. In this context, when recreation theorists began to describe recreation as any activity pursued for the sake of individual enjoyment, they were urging that recreation be reconceptualized to suit the focus on a free self that was deemed appropriately masculine.

Market relations, as conceived in classical liberalism, particularly suited this sort of individualism. A government service that opened up possibilities to 'all the people' increased the freedom of choice of the citizenry, just as provision organized by the private market supposedly does. By contrast, the offerings of charitably financed private agencies, such as the Ys, had been confined somewhat by the moral purposes they served. Others, such as the fresh air camps organized by churches, had limited their services only to those already designated as poor. Liberal recreation theorists proposed the removal of such barriers of moral judgment or means testing. All citizens, rich, middling, or poor, deserving or undeserving, had a right to enjoyment, and government had a role to play in increasing the range of opportunities from which citizens could choose. When the public recreationists framed their goals in terms of augmenting the choices already available by means of the market, the subjects implied in their theory were not the deviant or vulnerable class of the 'less fortunate.' Rather, this liberal theory imagined the citizen whose play the state should serve as a consumer-like, freely-choosing, self-satisfying individual. Treated as genderless, this figure was implicitly masculine.

As recreation theorists moved away from the legacy of the 1930s, they sought to put behind them the definition of recreation as paternalist or, more appropriately, maternalist moral regulation. Left to the past was the solidarist vision of reform-oriented private recreation, serving therapeutically defined communities. Ahead lay the project of providing services to 'all the people,' with each person an individual and a citizen. This new project gave recreationists a language by which they could claim a place for their programs in a liberal democratic state. For women, a danger in this language was that two of its key terms – 'individual' and 'popular demand' – were devised with masculine referents apparently in mind. In a world where men's and women's 'jobs' were normatively different, the former bounded by paid hours, programs defined for 'off-the-job' living seemed destined to fit better with men's and boys' experience. But individualism made enticing promises to women as well as to men, and an openness to popular demand offered real hope of a service that would serve citizens universally. The combination of the problems and potential of liberal democratic recreation theory thus presented a newly enlarged, though not unbounded, space in which Ontario citizens could voice their recreation needs.

Expressing Needs

'Expressed need' was supposed to define the scope and content of Ontario's new public recreation programs, begun in 1945. The harmonies and counterpoints in the expression of needs were arranged by the mix of constituencies that made up 'public recreation advocates,' which included men and women already active in recreation movement organizations, such as the Ys. They were joined by adult activity enthusiasts, from singers to softball players, newly incited to organize by the offer of government funding. Together these people, from varied backgrounds of class and culture, set up public recreation programs in nearly one hundred Ontario cities, towns, and villages between 1945 and 1948. Over the next nine years, that number would almost triple to 274 (see Tables 1.1 and 1.2). There was no difficulty in finding some kind of demand for public recreation.

What exactly this public meant when they expressed a need for recreation can be inferred from program proposals, tastes expressed through participation in public programs, and debate about deficiencies in programs. All these sources involve representations, framed to explain and to persuade. Far from telling us exhaustively about leisure preferences of Ontarians, they tell us about the needs people perceived – their own or others' – as legitimately deserving of public response. Even information on patterns of participation is dubious as evidence of 'true' tastes. The data was reported, after all, by people intent on improving, celebrating, or justifying the kinds of tastes the evidence apparently showed. Clearly visible through these sources are both old and new rationales for the need for recreation. The older ones expressed the welfare/solidarist tradition; the newer ones were framed in the terms of the more individ-

Table 1.1
Public Recreation Programs in Municipalities in Ontario, 1948

	Population (number of municipalities in category)							
	Over 100,000 (4)	50,000– 100,000 (1)	20,000– 50,000 (15)	12,000– 20,000 (11)	8,000– 12,000 (14)	4,000– 8,000 (35)	Under 4,000 (245)	Counties (54) and townships (662)	Total (1,041)
Programs with directors	4	0	9	8	8	10	10	6	55
Programs without directors	0	0	1	2	4	7	19	8	41
Total number of programs	4	0	10	10	12	17	29	14	96

Source: Ontario, Department of Education, Report of the Minister, 1949, in Ontario, *Sessional Papers,* 1951

Table 1.2
Public Recreation Programs in Ontario, 1949–57

	Receiving provincial grants	In existence
1949	105	140 (est.)
1950	138	163
1951	140 (est.)	168
1952	150 (est.)	179
1953	150	215
1954	170	–
1955	129	238
1956	196	255
1957	274	274

Source: Ontario, Department of Education, Report of the Minister, 1949–57, in Ontario, Sessional Papers, 1951–9

ualist liberal recreation theory. Within both traditions, there were distinctively masculine and feminine voices.

Playgrounds were the paradigmatic concern of the welfare recreationists. When the provincial government began to subsidize recreation programs, many towns, villages, and suburban communities were able to finance new playgrounds or to renew programs and equipment that had been allowed to deteriorate during the Depression. Local Councils of Women were active in developing and supporting playgrounds in the 1950s, as they had been since 1902. Other women's organizations – the Women's Institutes, the Business and Professional Women, and the Home and School Associations – also helped start and maintain playgrounds programs for children, especially for younger ones. Men's clubs developed playgrounds mainly as playing fields. In one rural town, for example, the recreation club organized sports (especially softball) and games with 'support' from the local Women's Institute, which provided playground equipment for 'the smaller children.' One male parks board chairman in the early 1950s wanted playgrounds programs to provide only for sports. Contemptuous of activities like leathercraft and 'dabbling with plasticine,' he protested that 'we want our children to be sportsmen.' But for the women's groups, playgrounds were not merely playing fields. Rather, like day nurseries and playschools, they offered enriched child development opportunities along with help for mothers in their daily work of entertaining and civilizing their children. This connection to child care made one male member of a recreation commission in the late 1940s question whether a nursery school was not more properly funded by the Department of Public Health and Welfare than by the provincial recreation authority.[38] His doubts were not shared by women's groups, for whom children's play activities – whether sports or parties or nature study – had long been essential to the solidarist, regulatory goals of the recreation movement.

After the Second World War, this already-familiar moral regulation logic seemed to many community organizations the best basis for a claim to the newly available public recreation funding. For many, perhaps most municipal recreation programs, recreation was understood to be sports and 'physical culture,' and its purpose was to prevent delinquency.[39] They emphasized athletics for adolescents in terms that echoed the rationales that had been offered for Depression-era boys' work. For instance, members of an organizing committee from one of the larger northern Ontario towns, calling themselves an athletic association, wrote that they wished 'to bring up' young athletes and thus to do away with 'the greater percentage of juvenile delinquency.' The link to boys was made specific by a member of the National Council for Physical Fitness, when he reported on the success of British Columbia's program of physical fitness. This program served both sexes, but the report drew particular attention to the success of the sports program in keeping down delinquency among boys. When a boys' gang disrupted Toronto in 1949, the *Financial Post* found that most of the responses to its survey of 'informed Canadians' about a 'cure for hoodlumism' favoured not only stern treatment of offenders, but also prevention of delinquency through provision of sports and recreation facilities.[40]

The theory that linked sports to crime prevention also offered a peculiarly cold war rationale for a state role in recreation. Recreation was said to guard against Communism. Both Communism and crime were seen to be encouraged by poor mental health, specifically, by uncontrolled aggression. A professor speaking in 1949 to the Ontario Recreation Association drew this connection, and his analysis was quoted in the Canadian Congress of Labour brief in 1951 to the National Council on Physical Fitness: 'Many psychiatrists feel that the only real way of combatting the Communist and the revolutionary is to avoid too much frustration of individuals – and to provide – adequate means of expressing their aggressive tendencies through play and recreation – wholesome recreation is an antidote to strife at the community, national and international level.' Premier George Drew told recreationists at their meeting in the spring of 1948 that his 'Youth Plan [was a] Means to Combat Reds,' thus justifying public recreation as a way to shape bad boys into good, non-Communist citizens.[41]

The interest in delinquency prevention, anti-Communism, and their link to a preference for sports programs may be called the 'prophylactic' agenda in the post-war recreation movement. It attracted the efforts of men's community groups. One of the Kinsmen Club's earliest projects was the Hamilton Boys' Council, founded during the inter-war years as a 'junior edition of civic government.' A new, mixed-gender descendant of this form of club, called the Teen-Town, was widespread after the war. The Kiwanis Club started a national recreation periodical called *Young Canada*, and it promoted the view that, because of 'help received through re-creation in expressing latent abilities during leisure time, people find greater happiness and consequently appreciate more our Democratic Way of Life, and are less liable to lend an ear to "sales-talk" of foreign doctrines.' In various Ontario communities, these men's clubs, along with the Lions, Knights of Columbus, and the Canadian Legion, were common contributors of money, labour, and program direction to municipal public recreation plans. Often, when these clubs initiated publicly supported recreation after the war, their goals were inspired by a grand political agenda – 'fighting foreign 'isms.'[42]

While this agenda seems to have driven men's groups and to have been directed primarily at boys, mixed sex recreation committees and community groups also promoted teen dances for boys and girls, with an eye to preventing delinquency. Various recreation experts spoke of teen dances as providing 'healthy social growth' or as teaching teenagers 'how to get along with the opposite sex in a wholesome and acceptable way.' Perhaps because dances were easier than league sports to arrange, they were a commonplace item in municipal recreation programs, as they had been for private agencies such as the YWCA since the 1920s. With few costs other than the time of volunteer chaperones and the use of a hall, dances evoked little in the way of an elaborate or intense ideological justification from municipal recreation's 'public.' Nonetheless, as Mary Louise Adams has argued, the sexual development of youth and not just the training of boys for work and politics was part of what 'the people' expected recreation programs to address.[43]

Women's groups shared with the men's groups an interest in providing recreation for children and youth, but the priorities of the women constituted a 'reproductive' agenda that sometimes led them to criticize what was offered as recreation. When sports compromised the safety of younger children at play, a Brantford woman asked for restrictions on sports. In a northern Ontario town, women protested against the sports-dominated youth program and sought financial support for activities they felt would interest young girls. As a result, in the years that followed, a ladies' program director was hired and new programs began for both women and girls. Women were also at the forefront of objections to male-led, sports-only recreation programs in an eastern Ontario town. In a conflict that was fought on a Catholic–Protestant division as well as on issues of what recreation should be, a woman social worker joined with a municipal councillor to organize opposition to the appointment of a popular sports leader as recreation director.[44] Expressions of demand for recreation by women were often critical of the way sports and recreation were conflated in the discourse of delinquency prevention.

It may be that women's organizations also objected to the passion for arenas that was prevalent in many towns.[45] Children who used arenas were mainly those old enough to travel across town by themselves, although younger children would often be taken by their parents to special events or by their school teachers to scheduled classes. By contrast, playgrounds and small, natural ice rinks in vacant lots, supervised by neighbourhood parents, were safe places for younger children to go to. In some towns, money spent on an arena meant that no money was available to resurface playgrounds, provide drinking fountains, or set up new neighbourhood rinks. Arenas could be in direct budgetary competition with playgrounds or other programs, and were enthusiastically promoted by men's service clubs.[46]

In expressing recreation needs, even narrowly conceived as 'for our children,' the specific contribution women made was to speak for younger children, mirroring the reproductive values that were understood as maternal. Men's voices addressed the role of leisure in converting youth, especially boys, into adults able to work, to vote, and to form families. Episodes of tension and incomprehension between men and women recreation volunteers suggest that gendered voices may well have represented genuinely divergent perceptions of need. But for women, at least, the reproductive preoccupations of their rhetoric may also show that they knew well that they would be heard on these topics, and not on others. This point will be discussed further in Chapter 6.

Just as images of fatherhood and motherhood structured the expression by adults of the needs of children, so too did gendered norms (and patterns) of labour shape the contours of adult recreation demand.

Needs were obviously being defined by work when men in rural Ontario were attracted to 'recreational' adult education classes in practical farm topics, such as farm machinery repair, motor mechanics, farm engineering, and electricity. Similarly, women's work as mothers helps explain why women were the chief customers for the parent education classes that were frequently co-sponsored by municipal recreation departments and Home and School Associations.[47] When women asked for parent education classes, and men sought farm machinery courses, they were expressing an interest in 'constructive' leisure. Their recreations were simply a relaxed and perhaps stimulating appendage of their work. They were using leisure time to learn skills that would make their work easier, maybe even more enjoyable.

But in other forms of adult recreation, work and leisure were linked in less earnestly constructive ways. Organized by gender because it was related to gendered patterns in work, some public recreation demand was, nonetheless, primarily about 'gratification,' just as recreation theorist Romney would have wished. Arts and craft classes were more like playtime pursuits than were courses in machinery repair or parent education, and undoubtedly the women who formed the vast majority of clients for these classes took them for fun. Women learning crafts reported having a good time socially. They took pleasure in making attractive things for their homes and for gifts. That they were also aware this form of play saved them from having to buy presents or home decorations, or that they could even sell their quilts or other crafts for extra income, does not mean that these useful classes were not largely pursued as sources of pleasure.[48] Similarly, the expression of interest by married women in having recreation activities available for the family 'as a unit' may have reflected a desire for help in their work as mothers, but it surely also indicated their hopes for some sociable time with their families.[49]

Family recreation activities were just one form of what recreationists in the 1950s labelled, pseudo-technically, 'social recreation.' Publicly funded social recreation included dances, singalongs, meals, and card parties, exactly the sorts of activities that were sponsored by many private clubs, both women's and men's.[50] In public recreation, these events were rarely, if ever, segregated by sex, and they were presumably enjoyed by all (or at least most) of those who attended. Women, however, were more likely to have their enjoyment of these events combined with the 'joy of effort': the 'social convenors' on local recreation committees were almost always women. This arrangement mirrored the expected gender division of labour in married couples, with the wife responsible for hostessing. In public recreation as in churches, unions, and service clubs, the ladies auxiliaries were most often the organizers of meals and social hours. (When the men in mixed groups took on the catering and serving duties in special annual events, it was an occasion worthy of note.[51]) In social recreation, then, as in the other public recreation programs women apparently enjoyed, there remained something of the blending of family work and play that marked the pleasures prescribed for women in Depression-era recreation theory.

That the most common of expressed needs among Ontario men was for sports facilities comes as no surprise. The lighted playing fields many communities built with the aid of the provincial recreation program helped make possible a greater number of adult baseball teams (with men's teams being larger and more numerous than women's). Hockey (mainly but not exclusively a male sport then as now) was notorious among recreationists for how its supporters and players dominated facilities committees. Businessmen promoted arenas, not only for recreation, but as revenue-generating, possibly profit-making venues for semi-professional sport and touring shows. While activity enthusiasts eagerly claimed public funding, some of the demand for sports facilities also came from social agencies concerned about the dangers of men's leisure.[52] The men who only came to these facilities to play could, and undoubtedly did ignore the motives, high or low, that moved social workers, unions, and businesses to express what they thought were adult men's recreation needs.

The recreation needs that adult Ontarians gave expression to were shaped by gender relations and by the tastes that were prescriptively deemed normal. But we should not forget the limits on the power of social prescription and the varieties of cultural traditions that might prompt apparently unusual (but in their own terms perfectly 'normal') hobby preferences in both men and women. There were, in fact, a few men in many crafts – some in painting and leatherwork and a few in rug hooking. Perhaps some of these participants came from cultures less likely to label amateur artistry as a feminine pursuit. The women who took woodworking classes – and there were some who did – may just have been adventurous individuals, or they may have had as role models mothers or aunts skilled in craft work other than sewing and knitting.[53] Adult women played some sports in sex-segregated teams and leagues – mainly curling, softball, and bowling, figure skating among younger women, and, in larger communities, basketball and hockey.[54] These exceptions indicate, of course, that the provision of recreation services need not have been as patterned by gender as it was. There existed the possibility of more diverse tastes, and a public recreation service committed to equality might well have sought to encourage these. But there was no compelling moral rationale to invoke in support of making adult men more 'sensitive to beauty' or grown women more 'sportsmanlike.'

However, the innovative liberal trend in recreation theory had a real potential to support a more purely hedonist understanding of the recreation needs of adult women. By insisting that all individuals had the right to pleasure, theorists such as Romney put claims by women for recreation services on the same footing as those by men. The opportunity that this kind of recreation theory afforded to women to claim rights actually was recognized by some women active as volunteers in the public recreation movement. The female president of the Ontario Recreation Association in 1951 urged 'the recognition of the rights of women and girls in Recreation,' concluding that 'the first consideration in our work with women and girls is that we think of them as *INDIVIDUALS.*' That is, not as mothers. A woman on the Fort Frances Recreation Commission wanted to see her community redress the inequality of service to women and girls; no longer should they get 'the short end of the stick.' In these and other, sometimes subtler, turns of phrase, equality language and rights talk helped justify expenditures for women's sports, craft classes, and clubs.[55]

When, in the late 1940s and early 1950s, Ontarians expressed recreation needs through new public recreation programs, they used language shaped by recreation theory and by perceptions of the proper 'jobs' in life of men and women. Promulgated by schools, churches, service clubs, and private recreation associations, recreation theory (both old and new) gave Ontarians the terms with which to express leisure needs. Recreation theory's imagined subject was most often masculine – the industrial worker, the consumer of commercial recreations, or the boy in need of guidance or of discipline. Women and girls in parallel social positions were understood as quasi-masculine; only maternal and familial recreation needs were distinctly feminine. In the face of recreation theory's focus on masculine experience, women's voices sometimes had a corrective tone, as in the attack on sport in playgrounds and in the assertion that women, too, were individuals. The former charge drew on the older recreation theory, which made room for women to speak as mothers; the latter criticism came from the new recreation theory's assertion of universal rights to individual enjoyment.

Both of these sources of critique found support in a provincial agency committed to universality of service and to a democratic responsiveness. But, as it turned out, it was not easy in the context of the 1950s to devise programs and administrative policies that addressed women both as mothers and as individuals. Part of the reason for this difficulty was that, provincially as well as municipally, the paid leaders of the recreation movement were torn between the welfarist conception of recreation and the liberal, hedonist one. Each understood women in distinct terms, and each offered specific possibilities for providing benefits to them. How the needs of women and girls would be defined and met as public recreation grew would depend on more, therefore, than just the expressions of need of individuals or even groups. Whether a wide variety of such expressions would be encouraged, or even heard, would depend on the relative fortunes of pleasure and disciplinary purpose in the rationales for specifically state-funded recreation. Central in shaping these rationales were the odd characters who made up the province's Community Programmes Branch, to whose early years this story now turns.

2

Making a Democratic Bureaucracy,
1945–1949

A very hardworking group of civil servants toiled long hours during the first four years of peacetime to arrange new opportunities for other Ontarians to play. More than any other institution of the recreation movement, the Department of Education's Community Programmes Branch (CPB) did the ideological work of securing recreation's place in the welfare state. As unelected officials, they might seem to have been beyond 'politics.' But if politics means devising a policy vision and selling it to the public, their work was politics. If it means managing sensitive relations with their federal and municipal counterparts, these men and women were political actors. And if it means wielding authority to achieve social change, these idealistic bureaucrats were as much engaged in politics as any of their contemporaries in social movements. Their approach to these political pursuits determined how public money was spent and how information circulated. They had real power and real opportunities to use it coercively or responsively. Much of what public recreation would become depended on how the CPB staff understood their jobs.

In fact, within the CPB there were two competing visions of how public recreation might be democratically administered. One was a technocratic liberalism, of the sort Doug Owram argues emerged in Canadian public agencies in the inter-war years. This view of public administration had strong affinities to Chicago's 'human ecology' school of social thought.[1] Its proponents in the CPB believed that empirical social research would identify recreation needs whose fulfilment would produce social well-being. Unlike more openly moralist reformers, they did not claim to know, on the basis of general principles, which recreations would have this effect. The other vision that was current at the CPB was at once more populist, hedonist, and individualist. Instead of offering a program determined by research, the ideal in this vision was to support community organization around expressed needs. This norm represented a shift away from rule by those with expert knowledge. The democratic civil service, in this formulation, responded to public demand and did not impose programs from above, ultimately deferring to the authority of individual choice. In the words of one CPB director, the policy was 'based on the strong belief that it is the right of the individual to choose his leisure time activities.'[2] Such a policy reflected the public recreationists' sensitivity, as liberals, to criticism that their work illegitimately invaded the privacy of civil society. It also expressed their aversion to their predecessors' reputation for stuffiness and Victorian prudishness. As leisure reformers, they wanted to change Ontarians' experience of spare time. But as liberals, their conscious purpose was to achieve reform without coercion or condescension.

What follows in this chapter is an account of how the connected fortunes of these two visions shaped the beginnings of the CPB. By 1949 it had assumed the institutional form that was to last through the 1950s. Similarly, by 1949 it had come to contain within itself, in tense conjunction, advocates of service to 'the people,' directed chiefly by private leaders, and promoters of service to social purpose, directed by government experts. The policy wrangling that this conjunction produced was a family quarrel about democratic methods among liberals. As I argued in the previous chapter, the more populist of these visions endorsed some kinds of feminine entitlement to public recreation services. But this same view, in its individualism, disparaged the moral and social reform tradition from which many demands among adult women arose. The more technocratic liberalism, which was explicitly sympathetic to social purpose, offered legitimation for service to women and girls through the findings of social research. At stake in this family quarrel among liberals, then, was the basis on which women and girls could claim public services.

The Two Elements

The CPB was the union of two Ontario government programs that had both started in the 1940s. One focused on adult education programs and the other on physical fitness, but both were responses to the National Physical Fitness Act of 1943, which established a physical fitness program that was intended to be part of a proposed national health insurance system. Its advocates argued that if the state was to secure its citizens against the financial risks of ill health, then it had an interest in promoting good health. The state also had an interest in fostering a healthy military force. Armed forces recruiters had rejected between 16 and 33 per cent of applicants for basic training during the Second World War. Ian Mackenzie, minister of pensions and national health, claimed that a physical training program like the popular Pro-Rec program in his home province of British Columbia was therefore in the public interest. Not only would Canadian men be better suited for war and for work, but, as an afterthought he argued, as well, that more physically active women and children would enjoy improved 'intellectual and social morale.'[3]

A key component of the new national physical fitness program was the promotion across Canada of an ideal of 'total fitness.'[4] For this task, Mackenzie hired a Pro-Rec man from British Columbia, Danish athlete Ian Eisenhardt. From 1944 to 1946, Eisenhardt travelled across the country to promote fitness programs that stressed broad participation and a notion of physical fitness that included not only 'brisk exercise' but also community singing and good health habits. As he explained, the goal was to 'inculcate in our youth a desire for greater physical strength, better mental alertness and a certain spiritual discipline.' In his recollections, a former municipal recreation director in Ontario recalled that Eisenhardt did a lot to 'excite people.'[5] As early as 1945, according to an Ontario physical educationist, numerous organizations in Ontario were putting pressure on the provincial government to take part in the national fitness plan. The president of Lewis Craft Supplies wrote to Premier George Drew in May of that year to say that the comments of a speaker in the Opposition on the virtues of the National Physical Fitness Programme had 'registered very strongly in the mind of many folks whom we know ...' By no means a disinterested party, this manufacturer of hobby materials wrote that 'physical fitness and Recreation will stimulate a common interest, and go a long way toward bringing about an ideal relationship between Capital and Labor.'[6] Like other programs of the welfare state, this one derived some of its appeal as a mechanism of social integration.

Drew was hesitant to get involved in the national program because he disliked federally led cost-shared programs, not because he doubted the value of public recreation. In fact, he was known as one of its keener supporters. Like Ian Mackenzie, Drew was familiar with a popular recreation-related program in his own constituency. As MPP for East Simcoe, he was aware of the success in Simcoe County of the Community Life Training Institute. This University of Toronto–based extension program worked closely with the county's active Federation of Agriculture to organize adult education, including recreation. Perhaps because of such organizations in Ontario, Drew, unlike Mackenzie, understood that recreation was more than a means to physical fitness. Recreationists recall that Drew had reportedly not only been impressed during the war by the British Central Council on Physical Recreation but also pleasantly surprised by the interest of Canadian servicemen in the 'educational and recreational' programs offered them in England. As early as 1943, at the beginning of a five-year stint as minister of education, Drew had acquired a reputation among some adult educationists as an ally. When Eisenhardt's promotional work began to arouse organized interest in recreation, Drew responded by establishing Ontario's own recreation and adult education programs. The regulations for these were drafted and approved in September 1945. The adult education program was not a wholly new creation but instead was a reorganization under government auspices, with government funding, of existing adult education organizations.[7] By contrast, the Physical Fitness and Recreation program within the Physical and Health Education Branch was entirely new.

Established in reaction to Ottawa's initiative, the Ontario fitness program benefited from Eisenhardt's publicity work. Even before there were regulations defining the program, its new head, J.K. (Johnny) Tett, fielded inquiries made to the 'Director, Physical Fitness Program.' When the regulations were in place, he and his program still retained the image of physical fitness that had been established by Ian Eisenhardt. Operating under this image, Tett, with no full-time field representatives to promote the program, was nonetheless inundated with more proposals for recreation committee by-laws and more requests for personal appearances than he could accommodate.[8] Because of the federal program's name, the national program's trailblazing publicity identified recreation with physical activities, even though Eisenhardt's 'total fitness' concept meant more than that. Tett also intended something much broader by 'recreation' than merely a non-elite form of sport.

Although Tett's own background was in competitive swimming and boy's camps, he soon became familiar with contemporary recreation theory. Assigned the task of developing regulations for the new program, he went to the United States to research municipal recreation organizations. He came back from this experience with a view of recreation as more than the physical complement to adult education. Recreation was to include activities of all types for all ages. In his first memorandum to Drew, Tett marked out the new territory, distinguishing his recreation program by its hedonist goal: 'whilst the Federal Government are fostering a sports and physically active programme with a goal of physical fitness, this province is fostering an all round recreational programme *with a goal of happiness,* including a high standard of physical fitness' (emphasis added).[9]

Part of his job became selling this more inclusive concept of recreation to those members of the public who were interested mainly in sports for young men and boys. He was personally well-equipped for this job. As a young male athlete and a war hero, he was acceptable to the sporting interests. But he was also manifestly representative of a new start, a fresh beginning. He showed up for public occasions casually dressed in his old pilot's jacket, and put across his message without making a formal speech. A friend recalled him fondly as 'a bit of a psychopathic, hard-drinking, wild-living character who in one half day had more imaginative ideas than 90% of the recreation personnel I've run into since ... He was an idea man and a promoter and [had] enough wisdom to get people who were capable and [had] enough personal security for all his schemes.' Even those who sometimes found him frustrating to work with acknowledged that he was 'quite a card,' who 'always had a gimmick to attract attention.'[10]

Tett helped change recreation's image from the prim and class-biased one of 'wholesome' and 'constructive' activities to a more inclusive one of popular fun. A newspaper report on one of his speeches represented him as free from condescension and from commitment to any supposedly 'higher' purpose: '"You can't just go home and look at your wife all evening, no matter how lovely she is," said Squadron Ldr. Tett in a Toronto address yesterday, outlining the recently introduced regulations for encouraging physical fitness programs in Ontario. "People sit around in the evening just looking at each other until they almost bust," he said. "What they need is some form of recreation."'[11] With comments like these, Tett said that he was fighting, not the intemperance or delinquency of a deviant few, but a common condition of boredom. His picture of a husband and wife, without children, drawn from the man's perspective, offered flattering reassurances to the woman. The solution he offered for boredom was not simply the man's escape to a tavern or a pool hall. Both the husband and the 'lovely' wife needed recreation. The reporter implied that recreation was physical fitness. Tett, however, was apparently encouraging any recreation that would relieve the tedium of an idle evening.

Tett's unconventional style and his openness to a broad definition of recreation indicates that he brought to public recreation the populist hedonism of the new recreation theory. But he also represented another key difference between public recreation and the old-style promoters of private recreation agencies. Unlike, for example, the community leaders who campaigned for the Ys, he was offering money instead of asking for it. Under the regulations he administered, municipalities were eligible for annual grants of up to thirty-five hundred dollars, mainly for salaries, if they appointed a local committee and conducted a non-profit 'community programme of training in physical fitness and recreation.' These grants accounted substantially for the popularity of Tett's program. Even though the grants were to cover only one-third of the salaries paid to employees, they were an incentive for starting programs.[12]

With the offer of financial help, channelled through municipal governments, Tett was able both to promote and, subtly, to threaten to enforce his vision of recreation. He carefully disavowed any intention of tying grants to a required program. He described the CPB as 'primarily a service organization'; its policy was to provide 'services on request and in response to expressed need.' However, he also drew the attention of municipal representatives to the inclusion in the regulations of terms such as 'recreation' (as well as physical fitness) and 'persons' (instead of just boys or youth). The subtlest hint of this sort was sufficient to make clear to representatives of municipal government the possibility that grants could be refused if programs were not, in the all-encompassing phrase of the regulations, 'approved by the Minister.'[13] In later years, the coercive power inherent in the grant system would be used, but at the beginning it was not. Tett's recreation program incited municipalities to offer recreation services, and it promised that all Ontarians would be served by them in new ways, according to their expressed needs. In using liberal democracy's universalist language, Tett encouraged municipal governments at least to attend to women's and girls' expressions of recreation needs, and he provided the terms under which such needs might be framed.

Drew's adult education program, the Ontario Adult Education Board (OAEB), had rather different beginnings, staffing, contact with the citizenry, and funding.[14] It originated in existing university extension departments: its chairman was Dr W.J. Dunlop, director of university extension at the University of Toronto, and its first staff member, the director, had held the same position at Queen's before the war. Lacking the novelty of the health-linked national initiative and not having much appeal to Ontario's numerous sport enthusiasts, the OAEB staff faced a different promotional task. They were offering self-improvement with more an intellectual base than a physical one. Their purpose was to cultivate directly those social qualities that, for physical fitness advocates, were by-products of good health and good sportsmanship. In 1948, reflecting on their accomplishments up to that point, the staff of the OAEB wrote that 'good citizenship is the underlying objective of all recreation programmes.' A good citizen would be altruistic and socially responsible, tolerant of conflicting opinions, and capable of clear thinking. In a phrase redolent of post-war liberal values, they wrote that a good citizen would 'prefer methods of discussion and persuasion to methods of force.'[15] With this in mind, the OAEB promoted various leisure-time pursuits, because they were thought to help develop these qualities, not for the inherent enjoyment they offered.

For some of the staff members, this distinction between pleasure and social purpose was unambiguous. One OAEB staff member, a woman who handled the parent education classes and the Ontario listeners' group of the *Citizen's Forum* radio show and who had been the provincial secretary of the Federation of Women Teachers Associations of Ontario between 1924 and 1944, later described 'all the work' she did with the OAEB and then with the CPB as 'training people for citizenship.' She distinguished clearly between recreation and adult education, and she also seems to have shared the view of another staff member in those early days, who said that the adult educationists 'were superior to the recreation crowd.' She characterized recreationists like Tett who saw themselves as fostering 'happiness' somewhat dismissively as 'people who just wanted fun.' By contrast, adult educationists, in her view, were saying to people: 'we can help you to grow, mentally and physically and every way.'[16]

Her commitment to individual improvement through education was probably shared by other OAEB staff members. Five of the first seven assistant directors were former teachers, and one was an Anglican minister administering an adult education program.[17] Very likely, the one whose background I have been unable to determine was also an educator. The teachers were all experienced administrators, having been principals, school inspectors, education officers during the war, or directors of extension programs. In his recommendations for hiring the first two of the assistants, both men, the director linked their personal qualities, credentials, and administrative skills: the men were 'deeply interested in adult education, had high academic training, were excellent organizers and administrators, met people easily and had lengthy experience in education.'[18] Thus, the new OAEB staff were older, more highly educated, and more experienced in the professional role than Tett. They were undoubtedly accustomed to exercising authority over those they served.

From this kind of experience, it was comparatively easy for the staff to assert that recreation was not 'just having fun' but a means of helping people to a higher level of culture. Fostering enjoyment was one of their goals, but so, explicitly, was social improvement, represented by the making of 'better citizens, better communities, a better country.' Even the formulation of their educational goals indicated that the OAEB staff judged those whom they sought to serve. Popular commercial entertainment was dismissed gently as 'somewhat standardized ... radio, easily read literature (magazine), easily digested music, easily taught hobbies.' Sporting activity was approved, but deemed in need of 'careful training' in order to 'ensure the development of real sportsmanship.' Mere involvement of 'a majority of our population into activities suited to their age, taste and condition' might be 'statistically' a 'successful job of promoting recreation,' but 'socially and psychologically, it could be a dismal failure.'[19] The adult educationists' job was not simply to provide opportunities for recreation of all kinds, but to help people to achieve better kinds of recreation.

Unlike Johnny Tett's agency, the OAEB had in its mandate the requirement that it determine which kinds of adult education programming were best for Ontario's citizens. The board's defining regulations required that it 'formulate ... a comprehensive plan of adult education for Ontario.' To do this, the board proposed to 'survey the needs of the people' and, by supplying free programs that imitated the 'simple' or 'popular' commercial activities, to increase participation. From this basis, its staff would be able to take participants forward to 'a deeper appreciation of cultural arts.' This program sounds, of course, very much like the welfarist, moral reform tradition, but the adult educationists were more accepting of popular recreational forms than their predecessors had been. They condescended to commercial amusements, but did not pronounce them anathema. Rather than offering just moral censure, they designed a program of research and social planning to advance popular tastes. To this end, the OAEB held workshops in some of the large municipalities. From the data collected at these, its staff developed a list of needs: basic English and citizenship training, parent education, current events programs, and elementary skills courses in arts, crafts, drama, music, sports, playground supervision, the conduct of meetings, public speaking, and basic leadership.[20]

Without disputing the possibility of a real interest in, or need for, such programs on the part of some people, one may wonder how much the workshop process structured the resulting list. By comparison, a woman recreation leader in the 1930s gave a quite different list of activities as those most popular in the business girls' clubs she had directed. Based on her experience, a list of 'expressed needs' would have included tap- and clog-dancing, social dancing, personal hygiene, social etiquette, and lectures on art, travel, and history; the only items in common with the OAEB's list were dramatics and current events.[21] Compared to her list, the OAEB's reveals a bias towards serving needs in the areas of politics and productive work, as opposed to social skills. The main emphasis in personal relationships is on the interaction between parents and their children. Considering what was left out of the OAEB staff's list, it seems likely that their workshops were attended mainly (but not exclusively) by older married people. The interests of women as mothers were well represented; arguably, even the skill courses in sports and music, set at an elementary level, might have been designed to train adults to lead activities for youths. On the other hand, the business girls' list is more simply about a desire to have fun and, in particular, to have romantic, probably heterosexual, fun. This was a taste whose expression liberal recreation theory recognized and endorsed more readily than did the OAEB.

The survey method the OAEB used allowed it to sideline whole categories of need, whether women's or others. For the OAEB, the public's 'expressed need' was the adult educator's raw material; needs that did not lend themselves to a higher purpose could be dismissed. For example, when, in 1947, the OAEB became part of the new Community Programmes Section, the name called forth the expression of a certain need that, to one of the staff trained in education, seemed absurd. In a 1971 interview, he called the name 'a bit of a joke': 'When people heard about the new name, the Scottish people would call us up and ask us if we could find some Scottish comedian person and a good pipe band for Robbie Burns night and the Irishmen wanted something for March 17th ... They thought we were an agency for these fancy special do's.'[22] Later, multiculturalism policy would lead civil servants to take such requests more seriously, but for the OAEB, Scots and Irish variety nights were not 'community' programs. Encoded in the word community was a particular image of a citizen subjectivity whose development required the intervention of state-funded, professional leadership by recreationists.

Rather than following popular taste, the OAEB studied it and sought to use the information strategically to direct cultural change. From the beginning, it granted funding support only to agencies whose programs suited its 'comprehensive plan.' Most of its budget went to pay the salaries of field representatives, who entered the field with an array of services to offer. 'In the beginning,' one of these field workers has recalled, 'we went out and knocked on doors. We used to have to recruit people for weaving courses and parent ed courses by literally knocking on doors and selling an idea.'[23] However interested in democracy the OAEB staff were, their version of a democratic civil service was far more directive and prescriptive than was Tett's. But through its comprehensive plan, the OAEB did try to appeal to some conventionally feminine tastes and interests, and thus it, too, provided terms through which women and girls might claim recreation services. In defining certain feminine leisure pursuits as properly in the public interest, the OAEB's plan explicitly welcomed women and girls into social citizenship, though in a limited way.

The Union of the Two

In spite of, and also because of their differences, the efforts of the OAEB and its field staff and comprehensive plan dovetailed with Johnny Tett's less expert-driven program. Although he was committed to 'overall' recreation, Tett himself was best equipped to serve sports groups. He was in a physical education branch of the department, his background was in athletics, and his program was, at the start, publicly identified with physical fitness. But the OAEB, unlike Tett, had the staff to train and supervise the recreation directors hired by municipal recreation committees under Tett's program.[24] If a community leader wanted an inspirational speech to help start a program, he or she would likely invite Tett. But in a program's ongoing development, the OAEB field representatives could supply speakers on special topics, performers in the arts, or course instructors.[25]

Given the connections between the two programs in their daily work, it is not surprising that, on 1 May 1947, the OAEB ceased to exist and the field staff became members of a new entity, the Community Programmes Section of the Physical and Health Education Branch. Suppos-

edly, the former OAEB staff were to become the first line of contact
between the public and the newly formed section. However, Tett somehow managed to avoid being relegated to a back room. In October 1948
he informed municipal recreation committees that he was now the province's 'Recreation Advisor,' available for consultation on organizational
problems. Also, he said he would continue to be their contact for the
grants-in-aid scheme. Yet in another respect, the reorganization confirmed in the Community Programmes Section the prescriptive bent of
the OAEB. The new (designated 'acting') director was the head of the
Royal Ontario Museum's extension department, E.C. Cross.[26]

Clearly, the OAEB's comprehensive plan for cultural improvement
would still have a role in guiding the new agency.[27] A report on the first
six months of the section's activities revealed the plan's continuing
effect. The activities listed matched the needs identified in the OAEB
survey: courses in crafts, public speaking, and citizenship; leader training in parent education, crafts, and recreation; *Citizen's Forum* listening
groups and radio broadcasts on 'local problems'; and groups for drama,
choral singing, and orchestral music.[28] But, at the same time, Tett's
influence was far from extinguished. In the fall of 1947 a conference of
the province's recreation directors gave Tett an opportunity to mount
some resistance to the adult educationists' prescriptive agenda.

He invited the exponent of a market-mimicking model of public recreation, G. Ott Romney, to address the conference. What exactly happened at the conference is unclear. Those who were asked about it in
1971 spoke of violent disagreements and the productive working out of
differences between 'two sides' or positions, whose contents they did
not specify. The nature of these two 'sides' is suggested by the claim of a
former OAEB staff member that he and his cohort were able to talk Tett
into giving greater support for arts and crafts and drama. More direct
evidence of the two different agendas for programming, however, is
offered by Tett's letter of thanks to Romney, who had given a speech
presenting his non-judgmental, individualist, consumerist view of recreation. In his speech, Romney had remarked, for example, that 'Recreation does not have to seek justification – the dividends are self-
produced. It is a cafeteria of opportunity ...' As usual, he insisted that
'negative' definitions that labelled recreation as 'charity' or 'an antidote
for delinquency' were wrong. Tett's letter of thanks indicates the significance of Romney's perspective for the growth of the Community Programmes Section: 'Approximately three years ago I was given the
opportunity of assisting in the development of community recreation as

a part of the every day life of this province. My greatest problem and my greatest efforts were connected with the interpretation of recreation and the development according to the interpretation. I was delighted when your interpretation cleared the air in no uncertain manner. May I express my sincere appreciation.' Tett took a less instrumentalist, more simply hedonist view of recreation than did his ex-OAEB colleagues. His personality and background won him support among the sports-oriented recreation directors, but to convince the adult educationists he needed the intellectual backing of an American theorist.[29] Romney gave intellectual respectability to Tett's commitment to non-prescriptive maximizing of recreation opportunities. Trusting popular tastes was more than just 'looking for fun.'

On the ideological front, the 1947 conference gave Tett's populist liberalism new authority. Certainly, technocratic liberalism and its expert planning impulses continued through the 1950s to exert a vital counter-pressure against the populist variant of liberalism. But historical accident and administrative convenience gave particular influence in the CPB's formative years to Tett's ideological preferences, and especially to his dislike of explicitly prescribed programming. The course of events, more than the outcomes of debates, would make this corner of the civil service especially careful to avoid bureaucracy's authoritarian tendencies.

In determining Tett's effectiveness, the crucial fact was that he remained the administrator of the grant system. In municipal correspondence files of the section (raised to branch status after 1949), Tett's presence predominates. This was so until he left to join the RCAF in November 1952, even during the 1947–9 directorship of E.C. Cross. Of the ninety-six municipal recreation committees in existence in 1948, almost half had been organized by Tett alone, and with twenty-six he had some help from the OAEB assistant directors. Even after the amalgamation in the spring of 1947, Tett continued to be the person to whom municipal representatives and the former OAEB field staff addressed questions about eligibility for grants. He also received requests for help in finding candidates for recreation director positions. Because the regulations stipulated that municipalities had to have a local committee appointed by municipal council to be eligible for grants, Tett also fielded questions about the establishment and legal framework of these committees.[30]

Tett's close involvement with the grants system meant that he was in touch with events in many Ontario towns, cities, and villages. He was 'on the move all the time,' doing 'all the promotion,' according to one rec-

reation director. At least once, and probably more often, he wrote personally to thank a particularly effective supporter of recreation. Thus,
for the many Ontarians engaged in organizing recreation services, Tett
continued after 1947 to be the most important representative of the provincial government. It is not surprising, therefore, that even while Cross
was director, a complaint about the failure of the recreation program in
a town, allegedly the result of the lack of 'an extensive selling program
... from the top,' was sent to Tett, rather than Cross.[31]

Tett's response to this complaint expressed the image he wished his
program to present: provincial grants were to help programs initiated
and funded mainly at the municipal level; the provincial contribution
was to be responsive, not directive, to avoid interfering with 'community
initiative and autonomy.' As Tett wrote to a new recreation director,
nothing in the regulations would 'hamper [him] in any way from running the most complete programme of recreation for all the persons in
the community.'[32] In other words, the grants system would not specify
the program to be offered, but would support attempts to broaden
options for recreation. A recreation director or volunteer leader seeking
a deeper understanding of recreation's goals would be encouraged to
abandon a moral reform, social welfare orientation. Universality of service rather than an improving 'comprehensive' program was the con-
stant theme of Tett's advice.

The relative weight of Tett's influence by 1949 was indicated by the
new regulations that officially amalgamated the two programs that had
been grafted together two years earlier. The title for the regulations,
'Programmes of Recreation,' reflected the primacy of Tett's division.
More important, the new regulations continued the allocation of funds
to municipal recreation committees for their facilities and recreation
staff. The new CPB exercised less direct budgetary control over its clients
than had the OAEB. However, the adult educationists' 'comprehensive
plan' had left its legacy: the regulations now contained a definition of
recreation as 'cultural, educational, physical and social activities.'[33] A
rhetorical purpose was undoubtedly served by the order of this list.

In the spring of 1949, events would put more control into Tett's
hands after E.C. Cross fell seriously ill, and in August Tett was made acting director of the new branch. The deputy minister made it clear that
Tett was to consult on questions of policy with an advisory committee
composed of other CPB staff members. One of the adult educationists
on the staff recalled that pressures from higher up in the department
discouraged Tett from shifting the program too far away from a 'cul-

tural' focus.[34] And yet, when Cross died in February 1950, Tett was appointed director.

This appointment has nowhere been clearly explained. Depicted by some of his previous co-workers as wilful and eccentric, Tett would seem to have been an unlikely candidate for increased responsibilities. The more predictable choice would have been Ken Young, a man older than Tett and highly respected among the adult educationists who formed the majority of the staff.[35] Indeed, Young became acting director when Tett left in 1952, and in 1954 he became director. In 1949, however, Young was one of several field representatives, whereas Tett was administering the grants system, a job he had done since 1945. This difference probably accounts for Tett's promotion. Tett had never ceased to control grants, and thus had established himself as a key administrator. However brash and youthful he may have been, he was the author of the system of grants to municipalities and its most experienced manager. With his promotion, his ability to enact his vision of democratic public administration was enhanced.

Liberalism and Democratic Welfare Policy

Tett and the OAEB both claimed that their programs for Ontario citizens' leisure time were innovative by virtue of being democratic. The OAEB's claim was based on its use of the survey method as a diagnostic tool and its commitment to fostering citizens worthy of democracy. Tett's claim was based on maximizing the conditions for choice in leisure-time pursuits. The OAEB's methods led to a compensatory program that responded to unmet 'needs' rather than to the greatest popular demand. The comprehensiveness of its program was limited by the biases of its survey research and by a continuing allegiance to the view that a recreation interest was not a recreation 'need' unless it was conducive to cultural improvement. A broad streak of solidarism and its fundamental idealism made the former OAEB in the CPB unconsciously illiberal in their unwillingness to respond to some choices.

Tett's idea of democratic service privileged universality of choice over a prescriptively complete program. He appears to have hoped that, given public funding, municipal governments would feel obliged to provide services to make recreation available to everyone. Because public money was everyone's money, recreation programs funded in this way would be open to claims from all citizens. In effect, market-like forces of demand would invisibly produce a program that served everyone's needs. This classically liberal faith in 'consumer demand,' so to speak, contrasted with the views of the adult educationists, who came from a social liberal milieu that endorsed planning as the way to a better life for all.[36] Thus, two models existed within the CPB of how public recreation might democratically serve 'all the people.' On the one hand, the OAEB orientation, frankly regulatory (however much it claimed to be based in objectively recognizable needs), looked back to the moral reform, social welfare tradition. On the other hand, Tett's methods were in tune with Romney's 'positive approach to recreation.' The fortunes of Tett's career, enhanced by the unhappy accident of E.C. Cross's death, meant that this 'positive' approach was reinforced within the branch.

In their reliance on social science instruments, the OAEB's methods resembled the technocratic liberalism that Doug Owram has described in *The Government Generation*. Instead of Keynesian economics, the adult educators drew on University of Chicago–style sociology. But they shared with federal civil servants the view that the best hope for social welfare lay in knowledge rather than moral exhortation. Tett's liberalism cast the power relations between state and civil society in a different mould. Just as secular as the OAEB members, Tett was less enamoured of professional control. While the abandoning of moral-religious discourse isolated economists from non-experts, as Owram has argued, the same secularization had the potential to lessen the difference between professional recreationists and the people they advised. Tett's perspective opened up the way for popular tastes and preferences to be the primary force for defining services, with expert analyses of social value taking a secondary place. If public recreation were directed in these terms, it might have the charm of cheap amusements, especially if it were combined with the universal accessibility of a municipal service. For a few years, while Tett was director of the CPB, the slender promise that individualist, hedonist liberalism offered to women in recreation became sturdier. Attenuated, at least temporarily, was the support the provincial agency would offer for recreation programs that reflected and supported women's maternal role as cultivators of higher tastes and better values.

Although it was allegedly non-directive, the CPB in Tett's years actually attempted, by non-authoritarian means, to shift community recreation demand away from an exclusive focus on the moral and social reform projects requested by citizens schooled in the maternalist welfare tradition. The domination of public recreation by such projects – the 'negative definition of recreation' – threatened to discourage the universal participation that Tett believed was public recreation's particular goal. Between 1949 and 1952, when Tett resigned, the CPB's efforts to encourage universal participation showed one way that a civil service agency might be both liberal and democratic. But in another way, liberal methods of regulation subtly undermined something that was valuable to both liberty and democracy: equal access to employment in public positions. As I will argue in Chapter 3, attempts to manage public demand in liberal ways helped exclude women group workers from the new profession of public recreation director.

3
Regulation and the Gendering of a New Profession, 1949–1954

In the twentieth century, following on the heels of the women's suffrage victories, the doctrine of separate spheres gave way to the doctrine of the equality of the sexes. Although the new norm, like the old one, has been frequently belied in practice, nonetheless the affirmation of women's equal citizenship as a value was a significant change. The new doctrine was fundamentally a liberal one, supposedly freeing women to be full members of the polity, to participate fully in public life. But even for the middle-class, respectable, white women for whose benefit this liberal feminist victory was most clearly intended, the new possibilities came at a price. The prescribed opening of opportunities to women also closed off certain options that the Victorian norms of gender segregation had allowed. As Nancy Cott has argued, women professionals of the first post-suffrage generations were not supposed to think of themselves as women facing specifically masculine competition. In this previously sex-segregated job market, as in the political arena, women of the new day were meant to engage as members of a universal category, as human beings, who competed with other, like individuals in contests of merit.[1] To think otherwise was to revert to a Victorian world of sex difference, and thus to betray the sex-neutral personhood supposedly won by the suffragists. Thus, women interested in professional employment found that the doctrine of the equality of the sexes committed them to a meritocratic engagement on terrain that unfortunately assumed socially masculine contenders.[2]

Both the spirit of this new liberalism about gender and work and its unwitting subversion were apparent in the making of public recreation director into a man's job. The civil servants who oversaw the profession's early years apparently assumed that men or women were able equally to fill the job. For example, in describing the province's first rec-reation program at its founding in 1945, the chief director of education, Dr J.G. Althouse, told the minister of education that governments should train 'ex-service men and women in practical physical education and recreational leadership.' Similarly egalitarian assumptions were implied in the advice Johnny Tett gave municipalities: 'It is entirely up to the recreational committee to select the man or woman of their own choice.' In 1947 he again used gender-specific and inclusive language to refer to the pool of candidates for recreation director positions.[3] If the CPB's role in developing the recreation profession was shaped by sex-ism, it was not a simple sexism that excluded women as necessarily unqualified.

Not automatically excluded from consideration for this occupation, women, and especially young women, also seem likely to have been available for and suited to it. Many had had relevant training in social work or teaching positions, including teaching physical education, where women had been employed since the nineteenth century, and increasingly since the 1920s.[4] These occupations involved organizing activities and fostering citizenship values, mainly for children and youth, but sometimes also for adults. In addition, there was a long tradition of female employment in positions of leadership in recreation. American statistics for 1928 show that women represented only slightly less than half the full-time, year-round staff of recreation programs. In Canada in 1948 the staff rosters of the Ontario YMCA and YWCA show almost equal numbers of men and women in program direction (as distinct from housing branch jobs and administrative work), with eighty-seven women in the YWCA and eighty-six men in the YMCA.[5] In a variety of organizations, women were employed as group workers, leading leisure activities for boys and girls and informal learning programs for adults.[6] And yet, in 1949 of fifty-six public recreation directors in Ontario, only two were women, and fifteen years later there were four among a total of eighty-six.[7] There was also a lower status position of assistant recre-ation director. (See Table 3.1 for wage data that indicate the degree of status difference.) Less common a position in the 1940s than in the late 1950s, the assistant recreation director job was somewhat more accessi-ble to women. In 1963, one-third of Ontario's assistant public recreation directors were women.[8] With qualified women willing and able to head up public recreation programs, why did so few actually fill these jobs? What was it that disadvantaged women candidates in this ostensibly open competition?

Table 3.1
Salary Ranges* for Full-Time Public Recreation Employees in Ontario Municipalities
(excluding Toronto), 1946–59 ($ per annum)

	Directors		Assistants	
	Men	Women	Men	Women
1946	$1,800–$3,000	–	$1,200–$2,000	$1,500
1947	$1,800–$3,000	–	–	–
1948	$2,300–$3,710	–	$2,200	–
1949	$2,400–$3,500	–	$2,000–$2,600	$1,300–$1,800
1950	$2,171–$3,910	–	$2,200	$1,650–$1,800
1951	$2,700–$3,200	$2,760	$1,190	$1,190–$1,320
1952	$3,900+COLA**	$3,000	–	$1,235
1953	$3,100	$3,000	$2,600+COLA**	$1,900+COLA**
1954	$3,400	–	$2,160	$1,896
1955	$3,430–$4,000	$3,360	–	$2,040
1956	$4,000–$5,000	$3,600	$4,000	$1,566–$2,280
1957	$3,600–$4,400	$4,000	–	$2,825
1958	$5,250	$4,000	$4,200	$2,825
1959	$5,500	$4,400	$4,400	$3,300

*Where only one figure is quoted, only one salary datum was located for that category of
employee in that year.
**COLA refers to cost-of-living adjustments.
Sources: These data were collected from the AO, RO, ser. B1, municipality files; Brantford Recreation Records; published reports of the Simcoe County Recreation Service.

While these questions are similar to ones that have been posed about
other professions, the recreation case is distinctively interesting in two
ways. One is that its basis in expertise was very slight: aspirants were
spared the task of having to scale a forbidding mountain of legal scholarship or medical science. Few of those who became public recreation
directors had the advantage of privileged access to prerequisite, special-
ized education. Thus, we can examine the creation of the recreation
director's professional expertise as an almost unadulterated exercise in
the legitimation of the occupation's authority. And this exercise in creating authority is significant for the history of the welfare state, because
it involved distinguishing the new 'public' recreation director from an
array of related private occupations. As a result, this story is, in micro-
cosm, one of converting the provision of private welfare into a state-
funded form. Its second distinctive point of interest, therefore, is that it
points us to the legitimation problems of a social service that was specif-

ically public, as these were understood in the early years of Canada's welfare state.

Both this chapter and the next examine the events, actions, and circumstances that gendered the recreation director's job. The focus in this chapter is on the challenges that the CPB staff faced in achieving their democratic goals by legitimately liberal means. In the next chapter, I examine the legitimacy problem through the eyes of the directors themselves and of the communities that employed them. In both chapters my point is that making the profession masculine solved administrative dilemmas endemic to liberal methods of regulation. Ensuring that this welfare program served 'all the people,' and at the same time avoiding totalitarian intrusiveness, required that recreation directors be the most 'manly' of men, in a white, middle-class sort of way. To understand this connection between gender and the character of the state, we need first to consider the regulatory challenge the CPB faced in its early years.

The Regulatory Problem

In spite of its commitment under Johnny Tett to provide no more than a responsive service, the CPB nonetheless had certain goals for municipal programs. The first and most fundamental of these was their survival. Divided on some questions, the CPB staff were united in wanting municipal recreation organizations to survive and to expand. However they might disagree about the precise criteria of a program's 'success,' provincial recreationists shared a common distress when public recreation failed in a municipality.[9] They were conscious of recreation's tenuously held place in municipal priorities; CPB representatives would help in any way they could to ensure stability and continuity for struggling recreation programs. Grant money, advisory services, and administrative advice were all means of support. Providing training for volunteer leaders was also considered essential. But, most important was a good recreation director. The CPB wanted recreation directors who could provide continuity and sound administration, and who could defend their programs against budget cuts. And the defence of a program was often needed.

In the late 1940s and early 1950s the newly instituted municipal recreation programs were only one example of many reconstruction expenses. They were begun in a time of enthusiasm for the possibilities of a better life for everyone in the post-war world.[10] Taxpayer support for public recreation was also grounded in anxiety about the dangers of delinquency. By 1951, however, some of the several dozen communities that had initially organized programs in 1946 were reconsidering their commitment to recreation expenditures. Municipal finances, while improved in many cases by the return to a peacetime economy, had been strained by the huge demands of suburban sprawl. As Doug Owram has shown, the decision of many families to move to the suburbs entailed significant costs to the collective purse. Roads, sewers, and school buildings all competed with recreation centres and recreation directors' salaries for a share of municipal tax dollars. Recreation directors asking for salary increases to keep up with post-war price inflation were applying pressure to budget decision makers who were already worried about how to raise salaries for underpaid school teachers.[11] In response to such pressures, Canada's municipalities sought federal help in funding recreation programs.[12] But with the national physical fitness program itself under attack in the early 1950s, there was little chance that recreation's claim on municipal governments would be bolstered by help from above. Instead, some municipal administrators tried to deal with their budget difficulties by reducing expenses in recreation programs.[13]

Alan Klein, a social work professor and recreation advocate, toured the province warning mayors and councillors of the social costs of cancelling recreation programs, but despite his efforts a rash of program closures and near closures took place in late 1950 and early 1951. The cancellation of Barrie's program funding was particularly upsetting to recreationists. Although it operated on a budget of only $4,000 a year, the Barrie program was nonetheless under attack in mid 1950 as a 'frill.' In self-defence, the municipality's recreation commission successfully proposed to town council that the voters be asked in the December municipal elections whether they were 'in favor of the continuance of the municipal recreation program.' With the support of the local newspaper editor, the radio station, and the Lions Club, the municipal program garnered a four-to-one majority in its favour. But just over two months later, in spite of the program's substantial public support, the newly elected mayor cut recreation from the municipal budget in the name of economy.[14] News of such closures was reported in local newspapers and in the *Bulletin* of the Ontario Recreation Association (ORA), alarming recreationists and bolstering the will of municipal administrators to cut.[15]

In 1949–50, at the end of the first wave of organizing, the annual growth rate of municipal public recreation programs was still 16 per cent. Then, suddenly, in 1950–1, the rate of increase dropped to a negligible 3 per cent. The next year was slightly improved at 7 per cent, and

1952–3 saw a 20 per cent jump. The reduced growth in 1950–1 suggests that organizing efforts, though still successful, were almost being counterbalanced by program closures. Leaders in the recreation movement took anxious note of this phenomenon. Speaking at the 1951 meeting of the Ontario Recreation Association (ORA), Klein expressed concern about a trend towards the elimination or curtailment of recreation services. He urged that the recreation movement unite in defining recreation as socially useful, so that municipal taxpayers would not baulk at funding other people's fun. At the next year's ORA meeting, University of Western Ontario physical education professor Earle Zeigler told the recreation movement representatives that anxiety about levels of taxation now threatened public backing for recreation.[16] Support for welfare spending was not, even in the affluent 1950s, infinitely elastic. By 1951, neither the moral panic nor the commitment to universal social rights that surged briefly at war's end was proving sufficient to sustain recreation as a secure element of the welfare state.

With their province-wide perspective, the CPB officials were the group that was most aware of the need to protect and promote public recreation, but recreation directors in cities and towns throughout Ontario were worried as well about calls for fiscal restraint and possible program reductions. A former director in northern Ontario recalled in 1971 that municipal funding was distressingly uncertain in the early 1950s. Often at recreation conferences, some of her colleagues would be wondering 'whether their jobs were going to be there when they got back.' Poor job security undoubtedly contributed to a high rate of turnover, called 'the mortality rate,' among recreation directors.[17] While the CPB was concerned that the comings and goings of recreation directors compromised the continuity and stability of programs, the recreation directors themselves sought job security. This common concern with the survival of the programs formed a solid foundation for cooperation between the directors and the provincial authority.

The strategy the CPB adopted to help programs survive was based on the view that if they were of high quality they would more certainly survive than if they were inferior. In this way, the concern for the survival of the programs translated into a standard for them, in spite of Tett's attempts to leave municipalities free of regulation. The standard reflected a compromise within the CPB. With Tett both supported and constrained by his staff of adult educationists at the CPB, the market model and the comprehensive model of service were conjoined. The resulting hybrid standard was 'balance.' A balanced program was not the same thing as the educationists' 'full and comprehensive' one. This distinction could be strangely sensitive, still capable of exciting a sharp insistence from a CPB veteran twenty years later in a 1971 interview.[18] It was a sensitive point because the notion of comprehensiveness implied specific content – a list of required activities. But this prescription of content was exactly the kind of illiberal imposition of therapeutic activities against which the CPB's notion of recreation had been defined. 'Balance,' on the other hand, was about form, not content. Whatever the particular activities it contained, a program that was balanced, when viewed as a totality, required the inclusion of cultural, physical, social, and educational recreations.[19] The notion of balance responded to some of the prescriptive leanings of the former OAEB staff by ensuring a place for cultural and educational pursuits in provincially supported programs. At the same time, it did not define a set menu of correct recreations, but instead left ample room for local tastes and preferences by accepting any program that offered choices in all four categories.

This apparently non-normative standard was adopted tactically to help sustain and develop the support of taxpayers for public recreation. By defining a suitable program as one that served '*all* ages, *all* interests, year round,' the CPB expressed the ideal that recreation was a universal entitlement and not just one for children and sportsmen. Balance as a criterion was thus deployed as a sort of intellectual judo, using the strength of sport and playground programs as an argument for enhanced cultural and adult social programs. The criterion was also attractive because a balanced program would include the maximum number of participants in recreation programs. Such inclusivity enlarged not only the potential scope of taxpayer support, but also the pool of volunteer labour for municipal programs, which were practical considerations not lost on the provincial recreationists.[20]

Given that the balance standard was designed, in part, to help programs survive and prosper, to enforce it by withdrawing grants was counter-productive. Occasionally, and reluctantly, the CPB cancelled funding for programs that had 'degenerated' into mere 'sports and playgrounds' arrangements. To avoid such awkward and undesirable outcomes, the provincial authority made municipalities aware that eligibility for grants was contingent on meeting the standard of balance. In 1951 a warning letter from the deputy minister of the Department of Education to municipalities said: 'Note: a program *confined* to any one age group or to any particular type of activity *is not* considered eligible for grants as being within the meaning of the regulations.'[21] Using the grant system to enforce standards made CPB district representatives inspectors, a role that contradicted their preferred style as friendly helpers. For members of a group who prided themselves on their reputation as 'nice people,' pulling the plug on a struggling recreation program was to be avoided if at all possible. They defined their role as 'enablers,' not regulators.[22] As one of the CPB's key members since its origins wrote in his role as field services supervisor in 1956: 'We are enablers, advisers and consultants rather than Inspectors.'[23] In focusing its regulatory strategy on education rather than coercion, the CPB situated itself clearly in the liberal tradition of public administration.

Consistent with that tradition, the CPB valued the decentralization of state authority. It counted as 'successful' those programs that required little help with administration after their establishment. The field representatives and advisers saw their job as being 'to help people help themselves.'[24] But avoidance of coercion and intrusiveness did not mean that the CPB did not regulate municipal programs. Beginning with Johnny Tett's earliest promotional tours, the branch exercised a kind of positive regulation, regulation by incitement rather than prohibition. Power may be exercised effectively by making certain courses of action easy and attractive. A government body regulating in this way can appear to respect the privacy of citizens and jurisdictional autonomy while supporting its preferred developments through its resources. The character of this approach is evident in the comments of a former recreation director and long-time CPB representative who denied that the CPB ever 'applied pressure' concerning program content. But, he added, the CPB representative might 'point out' to a recreation commission that its program only served boys. Similarly, rather than offer criticism, a CPB representative might arrange for an inadequate recreation commission to visit a more successfully organized town.[25] By offering information about higher standards, the CPB representatives hoped to inspire better performance. In this strategy, suitable recreation directors played a crucial role. As an informal employment agency, the CPB helped supply recreation directors who would be able to 'balance' and thus to protect public recreation programs. In effect, the recreation directors became the CPB's chief regulatory instrument.

Shaping the Profession

From its earliest days, the provincial recreation authority acted as a hiring hall for recreation directors, and municipalities sought advice from

Tett and later the CPB in choosing staff. Tett circulated books of mimeographed applications; in 1947 he had the names of sixty 'young men and women' on file who were seeking recreation director jobs. In the late 1940s and early 1950s, CPB representatives wrote reference letters for and against recreation director candidates, with comments on their character.[26] By 1949, municipalities requesting approval (as required in the regulations) for hiring a certain recreation director candidate had to supply the CPB with four types of information: the names of newspapers in which the position had been advertised, the names and addresses of the applicants, the names of applicants interviewed, and copies of written applications from those interviewed. The purpose of this documentation was to provide evidence that the position of recreation director was not merely a patronage appointment. A later version of the approval process required, in addition to assurances about hiring procedures, a signed statement that the successful applicant could provide a program for 'all ages, all interests.'[27]

Experience had taught CPB staff that municipalities might hire unsatisfactory recreation directors if the CPB did not monitor hiring. Between 1946 and 1951 an eastern Ontario mill town with a well-established athletic commission sought to have its sports director's salary paid under the community programs regulations. Although the local MP and a majority of the population supported this man's candidacy, the CPB insisted (in accordance with the approval process) that the applicant supply information on his experience in non-sports recreations. The purpose of this insistence, as the intra-branch correspondence shows, was to avoid endorsing as a recreation director someone who was really a sports coach. This town was only one of many where the equation of recreation with sports produced candidates who, in the eyes of the branch, were unsuitable as directors.[28] In another similar town, even before the hiring approval process was in place, the shift from sports director to recreation director was clearly motivated by the grant regulations. The town clerk wrote that the town had intended to hire a sports director, but if more money was available for someone called a recreation director, then that was who would be hired.[29]

The CPB's concern about possible patronage appointments was also a response to the obligation some municipal governments felt about hiring local candidates in times of public anxiety over unemployment, which was experienced even in the prosperous early 1950s.[30] In some towns, training and experience were judged less important qualifications than being well-known and well-liked in the community, and, arguably, these traits were in fact more valuable than 'technical' skills. Chapter 4 considers this question from points of view other than the CPB's. Here, however, in a consideration of the recreation director as part of the branch's regulatory strategy, being of local origin appears as a potential factor in the degradation of the recreation director's 'expert' status. Not only were local individuals unlikely to be trained recreation directors, they were often linked with a service club or an activity organization. They therefore threatened the 'public' character of recreation. Public recreation was distinguished by being administered by municipally appointed recreation committees, preferably composed of representatives from many social backgrounds and organizational affiliations.[31] These committees were the institutional embodiment of universal instead of particular entitlements. The creation of one of these committees sometimes meant that private organizations, where they existed, had to give up sole control of facilities and program management.[32] To present one of their own as recreation director was a means of reasserting that control, and, in the eyes of the CPB, this strategy therefore made local candidates look like Trojan horses.

Not only sports directors but also social group workers were inappropriate as public recreation directors. The recreation director's mandate to serve 'all the people' was considered a prime distinction between a public agency and a private one. The CPB's balance criterion expressed public recreation's inclusiveness. An association with group work threatened the attainment of this standard. According to social work professor Chick Hendry in 1952, 'government organizations' in recreation displayed 'a great resistance to the term "welfare."' The basis of such resistance was suggested in the Canadian Welfare Council's annual meeting that year: 'The word "welfare" sounded like "helping needy persons"' whereas those who resisted the welfare councils' involvement 'saw recreation as requiring a positive approach more like that of education.' Welfare carried a stigma; recreation, like education, was to be a social benefit for everyone. This view of the public realm inspired a bit of sweetly earnest cold war sloganeering in one Gala Winter Carnival program, which announced: 'Recreation – A Symbol of Democracy. A recreation for every person, every person in a recreation.'[33] To lead in this project, a recreation director had to avoid targeting only the needy or people who were perceived to be deviant.

By seeking to ensure that municipalities hired 'qualified' and 'genuine' recreation directors, the CPB was attempting to guarantee that public recreation would be balanced and inclusive, in other words, truly 'public.' For grant purposes, the provincial authority had defined 'qualified recreation director' in such a way as to direct non-intrusively the development of recreation programs. To say that a recreation director was not a sports director was to insist that programs should include more than athletics, and to say that arena managers were not really recreation directors was to forestall the subordination of non-profit programming to the balance sheet of a building. Similarly, parks commissioners could not be made into recreation directors simply by a name change, because their priorities would be maintenance and the passive use of parks instead of programming. The playground supervisor, a common recreation leader of the inter-war years, no longer counted as a recreation director because recreation was to include all ages. Former private agency workers could become recreation directors, but they had to realize that, as public servants, they acquired a responsibility to involve 'all the people' as participants and organizers in order to coordinate private energies and public resources.[34]

In short, the CPB directors and staff believed that the recreation director determined materially the nature of a municipal program. Although they also held as a precept the view that the content of public recreation programs should be established as a response to people's expressed needs, they felt that only a professional recreation director would be able to respond even-handedly to all interests. Making recreation 'public' required a specially trained point of view, an expertise in grasping the same 'big picture' as the CPB. If recreation directors shared the CPB staff's understanding of recreation, it seemed that the CPB would have allies in its attempt to correct imbalances in programs.[35] However, because recreation directors came from diverse educational and occupational backgrounds, a shared understanding could not be assumed. Many had as their only training in recreation their experience as volunteers in church, school, army, or Y recreation programs. Their activity enthusiasms ranged from sports to drama, from music to crafts. If public recreation's ideal of balance was to be sustained, candidates for public recreation directorships had to be made professionals by being taught 'what recreation really is.'[36]

This line of analysis brought the CPB to the conclusion (warranted or not) that an in-service training program was needed.[37] No university was prepared to organize one, and so the CPB undertook the task. Such a direct involvement by a government body in educating 'private' citizens was, of course, well over the line that notionally distinguished the 'enabling' CPB from a regulatory body. The CPB generally was not supposed to provide program services, but only to advise and consult.[38] Without trained recreation directors, however, programs would not likely meet a common standard, and so the whole system of public recreation departments might not retain its fragile hold on legitimacy as a public service. To protect recreation's place in the state, therefore, the CPB committed itself to training recreation directors. This participation in the construction of the profession was thus an intrusion of government into what was understood to be the 'private,' non-governmental, world, and the CPB acknowledged this with some embarrassment. To diminish the appearance of government direction, one leading CPB official emphasized the participation of the recreation directors' organization in planning the curriculum. But with the CPB hiring the training adviser and compensating municipalities for the loss of their employees' time, the CPB was indisputably in charge of the course.[39]

After beginning in 1948 in the form of a semi-annual training course lasting approximately ten days, the 'In-Service Training' program developed into a three-year certificate course that was first offered in 1951. Certification regulations were written in 1953. In the certificate course, there were nineteen credits to be earned, and the course also required attendance at three annual week-long provincial institutes and six one-day district institutes (two a year for three years). In between these formal meetings, recreation directors were expected to work independently to complete assigned reading and writing tasks. Administration of Programme and Community (Applied Sociology) at four credits each comprised almost half the curriculum. Recreation Theory, with three credits, followed closely in the course priorities. Activity skills (Techniques) and Facilities Management rated only two and one credits respectively. Of equal priority with recreation skills were Government (Mainly Municipal) and People (Applied Psychology). One credit was devoted to 'speaking and writing effectively.'[40]

A recreation director thus trained was not an activities leader or a facilities manager, but an opinion leader and an administrator. In his or her relationships with municipal government, such a director would be able to legitimate recreation's claim on tax funds with arguments about rationalizing public expenditures and serving social welfare goals. With the public, he or she would be able both to seek out and to stimulate recreation interests, having learned the sociology and psychology of leisure-time pursuits. Equipped with administrative knowledge, the trained recreation director would not need to trade on the faded glory of athletic accomplishments or the old loyalties of arts and crafts hobby-ists. He (but not so easily she) could be a professional, with training specific to *public* recreation, recreation for 'all the people.'

The New Profession's Gender Identity

Given the nature of the challenge to their legitimacy that the CPB's recreation programs faced in the early 1950s, the professionalization solution inevitably favoured making the position of recreation director a masculine job. Municipal recreation directors, starting up programs in towns where non-commercial recreation programs had been provided by the do-gooders of recreation's moral reform tradition, sought to broaden recreation's appeal by carefully distancing themselves and their programs from social welfare.[41] This meant breaking popular stereotypes of what recreation was and of who was entitled to services. The CPB hoped that trained directors would be equipped to mark out precisely for public recreation the right terrain between commercial entertainments and therapeutically oriented private recreation. These bordering realms of leisure were, as I have already argued, gendered territories. As the CPB and recreation directors struggled to position municipal recreation programs, they sought to establish some clear difference between public and private agencies. The negative definition of the recreation director as someone who was 'not a social worker' was a key element of this difference. To social workers clung all the feminine associations of the work of private recreation agencies – its educative, nurturing, and therapeutic purposes.

The role of public administrator served as a masculine alternative identity to the feminine one of social worker. C.E. (Chick) Hendry argued as early as 1947 that welfare councils were unable to address 'the whole of leisure.' To plan properly for recreation, matters of facilities and finance had to be taken into account.[42] To be truly 'public,' recreation programs could not simply use public money; recreation planning had to be an integral part of routine public administration. In a speech in 1949 to the ORA, public recreation theorist C.K. Brightbill set out the administrator's role in a list of reasons why recreation 'executives' fail. If the reasons for failure are re-stated as the implied guidelines for success, they amount to a capsule job description. The recreation director must be a 'good' administrator, which includes being able to make 'the best use of subordinates.' As well as delegating to subordinates, the recreation director must motivate people in the community to 'work for themselves.' He must administer finances efficiently, understand municipal legislation and the means of legislative change, and take care to conduct good public relations with boards, committees, civic leaders, and 'other professionals.' Program evaluation and long-term planning are the recreation director's responsibilities, and must be conducted in the context of overall community planning. The recreation director must understand 'the fundamental principles of community organization for recreation,' and stand firm in their defence if 'politics' interferes. These same themes were reiterated in a 1951 'Job Analysis of a Municipal Recreation Director in Ontario' that was published by the CPB, with the qualification that 'in smaller municipalities [the recreation director] may personally lead one or more activities.'[43] To act as an activity leader was, nevertheless, a compromise imposed by necessity on the director's managerial role.

When the CPB sought to train recreation directors who would be administrators and not program leaders, public officials and not social workers, they hoped that, in training such leaders, they might secure certain standards of quality in public recreation programs. Excluding women from the profession was not their goal. Nonetheless, the definition of recreation director that emerged from this method of regulation coincided with 'man' more than with 'woman' in the gender division of middle-class work at the time.

As James Struthers has shown for social work as whole, the administration of social programs was deemed to be beyond the competence of women. These views appear also to have held concerning the specialty of group work. The suspicion was that women could not handle money responsibly, being too sympathetic to make the necessary hard choices about the use of taxpayers' dollars. As public administration scholar Camilla Stivers has suggested, there was in the Progressive-era origins of the municipal administrative state a conscious identification of municipal reform with tough-minded masculinity and with a revulsion against feminine sentiment. In a study of gender and professionalization in American settlement houses, Judith Ann Trolander points out that one reason for the employment in these houses of increasing numbers of professionally qualified male social workers in the 1950s was that their funding requests to male-dominated community chests were seen as more credible than those of female social workers. Another example can be seen in the relations between the Canadian Welfare Council and the Trades and Labor Congress, where the same argument was made: that for a social worker to be effective in persuading a male audience to support welfare programs, the social worker must be a man. Even women's-page syndicated columnist Ruth Millett, far from being feminist on most issues, was moved in 1952 to remark on how little credence, or simply attention, men in general were willing to give the speech of even 'an intelligent, educated, well-informed woman.' In this context, defending fledgling recreation programs to mainly male municipal councils seems likely to have been defined as a man's job. As welfare scholars Harold Wilensky and Charles Lebeaux wrote in the mid 1950s, 'the active, aggressive entrepreneurial behaviour needed to develop professional and community contacts and to gain access to men of power – both essential for [social] agency survival – is often deprecated for women.'[44]

If the discursive gendering of the role of public administrator made the new profession masculine, so too did assumptions about a professional's single-minded dedication. These assumptions structured the hours and conditions of the recreation director's work. Directors had to devote themselves unstintingly to their work. The meetings alone for maintaining good public relations with the wide range of activity groups and volunteer committees were almost continual. In this context, the government training program, as light as its workload seems to have been, was a barely supportable burden, one more activity to fit into lives on which work already made too great a demand. One director noted, with a touch of ironic bitterness, that the recreation director's job did not allow him his own personal leisure time, much less time to complete the in-service course. He expressed the wish that recreation directors might 'live at least part of the time as we preach ... to fulfill the relationships to family and Community above and beyond the call of [the] office held.' Some men, unable to tolerate the hours, quit the field.[45] Men willing to identify so extensively with their careers were few enough, but members of this small, dedicated corps at least were not entirely deprived of wife and children by the job's long hours.[46] Male recreationists were privileged in being able to devote their energies single-mindedly to work, if they chose to do so, without foreclosing the options of marriage and family. The few women who were long-term recreation directors or members of the CPB staff were all single or widowed.[47] Consequently, they occupied quasi-masculine social positions as independent workers or breadwinners, and their presence as recreation directors confirms rather than challenges the masculinity of the occupation. Their presence would not have been controversial in the way that, as Strong-Boag has shown, career-oriented middle-class married women's occupations continued still to be in the 1950s.[48]

Glazer and Slater have argued that some women aspiring to professional success in twentieth-century North America have adopted superperformance as one means of overcoming their disadvantages in a sexist society. But the large sample of professional women Kinnear has studied supplies little evidence of that strategy.[49] It may be that, like the recreation directors studied here, Kinnear's subjects found that overwork was simply the standard in their occupations. In the formative years of public recreation, superperformance was scarcely a viable strategy for a woman seeking a superior position. What might seem an excessive identification of self with work was deemed normal for recreation directors.[50] The CPB's field supervisor spoke condescendingly, even scornfully, of directors who thought they could get by with working a forty-hour week.[51] With such expectations, the CPB was likely to end up with male recreation directors who were either young and single, or married to supportive housewives, whether or not the CPB wanted in theory to offer equal opportunities for women.

Did the CPB itself share the view that men were more competent than women as administrators and more able adequately to serve as leaders in public recreation? The demonstrated abilities of individual women and the effectiveness of the YWCA were acknowledged by a number of the CPB's key men.[52] But the branch's own structure bespoke the view that women had insufficient authority to be the movement's professional leaders. Women were a minority in the CPB. Of the forty-seven individuals employed for the first time by the OAEB or the CPB between 1944 and 1953 as advisers, assistant advisers, supervisors, directors, or district representatives, nine were women.[53] When the staff complement (not including secretarial staff) was at its largest with twenty-four members in 1953, only three were women. The positions of highest authority were occupied by men: the directors and the assistant directors were always male, and surviving staff lists show only one woman between 1946 and 1961 as a district representative. Another briefly worked as a district representative's assistant (a position usually held by a man). Otherwise, women in the CPB professional staff were advisers: providing specific recreation activity skills training, leadership training for volunteers, and advice on conducting activities.

Women advisers worked in music, 'allied arts,' crafts, radio education, parent education, 'gerontology' (seniors' activities), citizenship, and rural programs. Some of these areas corresponded with recreational preferences common among women, as described in Chapter 1. But other 'women's' fields, such as social recreation, drama, and art, had male advisers in the CPB, and there were both male and female advisers at different times in rural programs and citizenship. In crafts, there were almost from the start both male and female advisers simultaneously, although at the beginning there was only one, who was male. This pre-dominance of men even in 'women's activities' suggests a preference for hiring them as leaders. The available information on male advisers in fields whose clientele was mainly female suggests that these men had administrative experience in publicly funded or national organiza-tions.[54] This kind of background imparted an authority that helped legitimate giving all citizens opportunities to participate in such 'triviali-ties' as amateur theatricals, folk dancing, and Sunday painting. By con-trast, women advisers, as women, might have had difficulty dissociating such activities from their identification in the popular imagination as feminine or effeminate and thus deemed to be limited in their appeal 'only' to women or to mildly eccentric men.

In its reliance on male leadership, the CPB thus replicated the gender pattern in the creation of municipal public recreation organizations. A crucial ingredient in the recipe for establishing a new program within government was authoritative leadership. The figure of the public administrator, coded male, carried more authority than that of the group worker, often female and always associated with the welfare stigma. To accomplish its regulatory goals, the CPB needed recreation directors who could deploy informal power, whose influence on both male and female civic leaders would be effective, and who could speak authoritatively as experts on the recreation needs of all the people. Gen-erally, because of both imposed gender roles and internalized gender identities, such directors would be men. In effect, to solve its regulatory problem, the CPB drew on a certain kind of social power and public identity available mainly to men in a male-dominant society. Gender hierarchy provided a resource on which this state agency could draw to ensure its prestige and the survival of its programs.

In drawing on gendered expectations about authority to enhance the recreation director's stature, the state (through the agency of the CPB) contributed to the masculinization of a previously mixed-gender, albeit gender-segregated, occupation. Supporting this dynamic was the larger pattern of women's and men's normative roles in domestic life. From this sphere arose gender-specific incentives and disincentives to the superperformance deemed necessary to make public recreation viable. Thus, in its new form as a government job, the occupation of full-time, waged recreation director was masculine.

Of course, making public recreation leadership a distinctively masculine job played only a tiny role in constructing the gender relations of post-war society in Ontario. Recreation directors were, after all, only a few hundred men and women. But more important, the process by which their newly masculine profession was constructed shows something about state formation. A new state agency relied in quite a large way on gendered power and gendered meanings as a buttress for its very existence. In this instance, therefore, the state not only acted on gender relations in civil society, but was itself shaped by gender. To secure a place within government for leisure services, a new 'man's job' was invented. As the next chapter shows, gender relations and discourse continued to shape that job throughout the 1950s, making a manly occupational culture available where none necessarily existed. In the process, public recreation's survival was assured, but at the cost of the recreation movement's larger democratic project.

4

Constructing Community, Legitimating Authority, 1946–1958

To provide a social service that was both liberal and democratic was no small challenge. Charged by the CPB with seeing that all the recreation needs of all the people were met, municipal recreation directors found themselves in communities where, when tax dollars were at stake, many disagreed on which recreation needs of which people were truly public responsibilities. As occupants of an entirely new municipal job, many also found, from their first day at work, that their very employment was a point of contention. Threading their way through the often personal nastiness of municipal politics, recreation directors did what they could to help their programs to survive. They wanted to keep their jobs, and even to improve their pay and earn some respect. And, if they took seriously the injunctions of Tett, the CPB field representatives, and, later, the in-service training course, they wanted to exercise effectively a peculiar form of leadership. Somehow, they had both to ensure that all recreation needs were met by planning a program in cooperation with other municipal authorities, and, at the same time, to avoid imposing values and tastes on those they served. The weight of these and other contradictory demands was far from comfortable. The early recreation directors, some of them equipped with training in management or with a university degree but others with just their experience as coaches or choir directors, built their profession virtually under fire.

Both the novelty and the oddity of the recreation director's job threw into high relief the challenges of liberal leadership in a supposedly democratic social service. When not just the notion of a right to leisure services was new but also the expertise of a specialist paid to manage those services was far from commonsensically understood, it was not at all clear what the standard of democratic service should be or what the appropriate authority of a public recreation official was. This was all new ground for recreation directors. But it was ground that, in general terms, others had already covered and were still navigating in the post-war period. After the First World War, social workers had struggled to create credibility and worth for the expertise of their new profession. In the 1950s, economists had only recently come to carry significant weight in public administration. The use of social surveys to determine social needs was, in Canada during the Second World War, a phenomenon barely forty years old. The whole notion of state-sponsored, expert-managed social and economic planning was just taking hold in Canada in the 1940s, amid an international debate on the need for and the dangers of an interventionist state.[1] Recreation directors could draw conceptions of appropriate public authority from the recent experience of other social science–based occupations, though in some ways they did have to construct their profession from scratch.

As they did so, they could also read in newspapers and the more thoughtful magazines about the risks to private liberties their kind of occupation was taken to represent. Similarly, debate about the legitimacy of the entitlements their services were meant to fulfil was part of a larger discussion. The right to leisure, however strange a concept, was probably no more odd to some ears in the 1940s than some of the other rights enumerated in the United Nations' 1948 Declaration of Human Rights. When, for example, the right to be free of religious discrimination was affirmed by the international community and embraced as essential to democracy, Ontarians familiar with day-to-day restrictions on opportunities for Jews and Catholics may well have found other new-fangled rights no stranger. Some people welcomed the enlarged idea of citizens' rights, and others objected, but none could have been free from the sense that the standard of democratic responsibility by which government was now being measured had changed. How this rejigging of democracy would affect the freedoms of citizens remained to be seen. In their small way, the challenges recreation directors faced were part of a larger remaking of democratic community and liberal authority.

One might well imagine that the more general issues of freedom and justice being aired in the immediate post-war period were only dimly understood by the recreation directors. After all, some were qualified for the job mainly by their past high-profile performance in hockey or football or some other popular sport, a background that might have produced a certain anti-intellectualism. But whether or not they reflected on the play of political ideas, they experienced in their daily work precisely the political phenomena with which contemporary intellectuals were concerned: defining social rights and legitimating (or contesting) government power. And sometimes, particularly savvy citizen volunteers or an especially thoughtful director would frame in quite consciously philosophical terms the nature of the struggles of the recreation directors or the goals they pursued. In the narratives of their battles in particular communities, in their analyses of their situation, and in the comments they received on their endeavours (whether friendly or not), as well as in their reflections in the 1970s and later, we can see how a profession was made from next to nothing, and how, for a time, making the profession was intrinsically connected to the recreation movement's social welfare goal of building community.

As Ontario's first recreation directors strove to attain job security, better incomes, and social standing in their communities, they at first necessarily employed tactics that linked their status-striving with the welfare goal of overcoming social divisions. Because a director could only hope for success if 'the community' approved of him or her, the recreation directors as individuals all had an incentive to build the broadest possible basis of united support in the community for recreation. But the correspondences between social divisions and leisure-time pursuits made this a difficult task. The diversity of recreation interests meant that tastes about what made a 'good' recreation director varied. Feeling the vulnerability of their position, some recreation workers sought to give themselves the sort of peer credentials on which 'real' professionals based their autonomous authority. By the early 1960s, this professionalization strategy had succeeded. Unfortunately, its success weakened the link between the occupational fortunes of recreation directors and the making of more unified communities. That link had helped prevent the bureaucratization of the movement, and so the development of the profession was intimately connected to the movement's decline.

In this process, gender role norms played a part. Intrinsic to the impulse that made professionalization attractive was a desire for manliness. To be sure, men brought masculinity to the job, and by the mere fact of their sex helped distinguish it from its mixed-sex predecessors in private recreation organizations and group work. But the job itself was potentially feminizing. On the most obvious level, any association with amateur theatricals, craft classes, or play groups linked recreation directors with the topics of the women's pages in newspapers. More subtly feminizing were the job's supposed leadership norms. In terms of the Parsonian gender typology discussed in Chapter 1, a recreation director had to display many feminine traits. As I shall explain in more detail below, the director's work made him constantly seek the approval of others, forced him to accept insults to his ego and to rebound cheerfully, and required that he make himself pleasing. By contrast, the methods adopted to make the job of recreation director a profession allowed a director to call his (or her) work a 'man's' job, basing the job's authority in supposedly objective standards and protecting the director's ability to take principled positions and to act with integrity. To the extent that the wish for these kinds of manly powers played a part in moving recreation directors towards professionalization, this gendered context eased the movement's decline into an ordinary social service.

Inventing 'Recreation' to Make 'Community'

Promoting a newfangled thing called recreation rather than particular activities like hockey, hat-making, swimming, or target-shooting, was no easy job. There was no historical or taken-for-granted 'real' basis for such different activity groups to see themselves as pursuing common goals, towards which they might willingly share resources. If a new public recreation director wanted to foster a coordinated program producing something called recreation supposedly for everyone, he or she had to fill an old abstraction with new meaning. To do this involved speaking and writing persuasively, to be sure. But it also meant playing with social processes. In the early days of public recreation in Ontario's smaller cities and in towns and villages, recreation directors used both sophisticated group work methods and, more simply, personal charm, to create community organizations that embodied the notion of 'recreation.' In doing so, they hoped to build enduring, effective mechanisms by which ordinary citizens would be linked and empowered.

Recreation organization was supposed to enhance community feeling, whether through activities deemed universally enjoyable, or by new physical or political juxtapositions. In an article in a farm newspaper, a CPB representative approvingly quoted the leader of a square-dance club who praised recreation's community-building effect: '"It's like one big happy family here," says Andy, who is president of the group. "It brings the area together more."' In *The Story of a Community*, a CPB publication describing the successful recreation program in a new Toronto suburb, the author praised the community centre for building a 'subtle kind of community consciousness.' This consciousness was said to be apparent when activity groups 'integrated' their own activities with those of other groups. Community consciousness was also expressed when the drama club, composed mainly of 'ladies,' was able to persuade the school caretaker to 'lend his fine Scots voice to one of the male roles' in a play.[2] Although no explicit comments about crossing class and gender boundaries were made in the CPB publication, the point was clear: the contexts created by a successful recreation program offered new possibilities for social relations, thus fostering a common identity of participant to replace divisive ones of status. In this sense, the new community centre's goals were indistinguishable from those of a settlement house, although this and other community-building recreation projects were no longer located only in the city's immigrant quarter. The problem of social alienation, once imagined to lie exclusively between particular 'Others' – immigrants, the poor – and the supposedly successful 'Us,' had been generalized as a danger to Canadian society as a whole. Everyone was at risk of social disorganization, and everyone could benefit from the state's assistance in improving social relationships.[3]

Because social divisions tended to correspond to activity preferences, the recreation directors' organizing around the slogan 'all interests' was an attempt to encourage social integration. Those who could successfully represent themselves as serving recreation instead of just hockey players or watercolour painters were able to moderate competition for municipal grants and facilities among activity enthusiasts. Men and women, youth and adults, Scots and Hungarians, everyone might continue to engage in distinct leisure activities, but a public recreation body was supposed to represent all of them in relation to government and to serve all of them as equal possessors of social entitlements.[4] As well as rationalizing resource planning in a democratic way, new recreation institutions were meant to increase public support for leisure pursuits. In very practical ways, public recreation's universalist principles promised to strengthen collective provision. The notion that a public program should serve all ages broadened recreation's potential pool of volunteers and advocates; rather than just drawing on the energies of parents of small children, energies that were often strained, a recreation program providing adult activities would also develop a cohort of older volunteer organizers and corresponding support in the municipal council.

In the early years of public recreation, the organizational methods of new directors were drawn from group work, sometimes consciously, sometimes not. All of their methods worked best in the hands of someone whose personal qualities would be read as those of a natural leader.

All were aimed at changing common-sense ideas of what recreation was or meant. In social work terms, this exercise was described as 'interpreting recreation to the people.' University-educated recreation directors tended to 'interpret,' or explain, recreation as a means towards mental health, suggesting in a Freudian way that 'our real needs are seldom easily recognizable' and that certain kinds of leisure-time pursuits were particularly beneficial.[5] Many directors promoted the view that quilting or Swiss yodelling had as much right to public support as hockey and water-safety classes. Every interpretation of recreation, whatever its emphasis, served two purposes: to promote acceptance of public funding for recreation and to encourage a broad social base of participation. Interpretation was sometimes described as 'selling' recreation.[6]

And who was 'buying'? Who were 'the people' to whom this interpretation was directed? Far from being simply a mass of socially disorganized individuals, the audience for new recreation ideology included existing leisure groups. The new recreation directors faced, in even the smallest Ontario village, at least some array of churches, clubs, social agencies, and commercial providers whose existing projects and interests had to be recognized. In many rural communities, men's and women's service clubs, farm groups, and church societies already provided 'recreation' and thought they knew what it was. Larger towns and cities often had YM or YWCAs, and some even had councils of social agencies with leisure-time activities divisions. Sports leagues or arts groups also had views on what recreation was, and no competent recreation director could fail to take his or her message to these 'special interest' groups. Finally, there were the owners of arenas, halls, and theatres – leisure capitalists.[7] Could some of these be public recreation's friends, or did their business interests necessarily compete with social provision? A really thorough recreation director would meet with all the private recreationists, as well as with church leaders, school principals, and police chiefs, all of whom had established connections to the regulation of leisure.

With each of these groups, the recreation director had to negotiate his or her position. Would a public recreation program compete with existing agencies for the support of participants or for space in facilities? Would private agencies lose support from private benefactors once a municipal program was in place?[8] Meeting 'the people' in this way was a matter of institutional politics, requiring a deft touch. As we shall see below, a tactless step in managing these relationships risked provoking lectures on the proper role of government. Leisure organization served many particular purposes and interests in Ontario towns; fashioning recreation out of these existing materials was no trivial political task.

In order truly to reorganize community relations, the liberally minded recreation director tried to connect with the citizenry in general. Social alienation could be remedied only by activating the broad mass of individuals as citizens. In pursuit of this goal, the new director had to go beyond the platforms offered by community associations. Newspapers and radio naturally provided avenues of approach to the people as a mass. Brantford's first long-term recreation director used the newspaper announcement of his appointment to invite all and sundry 'to drop in and offer suggestions pertaining to local playgrounds and recreational activities.' Some recreation directors adopted a meet-them-in-the-street style of community organizing. Evoking an alarming image of bulk bonhomie, one recreation director approvingly called his colleagues 'Ontario's greatest collection of professional extroverts.' A member of the Recreation Directors' Federation of Ontario (RDFO) wrote in its 1955 annual report that to qualify as a recreation director one should have 'a pleasing and friendly personality,' 'productive energy and enthusiasm,' 'a sense of humor,' and 'a sympathetic attitude toward others' opinions and personalities' – in short, 'the ability to get along with people.'[9]

To sell recreation, the director had to 'sell himself.'[10] For individuals applying to work as a recreation director in their home towns, this sales job was already substantially complete. The popularity of a local person 'with young and old alike' and being 'well known' made it possible, in the words of one recreation commission member, for such a person to 'get the utmost co-operation from everyone, which after all is a prime requisite in this type of work, especially so as we are a young organization just beginning to get on a firm footing.'[11] While the university-educated recreation director was perhaps more likely consciously to embrace the role of opinion leader, all of the directors attained some sort of reputation in the community where they worked. In part because their job was a new one and in part because of a certain occupational culture, the first generation of recreation directors were public figures: 'everyone knows him and he knows everybody.' Getting around and talking to people in stores and banks and post office lobbies gave the recreation director an opportunity to interpret recreation to the previously uninitiated.[12] In this process, personal qualities came to stand for the quality of the program being promoted. The director's ability to move easily across sub-cultural lines symbolized the social integration that recreation was supposed to foster.

Thus, interpreting recreation involved a recreation director with a wide array of people in the community. In all these interactions, recreation directors urged people to enter into new kinds of relationships – to meet, for example, on the basis of larger neighbourhoods. Community events were common techniques for bringing people together in new ways. Some community organizations began with an ice carnival on a local rink with figure skaters from the neighbourhood and refreshments provided by women's groups. Elsewhere, May 24th fireworks were the initiating event. Band concerts and community singing also brought out good crowds and gave recreation committees needed publicity. One recreation service put on annual review nights, with displays of dancing and crafts; the director reported on the year's accomplishments, and the evening closed with square dancing and refreshments, courtesy of women's groups. Local radio stations and newspapers routinely, even enthusiastically, publicized such events. As Brantford's John Pearson recalled, public recreation events 'pulled people out of [sic] the streets. Now television and everything else doesn't make it possible, but it was fantastic the people that came and [the] excitement.'[13]

More than just a means of spreading the word, some recreation events were meant also to establish an inclusive definition of recreation. The recreation director from one small town remarked: 'to have a large enough membership for an effective recreation program, you have to cut across the social structure of the community. It is most difficult to get the different groups to work together.'[14] One attempt to surmount this kind of difficulty was Brantford's Crafts and Recreation Fair. Initially held in 1951, it claimed to be the first such event to combine both a 'sports show' and a 'crafts and hobby exhibition' in order to give 'a complete cross-section of recreational activities' (Table 4.1). The chairman of the Brantford municipal recreation committee praised the fair specifically as an agent of social integration: 'this event [will be] a good means of improving and strengthening relationships between all the groups involved.' Through the fair, the municipal Recreation Department helped participating organizations recruit new members and enjoy recognition for their accomplishments. 'The displays [in] the armouries [were] so choked with people by 9 o'clock that you could only elbow your way around,' recalled the recreation director. And the Recreation Department also benefited, because the newspaper reported on 'this public recreation thing.'[15]

Another method of establishing a socially inclusive meaning for recreation, while at the same time fostering public support, was the use of

Table 4.1
Groups Participating in the 1951 Brantford Crafts and Recreation Fair

Polish Alliance	Eagle Place Community Centre
Girl Guides	Radio Clud
Kloudsters	Harlequin Rugger Association
Revolver and Rifle Club	Brant Bowmen
Community Committees' Council	Indian Crafts
Iroquois [Park] Community Committee	Boy Scouts Association
Boy Scouts Association	Brant Soccer Association
West Brant Committee	Echo Place Recreation Commission
North Ward Committee	Brant Camera Club
Sunday School Athletic Association	Playgrounds and Recreation Commission
The Entertainers	Ukrainian Club
Ex-Servicemen's Dart League	Hungarian Society
Canadian Youth Hostel	Brant Film Council
Junior Stamp Association	Senior Stamp Association
Golf Association	Optimist Club
Horticultural Society	Armenian Society
Brant Sanatorium	Drama League
Ontario School for the Blind	Archer Club
Irish Folk Dancing	Scotch Folk Dancing

Source: BRR, RC minutes, 17 April 1951

surveys. These could reflect the aversion of volunteer leaders to having a professional recreation director impose his or her own program. The 1949 Leaside survey was motivated by this aversion, according to the man who was then recreation director there. In spite of the origins of the surveys in anti-professional feelings, a recreation director who was committed to a democratic ideal of community organizing welcomed such a survey.[16] He or she might suggest a recreation survey, and say something like: 'The recreation program is yours, not mine. To be of service, I need to know *your* needs and interests.'

At the same time that they sounded out opinions, the surveys also legitimated recreation as a public service, demonstrating that a recreation department was basing its programs on 'scientific' knowledge about what 'the people' really needed. This was apparently the goal of a crude form of survey conducted by one arts and crafts organization in conjunction with its municipality's recreation service. The organization asked 'everyone who did *anything* with his or her hands to bring these items to the Library Hall' for an exhibition. The response was enthusiastic, but eclectic. The organizers concluded (barely suppressing a shudder of aesthetic horror) that there was a 'need' for 'expert instruction.'

Surveys might also be performed by recreation professionals from out-side the community, who could be seen as objective and whose recom-mendations would therefore provide an authoritative response to criticisms that public recreation was unnecessary or that the local recre-ation department was unfairly neglecting some activity groups.[17] Such reports helped recreation commissions in larger municipalities to feel as though they were genuinely serving 'all the people.'

Where budgets or staff did not permit real surveys, directors who were eager to enlarge popular conceptions of recreation might resort to methods of 'stimulation' or of 'introducing new interests.'[18] This was a more aggressive interpretive approach, a marketing strategy, so to speak, that sought to expand the market not simply by advertising but by offering free samples. The Recreation Directors' Federation of Ontario encouraged its members to develop their programs in this way. One recreation director recalls that discussions in the federation prompted some of its members to get *off* the 'sports bandwagon.' It was pointed out that organizing sports for children, and especially for boys, merely duplicated the work of existing community groups. A rec-reation department would be better occupied if it gave those groups the resources they needed and turned the director's efforts to 'arts and crafts and music and drama.' The recreation director might invite a CPB representative to give a course for potential leaders in square-dancing or crafts or public speaking. Another CPB service available to recreation directors was the demonstration of hobby activities. For instance, the CPB hired a male adviser in 1950 specifically to 'initiate and stimulate' courses in making and using puppets. If directors were interested in some kind of activity that was not already organized, they might put on a class or bring in a guest expert to get things started.[19]

By explaining, organizing, socializing, surveying, and promoting, Ontario's new corps of recreation directors in the late 1940s and early 1950s fashioned in hundreds of cities, towns, and villages fresh opportu-nities for social contacts and personal pleasures. Animated by an idea of recreation as a means to social integration, they enlarged the range of leisure choices available to Ontarians, particularly in towns and villages. Universal recreation entitlement, sponsored by the state, offered much to women and girls as well as to men and boys. But, while recreation directors were, in this way, altering something of what the welfare state meant to women and girls, they relied on and reproduced gender hier-archy in the development of their profession. The dilemmas of liberal democratic leadership seemed to demand that they do so.

Problems of Leadership

Public recreation directors stood at a dangerous institutional location where divisions of interest and perspective in the private world were supposed to be subordinated to a uniting public standpoint. To represent 'the people' as a united community, the directors had to convince competing or mutually hostile elements that they shared something in common.[20] But they often found that their efforts merely made them and their departments focal points for social tensions. This predictable development might conceivably have been embraced as a necessary moment in a process of social transformation. However, most new directors seem to have viewed with alarm the awakening of slumbering social animosities as a result of their work. Liberal democracy's demonizing of social differences as 'special interests' that are intrinsically opposed to the public good, prepared new recreation directors to regard resistance to their project with frustration, anger, and contempt.

Personal concerns must have played a part in shaping this response. Social politics posed multiple threats to the careers of recreation directors. Many quit or were fired as a result of having failed in the proverbially impossible task of pleasing everybody, or, more significantly, of satisfying certain strategic individuals or groups. Expected, as government representatives, to mediate fairly the distribution of the taxpayers' dollars, recreation directors faced competing claims for facilities, equipment, and operating funds.[21] The agents of this competition were often identified with particular classes or ethnicities, or carried the moral meanings that were associated with gender or age. Such identifications and associations gave these 'small' questions of municipal politics an emotional intensity that could and did lead to recreation directors being fired or quitting. In some cases, a director would simply withdraw from the movement's larger social project, and the program would be captured by a particular activity interest.

The challenge posed by liberal democratic ideals thus translated into real difficulties for the status, security, and income of recreation directors. Faced with these difficulties, a director who did not quit but who instead accommodated his or her practice to local social politics, risked becoming merely an activity leader. These were disparaged by other recreation directors as 'physical types' and 'babysitters,' and were seen as failing to merit the prestige or the income level that a professional public administrator could claim. Equipped with university degrees, some of Ontario's first public recreation directors entered the field expecting ultimately to attain the social standing and income level of a high school principal. Others came to the job with more modest aspirations; for instance, a CPR trainman with a background (probably unique) in both semi-professional football and ballet successfully sought a small-town recreation director position so that he could work outdoors and avoid the odd hours of the railway trades. Excepting the ballet experience, his background was typical of the non-university-educated recreation directors. An outstanding athlete, he was attracted to a recreation job, especially in a small town, in part because he wanted more stability than a sports career could offer.[22] Such hopes and expectations must be seen as specifically masculine, in a period when most young women's aspirations to status and security still centred on marriage. Attempts to redefine recreation and to remake community thus put in jeopardy both the survival of a male director's programs and his claims to successful manhood.

In its early years, this danger was especially intense because public recreation directors had so little strictly structural power. They were the property of the communities – 'our' recreation director. Like clergy in Christian denominations where ordination is conferred by the religious community, recreation directors were empowered substantially by the communities they served. Whereas doctors or lawyers obtain their credentials from professional peers and can work as long as individual clients can be found, recreation directors in the period discussed here were simply employees. Moreover, they were *public* employees, expected 'to do everything to please the people.'[23] Nothing seemed more unlikely than that a recreationist in that position could be an agent of state tyranny or could impose tastes and values on the people. The liberal and democratic leadership ideals expressed by the CPB were apparently appropriate to the structural position of directors. To be a responsive facilitator was the norm to which these leisure authorities were schooled. And, in many ways, this was a rational norm, suited to the movement's larger goals.

In their daily practice, however, and in their later recollections, many recreation directors revealed that the pressures of circumstances, the accidents of personality, and the force of gender norms made this liberal democratic standard of leadership impossible to attain. In a variety of creative improvisations, they sidestepped the requirement that they be, in some measure, passive. Some positioned themselves as having been, even in the early days, specially equipped with professional knowledge that authorized the active exercise of power. One such director welcomed programming ideas from 'lay people,' but felt that recreation directors might themselves introduce new programs if, as professionals, they believed that such programs were 'something ... the community needs.' This man was aware of the precept that a public recreation director should 'wait for the people to come up with the ideas and suggestions,' but he dismissed this ideal as 'a textbook approach' that 'doesn't really happen in the field.' The force of that textbook precept was nonetheless real, even for this person: he spoke of sometimes 'planting' an idea with a volunteer, presumably so that leadership might not appear to come from him as a professional.[24] In this same vein, the CPB endorsed 'interpreting' recreation by stimulating new interests, even though this practice amounted to a variation on the imposition of taste, something directors, as liberals, were supposed to avoid.

More ambivalent discomfort with the ideal of responsive leadership is evident in the recollections of other retired recreation directors. Dealing with their complex feelings and thoughts on how to lead in this way strained the language of even the most articulate interview subjects. Responding to a question about factors that influenced the growth of recreation, one man said: 'recreation activities were becoming a more and more important part of living and have to be. I've got to be careful, I say [activity has to be] programmed, I mean programmed, but programmed, has to be arranged, or budgeted for, leadership has to be provided, to see that opportunities are there.'[25] The plethora of qualifications and rephrasings in this passage indicate the sensitivity of the topic. This person was concerned not to stray from what one of his colleagues called 'the fine line.' Too much leadership by the director might kill the volunteers' sense of ownership of and responsibility for programming. To do so would be to take the first step towards bureaucratic planning. Insufficient professional leadership, however, might allow recreation programming to stagnate in a narrow range of activities and to jeopardize its standing as a public service. The tensions around this issue meant that even an honest acknowledgment that recreation directors plan for what 'people will be wanting five years from now' aroused in a former director the concern that he might sound 'immodest,' too much like the old recreation theorists who claimed to know what was 'best' in leisure-time pursuits.[26]

The ideal of responsive leadership did not eliminate the old do-gooder style, but became a point of critical reference. The comments of one YMCA-trained recreation director reveal the continuing influence of a prescriptive leadership style: 'in most communities, even today, we're dealing with a, pardon the phrase, a very unsophisticated group of clients, not sophisticated perhaps from our point of view. They find a great deal of appeal in things which are physically-oriented.'[27] Again, in interjecting 'pardon the phrase,' he made an obeisance to an ideal of leadership by 'the people,' the clients, the non-professionals. Equally, he acknowledged that sophistication is judged from a certain point of view. But such gestures of tolerance and acknowledgments of guilt only underscore the difficult position of the working recreation directors, especially when building new municipal programs. They sought to capitalize on volunteer energies and to build broad community alliances. Certainly, one sensible approach to doing this was to be responsive, but being merely responsive might allow recreation to fall under the direction of a well-organized group of activity enthusiasts whose programming did not serve 'all the people.' Such an outcome would be neither acceptable under the provincial regulations nor beneficial to a program's long-term prospects or the recreation director's own status. To actively take the initiative in order to avoid these results only made sense, especially, as one director observed, given that 'the way of western man ... our way of life requires that the individual has to make his mark. And many professional people in recreation can only make their mark on the basis of ... developing their empire at the expense of other people, the people they serve.'[28] This vision of the individual resembles one kind of masculinity offered as normative in the 1950s, the kind that has been described as 'combative,' equipped with the means to dominate.[29] It also resonates with the longstanding association of masculinity with activity, in contrast to femininity with passivity, an association carried into the 1950s by the influence of Freudian psychology.[30] Both material interest and cultural frameworks, therefore, worked to make the subtle concept of responsive leadership difficult for these men recreation directors to put into practice.

The recreation director's leadership problems were lived out most directly in the relationship with the movement's core volunteers: the members of the municipal recreation committees (MRC), often called recreation commissions. Appointed by the municipal councils, MRCs at first came in many forms, from a group of aldermen to an assemblage of men and women representing a wide array of interested organizations. After 1951 provincial regulations specified that MRCs have only seven members. After that, some towns established a representative advisory group to complement the MRC.[31]

MRCs might either support or challenge the recreation director.

When Barrie's recreation program was under fire in the early 1950s, its volunteer leaders were prominent in its defence. MRCs also interpreted recreation; for instance, Brantford's commission helped organize a civic swimming committee that had as one of its goals to attract more adults to the public swimming pool.[32] The MRC shared with the recreation director the role of mediator among competing demands for municipal dollars.[33] However, the MRC, which carried the authority of 'the taxpayers,' had a real structural advantage in any open conflict with its recreation director. Considerable political savvy, useful expertise, and personal charm were required of a recreationist who wished to lead, rather than follow, his MRC. Those among the early directors who survived in one place for a long period displayed these traits, but the conventions of class power and the vicissitudes of Ontario's annual municipal elections in the 1950s could sabotage even a very skilled recreation director.

When an MRC took positions different from those of the recreation director, the latter often faced the delicate politics of affirming the CPB's democratic standards of programming, while resisting the will of 'the people.' One director, who was university-educated and who subscribed to the 'all interests' standard, found himself working for a committee composed mainly of 'people of the labouring classes.' In his view, the MRC's class composition meant that 'their concept of recreation was very youthful, very physically oriented.' The representative woman on this committee was there on behalf of 'the mothers of the community,' and moreover the recreation budget was justified solely on the basis of solving youth problems. In all these ways, the volunteer leaders transgressed the CPB's new recreation theory. Loyal to the CPB view of 'what recreation really was,' this middle-class recreation director struggled against the priorities of his working-class MRC, and made use of the provincial regulations to justify expanding the recreation program to include adult and non-sport activities.[34] For him, the standard of service to the people was not set simply by populist means. Rather, democratic service had to be justified, illiberally, by the state, that is, by the middle-class, specially educated experts in the CPB. Other cases also suggest that, when a director and an MRC disagreed, the ability to wield the provincial regulations in support of a position was at least as effective as pointing to popular support.[35]

Using the authority of the provincial state was an understandable tactic, given that the ups and downs of town politics could wreak havoc with any principled style of leadership. Having arrived at a working relationship with one committee, a recreation director might find, after municipal elections, that a different group had been appointed by the new council. When the new committee's priorities diverged from its predecessor's, the recreation director might well be unable to respond easily to the abruptly redefined 'needs' of 'the people.'

The case of Chatham in 1954 illustrates the problems that could emerge after a change in the MRC. For its first seven years, Chatham's Recreation Commission had been a diverse assembly of male professionals, managers, small-business owners, and skilled workers. They had organized the building of the Memorial Arena and had overseen the creation of a wide variety of recreation programming, ranging from social clubs for all ages and both sexes, sports for youth and adults, dances, and children's theatre. Their recreation director was a former YMCA man, and the wide array of programming reflected the Y tradition. In 1954 the vicissitudes of town politics produced a new Recreation Commission. Composed entirely of small-business men, this MRC charged that too few people were using the arena and that two events had lost money because of the director's mismanagement. They asked the recreation director to resign. Faced with the new commission's 'bottom-line,' arena-focused priorities, he quit and went elsewhere to a job with the Y. Cheered by two thousand hockey fans at a big send off, he had undoubtedly been popular with at least some of 'the people,'[36] but he had been unable or unwilling to negotiate the shifting of agendas among Chatham's civic leaders. Competition among elements of a community's leadership, sometimes coloured by class perspectives, determined what kind of popular support mattered to a recreation director's career.

Both the intimately small scale of these politics and the peculiar requirements of the recreation director's job gave an intensely personal quality to the problems of leadership. Who the director was, and not just how he or she performed tasks, shaped success or destined failure in this job. In one community, a fired recreation director was described as having been in a feud with some MRC members over a period of several years. The MRC suggested that he might be better in a job where personalities were less material to success.[37] In another town, a young director's relentless enthusiasm for meeting people skirted the edge of brashness, and he was fired in part because his extroversion was perceived as tactless and intrusive.[38] More generally, recreation directors faced the criticism that they were either too silent in meetings or talked too much. Each had to negotiate appropriate manners for the job's many relationships. Probably the best strategy was to tailor a conversational style to the mode prevalent in a particular group. But in groups of mixed social composition, which recreation commissions often were, it was undoubtedly inevitable that, to some members, the director's way of speaking would have seemed too bossy or too meek, too 'stuck up' or too 'rough.' A similar ambiguity plagued decisions about attire. If there had been more women directors, the criticisms of women's dress would no doubt have been acute. As it was, a comment on this subject from the mid 1960s seems to have been directed more at men: 'If he is well dressed, he thinks he is a big shot. If he isn't, he isn't a proper representative of your important industry.'[39] For male recreation directors, choosing the right circumstances for wearing a tie and jacket and deciding whether a three-piece suit was appropriate involved making decisions about the class image of the job.[40]

These apparently small matters of taste or manners constituted part of the sign system that bespoke the recreation director's social place and determined that person's fitness as the symbol of a socially integrated community. According to Pierre Bourdieu, people in circumstances of cultural change set great store by 'the seemingly most insignificant details of dress, bearing, physical and verbal manners,' because such behaviours embody fundamental values and beliefs.[41] It is not surprising, therefore, when recreation programs were new, that directors encountered this prickliness about appearance and manner. To succeed, they could not wear their role lightly as one costume among many. Their suitability had to be deeply grounded in their very self, their subjectivity. This no doubt made especially painful the kinds of criticisms they encountered as representatives of a new and slightly dubious social service. They were lightning rods for suspicions of the state's role in the provision of leisure.

As the representatives of public recreation, directors met with all kinds of attacks. One variety centred on the utility of government spending on leisure. 'Tax-payers' money is being spent to afford teenagers a good time, with nothing to show for it,' complained some Ottawa folk. In Brantford, one day in 1951, a man ran over to the Recreation Commission's sound truck especially to berate the new assistant director who was driving it. He wanted to tell the young man that at least one citizen resented paying taxes to support his riding around the city engaged in 'a lot of foolishness.' Directors were also lambasted on 'constitutional' issues: they and their MRCs were accused of being a law unto themselves, seizing from city council the elected officials' 'rights and responsibilities' in deciding where public money would be spent.[42] Finally, some of the most wounding, and best organized, complaints came from leaders of private organizations, such as churches, craft groups, and Ys, on whose territory public recreation encroached. The recreation director who mishandled relationships with these well-connected groups not only met with apparently principled explanations of the proper role of public agencies, but also with coordinated campaigns expressing what one observer frankly called 'jealousy, suspicion, and hostility.'[43] Claiming openness as part of their method of leadership, directors could not easily protect themselves if debate took a personal turn.

In addition to being criticized for their personality, clothing, and policies, recreation directors sometimes had the very legitimacy of their work questioned. More than most professionals (or paid workers of any kind), they were likely to have volunteer helpers who believed themselves to be as knowledgeable as the paid staff, or more so. After all, volunteers were privileged as the voice of the people. One director recalls his assistant director's unhappiness at being told by 'community people' that 'we don't need you, you don't do anything for us'; they complained that they were 'paying him money for something that he should do for nothing because recreation isn't a work job, it's a picnic.' Those hostile comments came from recreation's friends; its critics added volume to the chorus that described the recreation director's job as play, not work. After putting in long hours at meetings every night of the week, many directors found it galling to be told they were not *really* working and they were not entitled to their pay.[44]

Such criticism was especially hurtful because recreation directors developed a high degree of personal identification with their jobs. As William Whyte observed in his 1956 study of corporate business managers, top executives worked extraordinary hours because their 'ego demand[ed] it'; self and job were identified, and work became dominant in their lives, to the exclusion of family and leisure. A similar dynamic was apparent among recreation directors: sacrifices by men of family time and women's celibacy and childlessness reflected and reinforced the significance of the job in their lives.[45] For people who identified so deeply with their work, charges that their work was somehow not real required some sort of response. For the few women directors, who had already departed from gender norms by not marrying, defending their job's status was not especially tied to a defence of their personal social standing. But for men, for whom full-time work conformed with gender norms, defending of their job's legitimacy was also in part a defending their masculinity, their authority as men.[46]

Subject to close scrutiny and empowered through an unstable set of work relationships, recreation directors adopted a variety of means as individuals to maintain their credibility, authority, and emotional balance. Being able comfortably to accept criticism, often of apparently minor errors, was an essential skill for the job.[47] A reputation for hard work was a source of authority: dedication and selfless service gave the recreation director's voice a touch of the martyr's influence. Another tactic was to start more programs. New programs provided tangible evidence of the director's hard work and long hours, 'results' that could be tabulated in annual reports.[48] To prove that they were doing 'a real job,' recreation directors were tempted to treat their constituents as consumers rather than as partners in the work of reorganization. A somewhat alienated bureaucratic relationship with 'the people' would provide provide the recreation director with a more real, manly job.

Although many recreationists tried, as liberals, not to impose programs, their commitment to serving 'true' needs could drift into disregard or even contempt for the criticisms of non-professionals.[49] One urban planner actively counselled this shift in leadership styles: 'Recreation professionals must develop more professional arrogance,' he argued, 'if they are to survive.' According to one recreation director, denying criticism was part of being principled: 'As to [my] being contrary, I heartily agree. My concern is not with [satisfying] individuals or individual groups, but with all people, regardless of status, sex, creed or color.'[50] The independent attitude expressed by this man was based in a robust confidence in his own standards. That self-assured stance was also redolent of the Parsonian masculine personality type: tenacious, aggressive, ambitious, 'planful,' responsible, and self-confident. Collectively seeking a similar confident authority was the essence of the recreation directors' professionalization strategy, as it emerged in the early 1950s out of the instabilities of public recreation's first five years.

Empowerment through Professionalism

Maintaining authority by force of individual personality had its disadvantages and difficulties. Some directors appear to have felt that the influence gained through overwork was purchased at too high a price.[51] The most 'masculine' of the personal strategies – legitimating the job and asserting authority by pursuing one's own apparently personal agenda – was also the most dangerous, as it risked alienating important sections of the community. And when the genuinely valuable traits of

Parsonian masculinity emerged as defensive reactions to insupportable stresses, they also risked degenerating into their illiberal variants. Tenacity became stubbornness, aggressiveness shaded into brashness, ambition produced egocentricism, planfulness rigidity, responsibility a tendency to over-control, and self-confidence easily became self-righteousness. To avoid their job's peculiar destructive pressures, some recreation directors, quite understandably, sought in professionalization a collective strategy for their empowerment.

The institutional agent of this strategy was the Recreation Directors' Federation of Ontario. Founded in 1946 at a directors' conference called by the CPB, it claimed a membership in the mid-1950s of between eighty-nine and ninety-nine, or about two-thirds of Ontario's municipal recreation directors, including assistant directors. Lists extant for the mid to late 1950s show a membership encompassing about two-thirds of the public recreation directors, from all over Ontario, including both women and men. From the beginning, the organization gave its members opportunities to share successes and to commiserate over troubles. At first, a common condition of inexperience meant that they had no particular plan for dealing with the occupation's characteristic problems. Their initial move as a group was, after 1948, to help the CPB to design the in-service training course. Their own history of their organization's first ten years described this course as having 'brought nearer ... the security and status for which all had been striving.'[52] By the early 1950s, the organization began to coalesce around the program of professionalization: creation of standards leading towards government-backed credentials.

Apart from the CPB-initiated in-service course, the first sign of this program was the code of ethics published in 1953.[53] Adherence to the code, a ten-item list of standards of conduct, was a condition of RDFO membership. The practices that were specified indicate the importance of reputation to the recreation director's success. Item 8 addressed the problem they faced as public personages, and offered the support and surveillance of the RDFO as correctives: 'I will consider my personal behaviour carefully with reference to the standards expected of me by my community, recognizing that certain liberties which I would claim as an individual cannot be exercised under all circumstances without harm. If I should find it necessary, for any reason, to depart from the normally accepted lines of conduct, I will seek advice from the R.D.F.O.'[54] Item 5 spoke to the difficulties inherent in the recreation director's many work relationships: 'I will maintain good relationships by scrupulously protecting all confidential matters and not repeating criticisms.'

As well as acknowledging the problems endemic in a job so profoundly structured by personalities and relationships, the code of ethics also reveals the aspirations of the RDFO towards status and job security based in clear standards of merit. Item 4 accepts 'the principle of appointment and promotion according to merit.' Item 2 commits RDFO members to 'ask for and give clear written job descriptions,' and to seek agreements with recreation authorities on conditions of work. Both of these practices would clarify criteria of evaluation. Item 9 indicates that, in the RDFO scheme of values, education conferred both merit and status: 'I will use every opportunity of improving my general and special education and will support others in doing so, because I recognize that the whole profession benefits from the respect in which its members are held and from their ability to move from place to place and upward in the scale of responsibility.' Status alone is the explicit goal of the behaviour required in item 3: 'I will recognize my obligation to do everything in my power to improve the status of the recreation department among municipal departments.' In this context, the recreation directors' commitments to standards appear closely tied to hopes for improvement in their collective status.

The CPB helped professionalization along by setting up certification regulations in 1954 to accompany the in-service training course. Certification was supposed to give recreation directors an incentive to complete the course. In fact, few were willing or able to attain certification under these permissive regulations. In general, overwork explains the poor response to an arrangement that would seem to have offered improved job security and status. But some recreation directors ignored the program (and the urgings of the RDFO) because their aptitudes and experience were in organizing and activity leadership and person-to-person public relations rather than in the reading and writing skills of formal education. After the code of ethics was published, there was a decline in membership. This may have been the result of the departure of people who rejected the RDFO's equation of education and upward mobility with competence. Ignoring the possibility that these departures may have expressed a principled dissent from the professionalization strategy, the RDFO's historian simply celebrated the education-centred certificate program as an expression of 'idealism.' Its idealism lay in the link he believed existed between the occupation's status and the fortunes of the recreation movement.[55]

In 1956 that view was endorsed by the organization of the whole recreation movement, the Ontario Recreation Association. At its conference that year, it passed a resolution crucial to the RDFO's professionalization strategy. The preamble deplored the fact that 'unqualified personnel' were able to get work in recreation and expressed concern that this state of affairs jeopardized 'the future of the recreation movement in Ontario.' The resolution itself called for the Department of Education to make regulations 'governing the employment of municipal recreation personnel.' This resolution was by no means the pure and authentic voice of the people. About one-third of the ORA members were recreation directors, and in 1955 this substantial minority's domination of the plenary sessions of the organization had occasioned discussion. But for the Department of Education, whose CPB director had been attempting to upgrade the status of recreation directors, the ORA resolution must have seemed a perfect warrant for state intervention.[56] Here was 'public demand' for regulation. Democracy *could* create bureaucracy.

The consequences of the resolution followed quickly. New regulations for municipal programs of recreation were issued in 1957, tying provincial grants to the level of training attained by the recreation director. Following its established style of regulating by the carrot in preference to the stick, the CPB offered grant increases of up to $400, contingent on directors attaining higher levels of certification through the in-service course. At the same time, the RDFO had drafted the Recreation Directors' Act to allow them to incorporate as the Society of Directors of Municipal Recreation of Ontario (SDMRO). The immediate effect of this act, which was passed by the Ontario legislature in March 1958, was to reserve the title of Registered Director of Municipal Recreation for the SDMRO's members. The purpose of the society, now enshrined in law, was 'to increase the competence, knowledge, skill and status of its members, to establish a high standard of ethical practice for its members and to promote all things relating to recreation in Ontario.'[57]

The RDFO's later report on the act acknowledged regretfully that 'full professional status was withheld' because true professions require university degrees and 'the society does not demand this qualification for membership at present.' Recreation directors still had to rely on the provincial government's grant regulations to enforce educational standards. But the act helped solve problems regarding the status of the recreation directors. It gave the code of ethics some legal force, empowering the SDMRO to suspend or expel members. Its constitution in 1959 included for the first time a clause concerning unspecified 'disciplinary action ... in the event of malpractice.'[58] In essence, the act declared that recreation directors, through their society, would determine who was competent in the occupation. The designation of 'R.D.M.R.' after someone's name would guarantee a standard of character and knowledge.

The recreation directors had not managed to attain full professional status, but they had succeeded in establishing a means of legitimating their jobs through a process other than by pleasing the people who employed them. Competence could now be claimed on the basis of peer evaluation and educational attainment. These supposedly objective standards were meant to guarantee a certain quality of service to municipalities. In practice, this was not necessarily so. On the question of child sexual abuse, for example, the RDFO in 1956 acknowledged that 'sex deviates' sometimes could become recreation leaders (and presumably even directors) because recreationists had no way of identifying potential offenders. Judging character remained a subjective matter, a realm where not only gender bias but also homophobia and race prejudice could easily operate – and did. In 1949 the CPB had blacklisted one aspiring recreation director because he reputedly had 'homosexual tendencies,' an inaccurate means of protecting against pedophiles, which no doubt continued to be used.[59] Similarly, racism could be masked as a concern about qualifications. In 1957 a 'Negro' recreation director, whose 'personal ability had gained him recognition' from those who had at first opposed his appointment in one Ontario town, found himself facing concerns about 'problems with tourists from the deep South' when he applied for a better-paid director's position in a cottage country community. He decided not to pursue his application, and thus the resort town lost the chance to employ a director with an exceptional record of past performance, a high profile sports background, and a university degree.[60] Conversely, some recreation directors laid claim to their 'skills' on the basis of less than rigorous standards of education. The markers for the in-service course – some of them recreation directors – respected the practical problem facing their adult students: 'you knew that here was a man's whole future dependent on this damn little bit of paper, so most of us were pretty easy, quite frankly.' People whose academic work in other circumstances would have been failed were granted certificates.[61]

This is not to say that the SDMRO had no genuine interest in improving the skills of recreation directors. After 1958 it began offering its own weekend courses. Designed specifically to complement the 'university or college level' in-service course, these sessions covered 'practical knowledge' that recreation directors needed on the job, such as telephone answering styles and filing methods.[62] However, such knowledge was not part of the course that provided credentials. Such low-status matters, linked to 'feminine' clerical work, would not contribute to constructing professional status.

The in-service course and its associated credentials served, like the RDMR designation, more to give recreation directors a status and a basis of authority outside the social and political networks of the villages, towns and cities where they worked than to teach them skills they really needed to know to do their job. Their vulnerability to criticism from many directions and to shifting priorities within local government makes it easy to understand why they found such credentials attractive. In retrospect, however, some recreation directors regretted the way the professionalization project directed their occupation's development. One man said that the struggle 'to be recognized as equal to doctors and lawyers and teachers' focused the SDMRO's energies on 'professional status rather than professional competence.'[63]

One of the female members, who recalls enjoying the SDMRO 'fellowship' during the 1950s and 1960s, came to believe by the early 1970s that the preoccupation with certification had been a mistake. In the spirit of the early 1970s, she asserted that such credentials 'should be scrapped completely ... people [should] be judged on the basis of what they are as human beings.' She implied that credentials did not necessarily produce good recreation directors. This theme was repeated by a long-time leader in both adult education and recreation. He recalled that the first post-war recreation directors were untrained, but were 'very interesting human beings,' whose performance compared favourably to the new university-educated recreationists of the 1960s.[64]

Professionalism had contributed to undermining the structural basis for a particular kind of leadership. Without the credentials of a recognized profession, recreation directors had had to exercise leadership by means of whatever personal qualities they possessed and community support they could muster. The association of power with masculinity advantaged men in this work. A director had to have 'qualities which [would] make him acceptable to the community in which he serves.'[65] If white, middle-class men were typically leaders in a given community, then women, people of colour, or working-class men had to overcome expectations about who was acceptable in leadership positions. Male athletes from working-class backgrounds drew on the prestige of their sports records, but only a handful of women and one, apparently mid-

dle-class, black man managed to make themselves sufficiently 'acceptable' to become full-fledged directors.[66] Being a 'natural' leader in
public recreation's early days was a (white) man's role.

But the link between authority and masculinity was weakened by the
perception of the recreation director's job as play. Behind the criticism
lay the question: 'Should *a grown man* be earning his living leading sing-
songs? (or organizing sandlot softball or teaching weaving?)' The necessity of being pleasing, combined with a lack of independent power, further compromised the masculinity of the job. Even the administrative
role, if practised according to the ideals of responsive leadership,
deprived recreation directors of the chance to 'make their mark,' to
exhibit the ambition and planfulness deemed appropriate in the Parsonian cultural ideal.

Professionalization offered a way to bolster the recreation director's
authority and status, and it did so in a way that emphasized 'competence, knowledge, and skill,' supposedly objective qualities, rather than
personal leadership abilities. In 1959, one of the recreation directors
most enthusiastic in promoting the 1958 charter, and himself a gifted
community organizer, warned that professionalism should be more
than just a certificate of educational attainments: 'to "be" a professional
involves more than academic study. *One must think like one, act like one,
and behave like one.*'[67] But the leadership qualities he saw as part of being
a professional were no longer the only route to job security and status,
once qualification by credentials became possible.

The consequences were apparent in the mid 1960s, when young people with degrees took over established programs and were able to
administer them without making extensive popular contacts or taking
personal initiatives in leadership.[68] Undoubtedly, among later generations of recreation directors there have been individuals who were willing and able to be public personages and, by the force of personality, to
make new connections across social boundaries. But by the early 1960s
such qualities and goals were no longer necessary to the survival of recreation programs. The creation of professional standards and a 'registered' status in 1957–8 were elements in a broad pattern of change in
the recreation movement away from community organization and
towards the provision of services by paid staff. Insofar as professionalization was an attempt to attach to the recreation director's role a masculine kind of authority, gender played a part in making this change.

The recreation directors, in pursuing job security and status by means
of state-supported credentials, played their part in turning recreation's

active partnership of state and citizen, embryonic in the late 1940s, into a more alienated consumer relationship in the early 1960s. For women, the irony was that the universalist notion of recreation provided them, and girls, with more leisure opportunities, but the professionals who were considered capable of defending that notion were increasingly defined in masculine terms. Recognizable in the common sense, practical considerations that determined this outcome is a paradox endemic to liberal democratic welfare states. In the context of liberal democratic values, the administrative authority of welfare reformers is produced by processes that reflect and reproduce the social hierarchies whose disadvantaging effects reformers seek to correct. Professionals appear to benefit from these processes, but if their welfare goals include some form of community organization, they face the mixed consequences of the paradox quite directly. The case of recreation organization in Brantford, to which we will now turn, shows how professional public recreationists aspired to remake community politics on more democratic lines, and how this project foundered on its liberal assumptions.

5

The Meanings of Citizen Participation: Brantford, 1945–1957

In 1951 an ORA conference speaker explained why recreation was important to citizenship or, as he put it, to 'our way of life.' Because people '*want* to participate' in organized recreation, he said, 'they are willing to co-operate, willing to take responsibility, willing to give a little.' These attitudes were, in his view, essential to democratic citizenship and were encouraged more by voluntary activities than by compulsory ones. In a world where people were obliged to go to school, impelled by necessity to work, and pressured by social convention into church attendance, recreation was, according to this speaker, a unique realm of freedom. Seeking pleasure through self-organized, collective pursuits linked leisure and democracy. Playgrounds, clubs, night classes, and sports were all means to foster active citizenship.[1]

While all Ontario recreation directors were taught these precepts, Brantford's first recreation director, John Pearson, had the reputation for practising them exceptionally well between 1945 and 1953. Among the various mid-sized Ontario municipalities, such as Guelph and Hamilton, that attempted to organize elaborate schemes of citizen participation, Brantford was one of the most successful. While its relative success made it atypical, the system of citizen involvement that was attempted in Brantford was, in general, the kind of social organization the government, through the experts in the Community Programmes Branch, meant to encourage. By getting ordinary people involved in planning and providing social services, the recreationists in Brantford hoped to accomplish Premier George Drew's goal of showing 'how free people live together.'[2] In Brantford, especially, the recreation movement's professionals resisted becoming bureaucrats and tried to foster citizen-led organizations that could hold at least municipal policy makers accountable to their constituents. In short, the recreation movement in Brantford, in its early years, was intended to make citizen participation part of the welfare state, so that the welfare state would be democratic. But after some initial success, the Brantford experiment failed in these political goals.

By the late 1950s, recreation in Brantford, as elsewhere, became only though not unimportantly, an efficiently (and professionally) provided municipal service. It ceased being a spearhead of citizen participation and, implicitly, of democratization in civic culture. In examining the causes for that outcome in this one community, we can see how the 'molecular networks of everyday power relations' were an essential part of the foundation of bureaucracy. Bureaucratization took place over time, and at certain stages of that process the hierarchies of the workplace, wealth, and family decisively determined whether citizens' attempts at participation would be rewarded with power. When participation did not empower, the ground was readied for the growth of bureaucracy.[3] This connection between social relations of gender and class and the formation of bureaucracy can be seen especially well in the Brantford case, where citizen alienation *preceded* a drive by professionals to limit participation. While the motivations of professionals contributed to Brantford's change in participation after 1956, the shift away from a relatively broad activism was already observably under way in 1953. Rather than being imposed by professionals, this shift came from volunteers' own experience of citizen activism. Finding themselves forced to accept a limited range of choices, ordinary citizens ultimately chose bureaucracy.

The Promise of Participation

The precise political potential of citizen participation depended, of course, on exactly how that broad notion was defined. Cold war idealism about democracy animated both conservative and change-oriented political projects. Within the recreation movement, and indeed generally, there were two strands of thinking about and practice of 'participation.' The first – and the one that was most likely Drew's – was rooted in the activities of service clubs and women's benevolent societies. For these groups, 'democratic living' meant a sort of organized helpfulness. Translated into the terms of the public recreation movement, such social involvement had the extra democratic virtue of being inclusive. Whereas private benevolent groups organized themselves as businessmen or as Catholic women or as farmers, in public recreation, the chance to help out was open to all citizens. Private groups performed valuable social services, but only through public recreation did this work become citizen participation in government. By cooperating in a public program, citizens of all sorts would be obliged to find common ground – in effect, to see social decisions from the brokerage standpoint of their elected officials. In addition to this indirect learning, participants in public recreation were also linked by the grant system to the leadership education programs of the provincial recreation office. In this way of thinking, then, citizen participation in public recreation was a means of expanding and informing citizen activity in a way that would tend to legitimate government. In effect, this kind of participation reduced the distance between government and private groups; citizen groups involved in public recreation became auxiliaries to a state enterprise. Indeed, this conception of participation in governnment might appropriately be labelled 'auxiliary.'

The political promise of participation was quite different when it was rooted in reformist social work and the labour movement. These were the sources of the second strand of recreation movement thinking and practice, which might be labelled 'insurgent.' In this mode, citizen participation meant cooperation among citizens *in opposition* to government. While still founded in a faith that democratic government under capitalism could be made to work, this oppositional notion of citizen participation assumed that, for the working class, democracy did not yet work at all well.[4] In the 1940s a recent and successful example of such citizen participation had been Chicago's 'Back of the Yards' Neighbourhood Council, whose purpose was to support the nascent packing house workers' union. The council's organizer, social worker Saul Alinsky, called it an example of 'the people's organization,' and intended it to be an opposition force against elite-dominated governments. This sort of organization shared with the auxiliary idea the hope that participation could overcome socially divisive racial and ethnic hatreds, but the insurgent conception accepted that the people were often at odds with their rulers. Alinsky's tactically inventive left populism became famous in the radical politics of the 1960s. Part of what is intriguing about the Brantford story is that it shows an Alinskyite idea of citizen participation at work in a moment, not of left radicalism, but of real optimism about liberal democracy.

When Pearson came to Brantford, he, like Alinsky, had a working-class background, a sociology education, and work experience in community organization. His previous job had been as the YMCA community secretary in Broadview, a working-class area of Toronto.[5] Once in Brantford, Pearson began to build public recreation on what he called 'the Alinsky formula,' or, as he modestly acknowledged in a letter to its originator, his own 'warped version of it.' The goal of 'the formula' was to generate in city neighbourhoods a form of popular organization that would bring people together and empower them in relationship to city government, large property owners, powerful merchants, and big businesses. Alinsky proposed that people reject 'charity.' He argued that a community could only get what it needed if its members together made their own decisions about what they wanted and collectively went about satisfying those needs, by whatever means possible.[6]

This formula implied the rejection of some of the recreation organizations that had previously existed in Brantford. In particular, an organization that was formed the year before Pearson's arrival violated Alinsky's idea of citizen participation. The city-funded Brantford Playgrounds and Recreational Commission consisted of middle-class women and men representing service groups such as the IODE and the Optimists.[7] Such elite leaders, doing good for other people, were the objects of Alinsky's scorn in his 1946 *Reveille for Radicals*. In this, his first manual for community organizers, he argued that 'the people's organization' had to be led by a community's 'natural' leaders, not its self-appointed upper crust, however benevolent the latter's intentions. The radical organizer's job was to get to know the people of the community and to find out which individuals had authority based in personality rather than position. The organizer could also help find a local issue that mattered to ordinary people, an issue that the fledgling people's organization could fight and win. Victory in 'battle,' followed by agreement on a democratic constitution, would form the basis of an enduring and empowering people's organization.[8]

That Pearson intended to use the Alinsky method is clear; how closely he meant to adhere to it is unknown. His actual organizing approach, as it appears in the documentary evidence, certainly resembles Alinsky's, especially in the way Pearson sought out new community leaders. The main difference seems to have been that Pearson was less combative, more willing to accept that, although the leaders of existing charitable and service groups should not dominate civic affairs, they could usefully contribute. Nonetheless, he clearly preferred 'natural' leaders. When, in retrospect, Pearson identified one man as 'the model for a volunteer person in the community,' his choice was not a service club representative or a YMCA leader, but a factory worker who came to the recreation movement by joining a neighbourhood community committee.[9]

Pearson's Alinskyite ideas met with a favourable reception in Brantford. Between 1945 and 1948, about three hundred other men and women, showed, by joining community committees, that Pearson's way of organizing public recreation worked.[10] Committee membership alone does not prove that these individuals adhered to Alinsky's political methods, but subsequent events, described below, show that there was an insurgent element in the volunteers' ideas about participation. And, given Brantford's history, it is not surprising that some of the recreation volunteers were attracted specifically by a populist-socialist style of community organizing. Situated in the rural heartland of the United Farmers Organization and the cooperative movement, Brantford city voters themselves had elected a labourite mayor, M.M. (Mac) MacBride, for eight terms in the inter-war years, and in 1946 had elected another left-labour mayor, stereotyper J.H. Matthews. Successful organizing in the 1940s meant that, by 1949, roughly 37 per cent of Brantford's paid labour force were union members. It is not surprising, then, that as Pearson's scheme of citizen participation unfolded, the ideas he brought to Brantford met with an appreciative reception, at least in some circles. Certainly, at the beginning, Mayor Matthews liked Pearson's novel suggestion that the recreation program should be generated from popular requests rather than be predetermined by the recreation director.[11]

Inclusiveness: The Community Committees

Like the experts in the provincial government, Pearson believed that for a recreation director actively to promote his own ideas about 'wholesome' or 'constructive' activities was to predestine citizen participation to failure. He described his role as a director as being initially like radar, finding out 'what's around' by sending out a wave of energy and observing the pattern of its rebound. He later recalled that to some people this looked like he was 'sitting on his fanny,' but in fact he was actively seeking a certain kind of initiative. More than individual initiative, Pearson wanted to foster community organization. A principle of 'No activity without a committee' complemented his stand of 'No program without public demand.'[12] He wanted to discourage the notion that, as the main employee of the Recreation Commission, he would busy himself in planning activities, coaching teams, and managing building projects. In his view, these were functions a well-organized community could perform itself. Consequently, if someone said 'We need more tennis in this town,' Pearson would ask, 'Well, what are you doing about it?' And he met demands for new facilities with suggestions that there were other – and better – routes to making more activities possible.[13] At the beginning of all these routes lay the formation of a community committee.

In Pearson's view, the best way to provide recreation was to mobilize neighbourhood energies, to build 'a sense of community.' 'Where do you live?' and not 'What budget do you need?' was his first question to an interested citizen. To illustrate what people could do on their own, Pearson wrote in his first *Recreation Bulletin* that one man, by flooding the lot near his house, had made a rink for the smaller children, and in this way had 'given a lead to [his] community for neighbourhood projects.' The first initiative that truly fit Pearson's ideas was a request from a self-organized neighbourhood committee for a playground rink. What was attractive to Pearson about their request was that, to supplement the city's contribution to their rink, they were willing to raise money to pay for instructors and program materials and event publicity.[14] Such efforts, Pearson believed, would help build community feeling.

In the years that followed, the example of this neighbourhood's committee was copied in other parts of the city. When they reached their peak in 1952, Brantford's community recreation committees operated in eighteen different neighbourhoods, scattered evenly throughout the city's residential areas (Figure 5.1).[15] The members of these committees raised money for recreation and shared the work of organizing and supervising activities. They even built some equipment.[16] And between 1946 and 1954, recreation volunteers also participated in a 'people's organization,' the Community Committees Council. This council was formed at a meeting Pearson arranged near the end of his first year's work, to encourage representatives from the community committees to plan cooperatively their winter programming. Through their discussion of joint activities, the representatives decided to form the council, which would meet monthly not only to plan programs but also to make representations to the Recreation Commission, the recreation authority appointed by the city council. From this beginning, citizen participation expanded and became more oppositional.

Grassroots citizen participation in the Brantford recreation movement, then, had two levels: neighbourhood committees and a city-wide council of committee representatives. Both levels contributed to the rec-

FIGURE 5.1

Map of Brantford, 1952, showing the location of community committees existing at various times between 1946 and 1952.

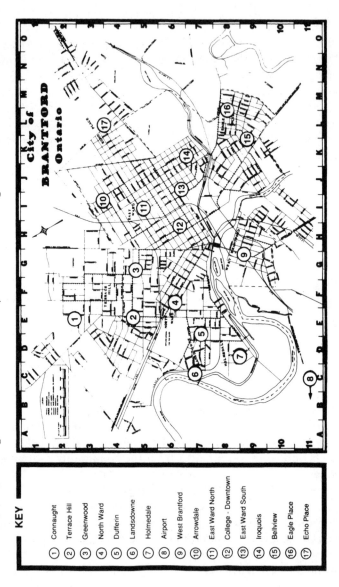

City of
BRANTFORD
Ontario

KEY

1. Connaught
2. Terrace Hill
3. Greenwood
4. North Ward
5. Dufferin
6. Landsdowne
7. Holmedale
8. Airport
9. West Brantford
10. Arrowdale
11. East Ward North
12. College – Downtown
13. East Ward South
14. Iroquois
15. Bellview
16. Eagle Place
17. Echo Place

Source: Cartographic and Architectural Archives Division, National Archives of Canada, NMC 12947 S. BRR, Community Committees Council, minutes, 12 January 1949, 1, 5 September 1951.

reation movement's democratization goals, but each did so in its own specific way. The council was more specifically Alinskyite, whereas the community committees served a purpose common to both the auxiliary and the insurgent notions of participation. The community committees were the primary sites for building a new sense of community, or, in other words, promoting social integration. They were to be inclusive and welcoming bodies that would help transcend social divisions. On a foundation of social integration, decision making would be more democratic, more able to serve common purposes. Every committee member would be a 'citizen.'

At the level of the community committees, this vision seems to have met with substantial success, carefully nurtured by Pearson. To encourage the inclusion of different social groups in the committees, Pearson started sending out a *Recreation Bulletin* in the winter of 1946 to people who, in his words, were 'actually or potentially leaders in the neighbourhood in which they live.'[17] That working-class leaders were among those who Pearson hoped to attract to the recreation movement was signalled in his first editorial: 'labour's demands,' he wrote, were leading to 'a better life for more people.' In the context of the labour climate of 1945–6, when the new industrial unions were fighting pitched battles against the attempts by major employers to hammer them back into Depression-era impotence, this mild observation amounted to a pro-union stance.

Clearly, Pearson was trying to get working-class people involved in the recreation movement. And surviving records indicate that the citizens who became involved in organizing recreation through these committees were, in fact, sociologically diverse, in class status and other ways. The committees included both women and men (slightly more men). Members came from all social classes, but the majority were working class (see columns three and four in Table 5.1). The women were more likely to be working class than the city's male recreation volunteers: 69 per cent of the women in the sample, including commission members as well as committee members, were working class, as against 58 per cent of the men. The committees were virtually uniform in one respect: 91 per cent of members were married people. The members' ethnicity is difficult to judge; however, the presence on committee lists of names such as Camilleri, Schwarzkopf, Papai, Barsotta, Szoke, Souliere, and Romanuk indicate that the 23 per cent of Brantford's population who were not Anglo-Celtic were among those involved.[18]

The degree of social mixing in the recreation committees was

Table 5.1
Summary of Class[a] and Sex Distribution of Volunteer Leaders in the Brantford Recreation Movement, 1944–61

	Recreation commission members[b] (n is 87)	Key people on community committees[c] (n is 50)	Community committee executives[d] (n is 127)	Community committee attendance[e] (n is 59)	Miscellaneous[f] (n is 59)	Total number[g] (n is 336)	M	F
Men (%)	91	70	60	54	59	65		
Women (%)	9	30	40	46	41	35		
							M	F
Working class (%)	33	73	81	62	61	62	59	69
Professional/ Manager (%)	47	17	16	30	29	28	31	21
Owners (%)	20	10	3	8	10	10	10	10
Not identifiable (n)	6	2	3	5	7	22	19	3

aThe class for men was determined by the occupation given for them in the city directory, and for women either by their own paid work or by the occupations of their husbands or fathers. This sample included only four women who were identified as paid workers in the city directory. Because only one occupation was given for married couples, the extent of married women's paid work is undoubtedly under-stated. Four occupations of ambiguous class status were classified as follows: the class position for salesmen was determined by the character of their neighbourhood and the type of commodity they sold; tradesmen who owned their own business were included in the 'owner' category; grocers were labelled 'owners' if their home address was separate from their store address, and, if not, as working class. Foremen were categorized as managers.

Table 5.1 (concluded)

bThis sample includes names of individuals (each counted only once) who served on the Postwar Recreational Projects Committee (1944) and the Recreation Commission in 1944, 1945, 1948 to 1954, 1957, and 1959. The names were taken from annual lists that were usually kept in the binders containing minutes and in the Brantford City Council minutes. Some mid-year changes of service club appointees may have been missed.

cThis sample includes names of individuals (each counted only once) who served as CCC delegates or representatives, or who participated in significant committees or special meetings, as follows: individuals chosen in 1948 to lobby aldermen; members of the 1949 constitution committee, the 1950 Community Centre meeting, the 1951 Community Centers Committee, organizers of the 1953 Crafts and Recreation Fair; attendances of the 1953 fall and winter programs planning meeting; delegates to the Recreation Commission from 1948 to 1952; and the Recreation Office's 1955 list of contact names for each Community Committee.

dThis sample includes the names of individuals (each counted only once) on surviving executive lists, for the years 1950, 1953 to 1956, and 1961, for the following neighbourhoods: Echo Place, Arrowdale, Eagle Place, North Ward, Bellview, and Iroquois.

eThis sample consists of fifty-nine names taken from attendance rosters in the minutes of four well-attended meetings in the first three years of the council (November 1946, January 1947, September 1947, and June 1948).

fThis category includes individuals who attended four event-related committees in 1946 and one public organization meeting in 1952.

gSome individuals appeared in more than one category; consequently, the total sample number is less than the sum of the sample subsets.

uneven, depending as it did on the composition of the committees' neighbourhoods. This is apparent in newspaper reports of the formation of three early recreation committees. Of the thirty-six committee members named, thirteen were women, and twenty-three men. Working-class men (twelve) and women (seven) were in the majority of those named, among the thirty-three identifiable individuals. However, the county crown attorney was also on one of the committees; he was one of ten men with professional or managerial occupations, and there were two women married to men from this social stratum. Fewest in number were the three small business owners and business owners' wives. In Connaught, a predominantly working-class suburban neighbourhood, six of the seven named committee members (two women, five men) came from working-class homes. More socially diverse was the committee centred on the Spring Street rink. Around this rink were two very different neighbourhoods: modest Victorian workers' cottages, many without telephones, were at the bottom of the hill, and at the top were mansions. Residents of both neighbourhoods were on the committee.[19]

Those who initiated the organization of the committees wanted them to foster social integration, that is, to establish cooperative relations that transcended religious lines, class differences, and narrow neighbourhood exclusiveness. Reflecting on a particular committee's success in building a broader community, one of Pearson's two staff organizers found that differences among the members in 'social mores and economic status' provided 'fizz but not disruption.' Some social divisions proved intractable: for instance, 'Red' Poles and 'White' Poles both helped with recreation organization in the North Ward area but were unwilling to attend the same meetings. However, other social gulfs were narrowed: in a neighbourhood of southeast Brantford, community recreation brought Protestant committee members for the first time into the Catholic Church hall, a step that required them to overcome a certain suspicious fearfulness.[20] Although we cannot assume that all of the community committees were equally successful in fostering social integration, most were remarkably stable over the period. Some expired, but only in one area did there seem to have been splintering.[21] Certainly, some of the committees accomplished at least one of the reform objectives of citizen participation, having acted as a means to constructing communities based primarily on citizen status. A state-funded program made this comparatively easy, because the activities these volunteers supported were funded with 'their' money as taxpayers.

Insurgency: Council and Commission

While the community committees contributed to breaking down social exclusiveness, the function of the Community Committees Council (CCC) was to modify power hierarchies. One might say that, while the committees taught cooperation, the CCC taught confrontation. At the beginning, its members saw themselves only as an advisory body. However, conflicts in the period from 1948 to 1952 would show that the CCC was where citizen participation became an attempt to empower subordinate groups. It was the CCC's fate by 1953 that spoke most tellingly to questions about the political meaning in Brantford of citizen participation.

The CCC was hindered more than helped in its democratic goals by its links with a government program. This was so because the CCC was incorporated into municipal government in a legally subordinate position. It had no power to spend public money; this power was held by the City Council and was delegated in part to the Recreation Commission and the Recreation Department's paid staff. (The Recreation Commission itself was a volunteer board, but was appointed by City Council. As can be seen in Table 5.1, 67 per cent of its members over the period from 1945 to 1961 were business owners, professionals, or managers.) In the constitutional arrangement that centred fiscal authority in these bodies, the mainly working-class women and men of the community committees could only exert power by influencing the Recreation Commission.

Their efforts through the CCC to achieve such influence were, to a degree, successful. When the committees began in 1946, they had no say in budget decisions. By 1953, the CCC had six seats on the twenty-four–member Recreation Commission that determined the budget. Also, by 1952 the community committees successfully claimed the authority to approve collectively in their council all requests for services and facilities. After 1954, when recreation commissions had only seven members, one was a designated woman representative and another a community committee representative. Notably, however, this representation was informal, not the result of delegation by the committees' own council.[22]

In fact, this success in achieving representation, although noteworthy, was counterbalanced after 1953 by a withering of the community committees' collective voice. Between 1949 and 1953 there was a series of conflicts over resources and methods of representation, conflicts that reduced the community committees from an organized council to unconnected groups of petitioners. An organizational structure that had approached participatory democracy was replaced by one with only token representation of women and community people on a mainly middle-class, predominantly male commission.

This change in Brantford's recreation-based experiment in municipal democracy was clearly a class one. Compared with the community committees, the Recreation Commission included relatively few members of the working class. Even more notable, however, is the disparity between the large participation of women in the committees and their near absence in the commission (seen by comparing the first column with the other columns in Table 5.1). These class and gender patterns are connected. When the mainly working-class community committees were excluded from the highest decision-making body, so were most of the movement's female members. As previously noted, women in Brantford's recreation movement were a more working-class group than were the male recreation volunteers. And it was in the CCC and on the local executives, which were working-class terrain, that women most frequently appeared. If the Brantford recreation movement taught democratic methods, it was in the CCC that women volunteers had their best opportunity to learn and to be empowered. As the CCC declined and disappeared, so did one of working-class Brantford women's avenues for an activist citizenship.

In part, this activism was about community self-reliance, but the conflicts between the CCC and the Recreation Commission showed that some volunteers came to share Pearson's idea about enabling local communities more effectively to direct city government. At first, however, the CCC members imagined their role in relatively modest terms. In a September 1947 statement on the CCC's relationship to the Recreation Commission, its members stated that, 'primarily,' their council was 'a place for the exchange of ideas and the review of local problems which might be solved by the experience of other members of the Council,' with the commission 'responsible for the overall policy of the municipal recreation programme.' The CCC would implement policy and solve local problems, making representations to the commission only when problems proved beyond its resources.[23]

This view of the relationship between the CCC and the Recreation Commission reflected manager–worker and breadwinner–housewife hierarchies familiar in daily life. The breadwinner supplies the budget, and the housewife makes it do for the family's needs. The manager sets production goals and quality standards, and the worker makes procedural decisions about how these goals will be met. If the budget is too small or the production goals unreasonable, the subordinates have the power of protest.

Underpinning this power, which is one of the 'powers of the weak' that Linda Gordon and Elizabeth Janeway have movingly described, was the fact that the members of community committees did so much of the work in providing recreation.[24] By 1948 the CCC represented three hundred volunteers, who organized street dances, playground supervision, euchre games, movie nights, craft classes, concerts, current events discussions, folk dancing, and garden parties. As many as six community centres, which were activity groups that met on winter evenings in schools, were managed largely by volunteers. On the basis of this labour, the members of the community committees could and did claim that they were as much recreation 'experts' as the paid staff or the commissioners.[25] But until 1948, they could only offer that expertise through ad hoc delegations to the commission.

In June 1948 this power relationship – part of Keane's 'molecular networks' – began to change, as the community committees began to push the limits of their advisory status. The catalyst for new developments in the CCC's relationship with the commission was dissatisfaction with hazardous playground surfaces and shortages of equipment. Convinced that the commission was neglecting 'pressing' needs at the playgrounds, CCC members decided to send a delegation to the commission. One of them, Vern Hamilton,[26] called for reciprocal membership between the CCC and the commission. This suggestion bespoke the CCC's desire for a real change in its subordinate relationship to the Commission. In a gesture towards satisfying this desire, the commission agreed to add to its membership one representative from the CCC.[27]

The presence of a CCC representative on the commission meant that those who did the bulk of the movement's volunteer work now had a voice in budget decisions. And the commission soon learned that some of the CCC's interventions cost money. In the fall of 1948, Stephanie Burliuk described to the CCC the problems of families living in her low-income neighbourhood in downtown Brantford, in particular the lack of safe, attractive play space for children. At the next monthly meeting, representing a newly formed community committee, she said that the downtown needed a rink, a nursery school, and salaries for playground supervisors. The CCC endorsed her request for funding and, at the Recreation Commission meeting the next night, a special CCC delegation told the commissioners that 'the work in their communities could not progress unless their needs were budgeted for.' This position was accepted by the commission, but only after unusual 'discussion.'[28] Securing the commission's support for increased spending by the community committees was a genuine victory for the CCC: five months earlier, in the summer of 1948, Pearson had told the commissioners that the recreation budget had 'reached its peak.'[29]

In spite of its supposed support for the CCC's budget, the commission continued to stymie improvements in the downtown. In June 1949 it refused an offer of downtown playground space that would have cost only the amount of the vacant lot's annual property tax. Shortly after this offer was rejected, Burliuk's Central Ward community committee broke up, presumably discouraged by the lack of progress in finding play space. Only after she again roused the CCC to action the following spring were playgrounds found for downtown children. No new land was purchased for park use; instead, an existing, dirt-surfaced park was seeded for grass and Central Presbyterian Church allowed its 'backyard' to become a playground.[30]

The problem of the downtown playgrounds showed the limits of the CCC's power on the Recreation Commission; with more CCC members on the commission, the June 1949 decision on the tax deal would likely have been different. The CCC, in its own meetings, had responded sympathetically to the downtown committee's concerns. The disparity between its response and the commission's fed into its feeling that the commission was not sufficiently amenable to suggestion. Consequently, at the 1950 spring conference of community committees, members voted to seek greater representation on the commission.[31]

The mover of this motion was Bert Morgen, the factory worker whom Pearson later recalled as 'the model volunteer.' Morgen was energetically involved in community work, not only in the recreation movement, but also as an active member of the Brantford CCF Association and as an officer of the employee credit union at his place of work. According to Pearson, Morgen worked 'like a dog,' and was 'one of the demanding elements in our Community Committees' Council.' Sometimes, Pearson admits, Morgen would 'get us uptight' and get the Recreation department involved 'in more than [they] were ready for,' but 'he had appeal' because he worked so hard.[32] Indeed, the documentary evidence shows that Morgen had considerable influence on the CCC until he left it in 1951. As one of two CCC representatives on the Recreation Commission in 1950 and 1951 (the other, Harold Williams, was also a factory worker), he attempted to increase the CCC's power.

The strategy of Morgen and Williams was to increase the proportion of the commission positions held by members of the CCC. From only one in 1948, the CCC had come to have two of the twenty seats on the commission in 1950, still a small minority. In the fall of 1950 the commission began discussing the possibility of becoming a smaller, 'more efficient' body. Three proposals were made: for a thirteen-member, ten-member, or nine-member commission. Notably, the thirteen-member proposal was the only one that satisfied the basic demand of the CCC representatives that 'one less than half of the Recreation Commission' should be CCC representatives.[33]

The politics of the CCC representatives are suggested by the fact that the proposal for thirteen members was, relatively speaking, the 'left-wing' one. It included six CCC representatives, omitted representation from the Board of Trade, and provided for two members at large. By contrast, the proposed ten-member commission did not even include a labour representative. The nine-member commission was to include a representative from Brantford's Labour Council to 'match' the Board of Trade representative; this last proposal was the only one to include a member of the Board of Trade but there were to be no citizens at large and only two community committee members.

When a new Recreation Commission constitution finally became law the following spring, the CCC got its six positions, but the new by-law was unfriendly to the CCC's aspirations for a greater voice. In its new form the commission was actually larger than the previous one. Its by-law provided for twenty-four members, making CCC representation only one-quarter of the total. The commission had rejected the thinking behind the thirteen-member proposal, which had explicitly challenged the subordination of 'workers' to 'managers' and had even privileged the former over the latter as representing 'the community.' Morgen and Williams had argued that CCC members were 'much closer to the work being carried on and are thus in a better position to serve on the Commission.' They had claimed that, in relation to the services offered by the Recreation Commission, they, as volunteer workers, knew more and could serve better on the Commission than, say, a member of the Rotary Club or the Board of Trade or the Knights of Columbus. The community centres were more truly 'community efforts' because they were run by the participants, as distinct from the programs run by service clubs for the benefit of client groups. It was the *self-activity* of the committees that made them 'the community' in public recreation.[34] But the influence of this political view on the revision of the commission's constitution was, in the end, insufficient. The equal share in policy making that Morgen and Williams had sought for the CCC was denied.

Both men served out their terms as CCC representatives on the commission, but had doubts about how seriously the other commissioners viewed the opinions of the CCC.[35] In the enlarged Recreation Commission, the community committees, as the users and direct contributors to public recreation, were subordinated to a larger taxpaying public. One suspects that the citizenship of the community committees was seen as insufficiently disinterested. If this was so, then their involvement in the money-spending commission was restricted precisely because they wanted to participate in a double-sided way, as both users and managers of public recreation. This suggests the operation of a principle that, in the early years of Ontario's liberal welfare state, people had to be either citizen-constituents or consumer-clients. In other words, using welfare services disqualified people who were in other ways citizens from participation in government as policy makers, who were defined as 'disinterested.' Certainly, in the Brantford situation, the Commission–Council hierarchy separated users from managers and subordinated the former. This power relationship invited the alienation of the user.

Some of the users challenged this relationship. Not only Morgen, but also others in the CCC, fought to get more power for the subaltern elements of the recreation movement. They took a series of steps to make the CCC more powerful. By revising its own constitution, the CCC attempted to give itself a quasi-legal form of authority. Its 1948 constitution required the Recreation Commission to go through the CCC in providing services to community committees. It also forced any community committee that wanted services from the city's recreation office to attend CCC meetings regularly in order for the CCC to endorse its requests. Adopting 'grievance procedures' helped deal with internal weaknesses in the relationships among the committees, and so made them organizationally stronger.[36]

As the relationship between the commission and the CCC became more oppositional, the latter further adjusted its political methods. In 1951, during the debate about the Recreation Commission's constitution, the CCC dropped its practice of rotating chairs, and adopted instead an annual term. Seeing themselves as policy intervenors rather than merely apprentices in democratic method, the community committees gave the chair power based in continuity instead of furnishing many members with practice in leading meetings.[37] At the same session, the CCC changed its regular meeting time so that the Recreation Commission's committees would not put off reviewing CCC recommendations until weeks after they were made.[38] Together, these measures suggest that, in general, the CCC had come to take a tactical, more than a collegial approach in its relationship with the commission.

Unfortunately, having failed to gain even near-equal representation on the Recreation Commission, the CCC was without coercive power. Notably, the community committees did not contemplate withdrawing their volunteer labour in support of the CCC representatives on the commission. Consequently, when serious disagreements arose, the commissioners could dismiss the CCC's objections. This power imbalance was demonstrated in September 1952 when CCC representatives objected to the sale of a city playground to the Board of Education for a building site, an event that raised conflicts over social rights versus property rights. In the debate that followed, the CCC representatives found their motions ignored. Options that would have protected the playground, such as the expropriation by the city of privately owned vacant lots, were bypassed. Whereas the CCC wanted the social right to recreational space to be given priority over private land uses, the commissioners, reflexively, in a class-conditioned manner, defended property rights. And the commissioners' legal position in local government gave them the one-sided power to conclude the issue.[39]

As relations between the CCC and the Recreation Commission developed, it became apparent that the latter welcomed the contributions of the community committees only when these were offers to raise funds, canvass popular needs, publicize activities, or help with supervision. Here, there were grounds for cooperation: the CCC and the commission alike wanted to see better provision for non-commercial recreation. On spending questions, however, the commission would not meet 'public demand' as articulated by the CCC. It also differed from the CCC on the definition of 'the community.' Rooted in the charitable model of community service, the commission welcomed the neighbourhood committees as one more recreation interest group, one that was perhaps not quite responsible on questions of budgets and property. The community committees, founded on an inclusive idea of participation by 'all the people' and directly engaged in providing public services, believed themselves uniquely representative of the community. In the end, their ideal of inclusiveness was used in a way they had not anticipated, to swamp the representatives of these participant organizations in a sea of delegates from service clubs. The community committees were denied policy-making power that was commensurate with the labour they contributed.

A Change in the Meaning of 'Citizen Participation'

After September 1952, events and circumstances discouraged any further attempts to make the CCC a vehicle for the exercise of power by participants. In March 1953, John Pearson resigned his position and left Brantford, to study with Saul Alinsky, among other things. Three months later, area director Helen Wilson, who, like Pearson's assistant directors, had worked on developing community committees, also left, her departure substantially reducing staff support for the community committees. The committees expressed appreciation for her past work in 'community organization,' but reported that they now wanted a staff member who would initiate and lead activities.[40]

These parting words reflected the fact that the volunteers had a part in enlarging the power of professionals. The division of responsibilities between volunteers and paid staff had been, at times, a point of dispute between Pearson and the community committees. Some committee members wanted Recreation Department staff to take over the administration and operation of the community centres, even to initiate new program activities. But Pearson argued that to use staff in this way would be to undermine community involvement in the centres. His idea had always been to make services contingent on citizen participation. Like Morgen and Williams, Pearson thought that citizen participation meant providing volunteer labour and getting, in return, a voice in formulating policy.[41]

For at least the first five or six years of his tenure in Brantford, Pearson had been successful in motivating recreation volunteers to participate on these terms. Even a volunteer who wanted to shift some responsibilities to paid staff expressed pride in 'our community set-up,' and was himself a reliable participant in all manner of meetings. Recalling his high school and university days as a seasonal worker under Pearson, another man said Pearson expected you 'to do virtually impossible things and you did them ... you beefed about it but you did it nonetheless.' Why? 'Because everyone believed [in] him.'[42]

Getting people working for the services they wanted was not necessarily the same as engaging them in political life, of course. After all, pitching in was part of the auxiliary idea of participation. The Brantford recreation movement included volunteers who were interested primarily in getting programs of activities for their children and themselves. Developments after Pearson's departure suggest that, in the absence of his assiduous pushing and pulling, many such volunteers became unwilling to work for the larger, Alinskyite project of claiming a voice in policy making. After 1953 the CCC, the voice of the volunteers in funding debates, ceased to operate.

Staff departures were only a part of the changing forces that determined the CCC's fate and, with it, the meaning of citizen participation. Militating against the CCC's survival were its earlier defeats on land and representation issues. There had been genuine attempts to exercise collective power, and they had been frustrated by the powers that be on the commission. The CCC had begun to suffer from creeping ineffectiveness; the CCC's endorsement in the spring of 1953 had certainly not helped the Terrace Hill community committee's request for swings and a drinking fountain, which was still unmet in September. A sense of this ineffectiveness must have helped discourage participation in policy meetings. In early 1953, few community committee representatives were going to Recreation Commission meetings, and attendance at the CCC's own monthly sessions was also poor.[43]

Poor attendance at meetings was hardly surprising when even participation in the committees' winter recreational programs was shrinking. The community centres, which had helped keep community committees active throughout the year, were only minimally active after the winter of 1952–3. Competition came from the school board's new evening classes, which required no supplementary committee work. One group of women interested in rug hooking had refused to cooperate when Pearson secured from a local carpet manufacturer a supply of free wool scraps, which needed 'only' to be sorted by hand to be useful. They suggested that it would be better simply to buy wool. Some participants had said they would go to classes held by the Craft Guild and pay its higher fees if it offered 'better projects' than the community centres did.[44] Persistent difficulties in organizing a babysitting service at the centres probably discouraged some women with young children from seeking recreation, and, by extension, from attending meetings.[45] The number of adults willing to 'work to play' was also undoubtedly reduced by the increasing number of families with television sets between 1953 and 1955. In 1954, the North Ward committee seems to have been typical in observing that it could not 'commit itself to very much – financially or otherwise.'[46] Pearson's view of citizen participation had required an intense pace of volunteer work. Reasonably enough, then, volunteers sought to reduce their effort. Participation in the CCC became a logical place to cut, once the Recreation Commission had made the CCC powerless.

Already crippled by November 1952, the CCC was dealt a death blow when, late in 1953, the Recreation Commission was remade in a less representative form, with no positions assigned to the CCC. The commission by-law was amended in order to shrink it to seven members, one of whom would be a city councillor and at least one other a woman.[47] With the CCC broken up, citizen participation had, in effect, ceased to be about policy making.

This change was consolidated, after 1956, when the purpose of the community committees themselves was deliberately altered. The new recreation director appointed in 1956 was keen on citizen participation, but he defined it in narrower terms than had Pearson. Later, reflecting on his time in Brantford, the new director said (in an unfortunately revealing phrase) that he had agreed with the idea that participants would ultimately 'grow up' to be members of policy-making bodies. He concluded, however, by saying that it 'never did happen really while [he] was there.'[48]

He had arrived in Brantford as an assistant director in the fall of 1953, at the tail-end of the CCC's existence, when it was no longer especially vital. After he became director in 1956, he redefined the community committees.

> They were no longer community committees, having [an] interest in the whole government process. I narrowed it down to be a recreation interest because I couldn't see this community committee thing. I know that John [Pearson] still thinks that community committees and community councils having a full concern with the full range of government are important; anyway, we narrowed it down. The people who participated in those committees were making community-building decisions. They helped select where the parks were going to be, what programmes the parks would offer, what kinds of things should be done on them, how they should be designed.[49]

This director, while valuing popular involvement in government, did not push volunteers as far as Pearson had. While the later director wanted to 'support and encourage' community committees, he assigned them a more limited, auxiliary role. This professional's view did, indeed, shape the development of Brantford's experiment in citizen participation, but by the time of his arrival 'the people' had already made their choices about participation.[50]

The volunteers in the later period were no longer especially interested in testing the limits of citizen participation. Many continued to be active in public recreation, but after the frustrations of 1950–2, those who had pushed the limits of social hierarchies turned away from the Alinskyite council model. Having genuine policy power appeared not to have been a real option. And so, after 1952, they redirected their hopes. Together with others in the community committees, they turned their attention to providing services for their communities within the limits set by higher authorities. Staff-supplied services took centre stage, supplanting the recreation movement's less efficient self-activity and political insurgency.

Undoubtedly, limiting the role of volunteers made the provision of services more efficient, saving time both for the paid staff and for the volunteer workers. But this sensible public administration strategy worked well in part because it did not modify the power relations many people took for granted. It used socially subordinate people in organizationally subaltern roles. When, in 1952, CCC representatives – factory workers and clerks – had differed with the Recreation Commission on clearly ideological lines, it was able to withstand the challenge. Later, volunteers were able to offer advice, but the commission's revised constitution put out of the question any exercise of coordinated power, by bloc voting or otherwise.

The post-1953 structure of the Recreation Commission did not prevent some working-class men and women from becoming commissioners, but they acquired their positions as individuals rather than as representatives of a grass-roots organization. The new structure confined significant budgetary decisions to the commission and to the City Council. Local committees were restricted to local matters. If, under this new arrangement, recreation volunteers disagreed with some large tendency in municipal policy, they had the usual recourses of voters – recourses taken, again, as individuals or, at best, as members of a neighbourhood committee. The possibility of a larger, collective power had been foreclosed, the project abandoned.

In its most radical dimensions, that project had been Pearson's. But the influence of a social democratic and labour element was apparent in some of the CCC's characteristics: its grievance procedures, its definition of the community's representatives, and its affirmation of social rights. That element, an influential one, had not simply been pushed along by Pearson's force of personality. Their oppositional stance was of a piece with the rest of their politics. And their abandonment of the CCC seems to have been motivated by a judgment that the struggle to

make the CCC a power in recreation policy could not be won. This dis-
illusionment, as much as Pearson's departure, led to the CCC's demise.

The end of the CCC was not the end of citizen participation, but only
a change in its political meaning. Other committee people carried on,
as they had before and during the CCC's life, as auxiliaries, helping out
the recreation office or extending municipal services by volunteering
their labour, whether by building a portable stage or sewing a canvas
shade for a sandbox. When the time came for municipal elections, perhaps they voted. As voters and helpers, Brantford recreation volunteers
in the later 1950s were certainly acting as democratic citizens. But they
were not intimately involved in the political process in the way that progressive community organizers – not only in recreation, but also labour,
education and social work – had hoped they might be, as part of their
aspirations for a better, more democratic world after the war.

Some volunteers readily accepted a limited expression of citizenship.
To describe that limit as 'accepted' is not to say that all the volunteers
made the choice to accept constraints under identical circumstances. In
particular, women and men volunteers acted as citizens in ways that
were shaped by the gender relations of their social world. The lower
proportion of women among the leaders of the community committees
(see column 2 in Table 5.1) may have reflected not only sexist assumptions about leadership in mixed-sex groups, but also the difficulty mothers experienced in attending meetings because of their diffuse and
fragmented leisure time.[51] For all volunteers, the time demands of com-
bining helping out and policy making were heavy. But the appeal of participating in the policy fray was reduced most substantially when those
volunteers (most often men) who were willing and able to practise
oppositional participation had been effectively shackled by the 1951
revision of the commission's constitution. Brantford's most basic power
relations of class and gender, more than the efforts of power-seeking
welfare professionals, had so narrowed the potential results of full participation in this part of government that insurgent activism was not
worth the effort.

The attempt to build a 'people's organization' around recreation services is part of our political history, even though prime ministers, pre-
miers, and MPs are invisible (or almost so) in the account.[52] The
community organizing efforts of the recreation movement were significant as part of a broader undertaking, in a moment of liberal democratic idealism after the Second World War, to remake the relationship
between government and the people. As the state expanded old pro-

grams or added new activities in welfare provision and economic regulation, more and more Canadians were becoming, in different ways, clients of the state. Whether, as clients, Canadians would also be constituents, that is, actors in the policy process, depended in part on efforts such as those of the Brantford Community Committees Council. In the reconstruction mood of the post-war period, such efforts seemed promising. That this promise was, in the Brantford case, only minimally fulfilled can be attributed primarily to the 'taken-for-granted' status of private property rights and to the persistent class and gender asymmetries in access to public administrative authority.

Constrained by these forces, the recreation movement activists were only partly successful. Undoubtedly, they succeeded in making recreation services a new government responsibility. But efforts towards the broader reform goals of democratic empowerment were largely frustrated. The spatial and social closeness of municipal officials to those they governed failed to prevent the effects of the social prejudices that post-war liberals disliked. The Brantford case should remind us that 'the community' (especially as some conservatives envision it) does not provide an easy alternative to alienated clienthood.[53] Indeed, the community's social hierarchies may help to ready the ground for welfare state bureaucracies. That is why democratizing political culture means tackling the hierarchies of daily life. As the next chapter shows, in the democracy of the 1950s these hierarchies allowed women a role as citizens, but only a distinctively feminine one.

6

The Feminine Mystique
in Community Leadership:
Women Volunteers in Public Recreation

Essential to the feminism of the 1960s and 1970s was the aspiration that women's experiences and concerns be taken seriously. The story of recreation services is a curious one in relation to this part of the history – and continuing priorities – of feminism. On one hand, a feminist might see recreation services as important because they were about what was understood to be mother-work: entertaining and educating children and helping to stretch families' leisure budgets. Also, feminists, even sedentary intellectual ones, may well recognize the rightness of sporting women's sense of grievance at women's second-class citizenship in leisure services. But, on the other hand, inadequacy of leisure services hardly rates as politically serious, compared with the life and death issues that emerged in second wave feminism's critiques of the welfare state: reproductive rights, universal public child care, services for battered wives, and rights for women on social assistance. These and other policy questions that directly and materially affect the very survival of women and girls are, rightly, the central foci of the history of women and welfare. But the recreation movement helps to explain an important part of the background to the struggles around these issues. To put those women's questions into the centre of political life, feminists had to combat a pervasive dismissiveness, even ridicule of women's issues.[1] This particular sexism had, of course, long roots. But its immediate origin, in the 1950s, lies, I would suggest, in the particular, limited kind of citizenship into which liberal democratic reform slotted even communities' most respected women. The role of women in Ontario's movement for public recreation vividly illustrates that construction of feminine citizenship.

As in Brantford, the devolution of the movement in most of the province into a municipal service positioned women as helpers rather than as policy makers. This ancillary position was not, of course, an entirely new phenomenon. But it went against the stated democratic aspirations of the movement's professional leaders. Moreover, in some cases, making recreation provision a service of government did actually unseat women who had previously been recognized as leaders. The reproduction in recreation of a subordinate, wifely, and maternal role, and the events that sidelined prominent women can be seen through public recreation's story in specific towns and villages and through the history of the ORA. In the political culture of 1950s Ontario, making volunteer leadership democratically 'representative' of the community seems to have entailed putting 'Dad' – men volunteers and recreation directors – in charge.

The Politics of Women's Place: Patterns and Episodes

Volunteers in the recreation movement everywhere were a mixed-gender group, but men and women, boys and girls typically did different kinds of volunteer work. In 1951 a physical education professor observed 'a current trend' to have volunteers do service work similar to their 'vocational' labour: 'lawyers ... serve as legal consultants, the homemakers ... supervise children in play centers, and the businessmen ... manage money raising campaigns.' 'Homemakers' actually performed more tasks than just child care. Extending their wifely role into community work, married women also helped out men's organizations. Imitating men's service clubs and unions, some recreation committees had ladies' auxiliaries.[2]

Whether separately organized in auxiliaries or active in mixed committees, women volunteers (married or not) were responsible for any work resembling a mother's or wife's domestic labour. In one Ottawa Valley municipality, this work was formally set out: '[The auxiliary takes] responsibility for the care and furnishings of the [recreation centre's] lounge and kitchen, assistance with the entertaining of out-of-town groups sponsored by the ... Commission, fund raising for those things the Commission budget cannot supply, acting as advisers and chaperones for teen-age groups, making recommendations to the Recreation Commission.'[3]

The wifely role of volunteers was supplemented by the low-paid women's work performed by waged activity leaders. Craft leaders (about two-thirds of them women in a 1950 Brantford sample) were urged by

Brantford's community committees to take 'the attitude of a volunteer' to their work; certainly, at $2.50 or $3.00 per night, the craft instructors had to be doing the job at least in part for the fun of it. Direct comparisons of men's and women's pay are difficult to draw from available sources because the actual hours of employment are not reported, only totals of wages paid. Summer jobs provide the one clear case of the wage differences between the sexes: where girls worked during the summer as playground supervisors and boys as swimming pool supervisors, municipalities often saved a few dollars by paying the girls $87 or $90 to the boys' $100. A similar division of labour in the winter between male hockey instructors and female figure-skating teachers may have also been accompanied by a comparable wage differential.[4] Certainly, women were welcome in low-paid, part-time jobs as activity leaders, and in this work as in purely volunteer labour, the division of tasks followed predictably gendered lines.

The few women who sat as Recreation Commission members also found that a women's niche awaited them. The committee lists of the 1951 and 1952 Brantford commission illustrate the pattern. No women appear on the Grounds and Property Committee. By contrast, two or three (in other words, almost all the women members) appear each year on the five- or six-member Publicity and Public Relations Committee. The other one or two women sat on the Programme and Personnel Committee, probably to represent the program interests of the women and girls.[5]

The prejudice against women as public administrators appears to have operated in volunteer labour as it did in paid labour. The executive committees of recreation commissions were frequently all male and always had a male majority.[6] For a woman to be the head of a recreation commission was infrequent. In the seventy-six communities whose CPB files I examined for the period covered by this study, there was only one female president. This one exception, a doctor's wife who was active in administering Girl Guides and the Home and School Association, was elected president of her town's unusually gender-balanced (four men, three women) Recreation Committee. She reported her new position rather apologetically to the provincial recreation agency: 'It also happened that I was chosen president,' she wrote, adding immediately that 'There are several young enthusiastic men in town but they haven't been here long enough for the people to know them. One of them is vice-president and is very dependable.'[7] She seemed to be reassuring the provincial recreation authority that recreation in her town of almost three thousand people had genuine male leaders, and that one of them would soon be able to assume the proper primary role in their organization.

While she described the young men as appropriate potential leaders, requiring only a longer period of residence, this woman represented herself (however objectively qualified) modestly as a temporary stand-in. These representations reflected her understanding of men's and women's relative 'acceptability to the community' in important leadership roles. This acceptability could be developed by an individual's activities, but the perceived inherent difference between men and women was such that a young man could acquire, in a few years, greater acceptability for a top position than could this experienced woman community worker.[8]

Women's niche in volunteer work, then, was to do wifely work, run programs as low-paid part-time staff, and advise on the specific program interests of women and girls. In a minority on most recreation commissions (if not completely absent), women were deemed inappropriate for the most responsible administrative jobs.

To some extent, no doubt, this pattern in women's volunteer roles reflected their choosing to serve where they felt their expertise was strongest. But not all women accepted this division of labour. The woman president of the ORA called for women to be 'in on the planning' of recreation facilities.[9] What happened when women were not included on these bodies was reflected in the history of recreation facilities in one northern city. There, the woman head of a longstanding arts and letters association recounted the failure of a decade-long fight, begun in 1944, to have rooms for her organization included in a proposed community centre.[10] Getting inadequate facilities might have indicated budget limits; not getting any facilities at all suggested strongly that this woman-led organization did not have an effective voice in that city's decisions about recreation facilities.

Events in a Toronto suburb indicate that the subordination of women volunteer leaders in recreation was sometimes the outcome of a struggle rather than an inevitability. In the late 1940s, this southern community saw a two-year-long campaign to wrest control of the community centre from the predominantly female Home and School–based council that had run the recreation programs before the war.[11] The first recreation director this council employed was a musically trained man who found the council 'very fine ... with a wide representation of people of importance on it.' In 1949 he left to take an advisory position with the CPB. The new director, a powerful personality with a sports and industrial recreation background, appears to have initiated a push for a newly constituted administrative council.

The idea was to include in the council representatives from a wider variety of organizations, and thereby to bring in more participants to the municipal recreation programs. A woman-led organization would have been seen as providing recreation only for small children and women; male leaders would establish recreation's claim to be serving 'all the people,' adults as well as children, men as well as women. The proposed restructuring of the council was an alternative to plans already formed by the old council to increase participation. In 1949, before the change in director, the council, worried about a declining number of program participants, had undertaken a survey, to 'identify needs.' At the time of the new director's arrival, the council was planning a reformulated program. Undoubtedly convinced that the present organization was already representative and already had a workable approach to expanding participation, the council resisted being restructured. Only after two years did they give way.

In addition to some representatives from the Home and School Association, the new council included delegates from the Board of Education, the municipal Council, and an unspecified variety of activity organizations. Although women served in most municipal bodies, the odds were against the representatives from the Board of Education and the municipal council both having been women. Similarly, although there were women-only activity groups, men's groups, notably sports associations, were typically in the majority.[12] Thus, the successful reorganization, whether intentionally or not, very likely reduced women in this community to a minority on the recreation policy-making body, as was typical of other municipalities.

This larger pattern of male-dominated recreation administration was described and deplored by community organization expert Alan Klein, a University of Toronto social work professor who travelled across the province on behalf of the CPB to promote public recreation. According to Klein, 'very few' recreation committees 'have seen fit to include a woman.' But to exclude women from recreation committees was not the intention of provincial leaders such as Klein. Indeed, he told a recreation movement audience in 1951 that the 'ideal' recreation committee had seven members, including 'at least one woman.'[13] Nevertheless, even this low standard of inclusiveness was rarely met. When the administration of community recreation went from being a private agency project to being part of government, it also became predominantly, though never exclusively, men's business. In the Toronto suburb, as in Brantford, women's organizations and the large majority of women volunteers found that public recreation assigned them a subaltern place. In effect, the shift to a new and, in some ways, more democratic 'public' style of organization either reproduced women's role as helpers or actually removed them from their earlier position of authority.[14]

This is not to say that recreation ceased to be an important area of women's community work. Just as private recreation associations needed volunteers, so did government-sponsored programs require unpaid workers to go to meetings, make phone calls, prepare reports, attend conferences, and help out at events. In their interests both as mothers seeking services for their children and individuals cooperating in organizing their own group recreations, women volunteers worked to develop leisure opportunities in government-sponsored organizations.

The history of a women's craft group in Simcoe County shows the positive contribution public recreation could make to women's leisure options. But one episode in that history also suggests that, given a choice between endorsing, on one hand, the claims of women for recreation services for themselves and, on the other, women's claims for services for their children, municipal government clearly gave the claims for children priority.

The woman's craft organization was the Simcoe County Arts and Crafts Association (SCACA). Begun in 1945 on the initiative of some women who wished to have support and encouragement in their creative pastimes, the SCACA was open to both sexes and had a handful of male members. Throughout the period studied here, however, it was overwhelmingly female in membership and leadership. From the time of its formative meetings, the SCACA looked to government bodies such as the Universities' Adult Education Board for financial support. Closer to home, SCACA organizers saw the mainly privately funded Community Life Training Institute, a flourishing adult education body, as a likely source of organizational advice. At the SCACA's organizational meeting, the institute's newly hired recreation director, Louise Colley, was elected secretary of the craft body. She had been a gold medallist at McGill University's physical education school in 1932, was an experienced group worker, and in 1945 had earned an MA from the University of Chicago. An intelligent, philosophical woman, Colley took very seriously the social value of recreation groups. Even after the Community Life Training Institute became the publicly funded County Recreation Service, Colley remained involved with the SCACA, becoming its executive secretary in 1947. She brought the SCACA not only her own organizational skills and labour, but also the mailing and research facilities of the County Recreation Service office. No volunteer had time for the expanding duties of the secretaryship, and Colley, judging the SCACA to be a valuable part of community recreation organization, chose to give this private women's group the support of the public agency.[15]

Colley helped the women of the SCACA create a vital institution, hospitable to women from many of the county's social strata. Disliking organization for the sake of 'Organization,' Colley urged the group to avoid 'structure, rigidity and formality.' This informal style, possibly based in Colley's admiration for the settlement house movement, helped make possible cooperation among women from different class and status groups within the county. She and at least some of the members were proud of the fact that the SCACA's membership drew on both rural and urban Simcoe County, and included both single and married women, from social positions as diverse as wife of a county court judge, self-supporting cashier, farm woman, and linoleum layer's wife.[16] On other standards of success, too, the organization did well. It organized a series of quilt and rug fairs and art exhibits that drew good crowds – comparable to the crowds attending the area's small-town fall fairs. These events brought a degree of fame to Simcoe County, and earned the SCACA its operating revenue.[17]

The SCACA benefited tremendously from Colley's enthusiasm and hard work as executive secretary throughout most of the 1950s. In return, the SCACA supported the County Recreation Service. When the county program was threatened in 1953, the SCACA was one of the groups that successfully lobbied for its preservation. In addition, the SCACA made annual donations to the Recreation Service, varying from $25 to $100, and reimbursed the county for office expenses.[18] Unfortunately, this happy collaboration was threatened in the early 1960s as the County Recreation Service began to outgrow its budget. Budget shortages put the SCACA directly in competition for staff time, and hence funding, with the summer children's programs and with the women's volunteer groups that supported those programs.

In January 1962, after several years of grudging and insufficient budget increases, the county council refused to raise the Recreation Service grant at all. Looking for places to cut expenses, the Recreation Board decided to ask the community committees in charge of the children's summer program to find ways to raise more money. In March, the Simcoe County Women's Institute convention protested against any increase in fees for the children's program.[19] Colley and her associates in the Recreation Service argued in favour of the cuts that the Women's Institute opposed, contending that the leadership training and advisory functions, which included Colley's work in the SCACA, had to be done by paid staff, but that the budget for swimming classes and day camps could be reduced by using more volunteers. As the Recreation Service came increasingly under attack, its supporters rallied behind it, as they had in 1953. The SCACA joined in this lobbying effort, but the Simcoe County Women's Institute decided, after a difficult discussion, that they could not support Colley's strategy. When, in November 1962, a new recreation by-law was passed, the Recreation Service was effectively redefined as being only for children. Judging this a backward step, Colley and the rest of the recreation staff resigned.[20]

A few months later, in June 1963, the Recreation Board formulated a new policy toward 'adult groups': the County Recreation Service would not give 'excessive assistance and privileges to *one specific group* or organization that would hinder the development and organization of recreation as a whole in the County' (emphasis added). That the SCACA in particular was seen as an unacceptable drain on the county staff's time and the Recreation Service's resources was clear when, after Colley's departure, the county council noted approvingly: 'The Simcoe County Arts and Crafts Association ... has now become a more independent adult group in the way of organizing, conducting and financing many of their own activities.' In the Simcoe County case, then, women's volunteer labour did not give them a secure entitlement to tax support, however minimal, when their claim to services for an adult women's group was seen as competing with the claims of mothers on behalf of a children's program. Nor, in the politicized fiscal circumstances troubling the county at the time, did Louise Colley's fifteen years of modestly paid service count for much. Ten years later, she speculated that some county councillors may have felt threatened by the achievements of a woman-led program.[21] Certainly, the success of the labours of both the SCACA women and Louise Colley did not confer on them, as it should have, effective authority.

The expansion of public recreation programs may not have enhanced the authority of women in the community, but it often added to women's existing burden of labour for leisure, which varied depending on a woman's economic circumstances.[22] Women who were fully supported by their husbands' or fathers' income might enthusiastically join the public recreation movement, but the obligation to help out at the new playground or rink was more onerous for wage-earning women with domestic responsibilities. Even though 'busy people' are proverbially the best folk for getting things done, a woman balancing the rigid hours of part-time jobs or clock-punching factory work with the imperative needs of young families or infirm elderly relatives had no time to volunteer.

In localities where demands on women's time were especially likely to include paid work, recreation services that were expanding could find themselves short of volunteer labour, as recreation organizers in one of Ontario's small industrial towns discovered. The CPB representative claimed that parents in the town were eager to have their children participate in a recreation program, but that they were unwilling to help with the supervision. He commented, disparagingly, that these parents regarded recreation as 'welfare' – an unearned benefit – 'for the children.' Ultimately, the community was unable to organize any program other than some hockey lessons and one figure-skating course, with paid instructors for both. The missing workers were playground supervisors, whether volunteer or paid, positions usually occupied by girls and women. Without playgrounds, the town's recreation program did not meet the CPB's standard for balance, and the grant application therefore was refused.[23]

According to the CPB representative, the town's shortage of volunteers probably resulted from the playground program having been initiated by 'leading citizens' rather than by 'the townspeople.' However, the Legion, the Lions, the Oddfellows, and the Masons all supported the program from its outset. This committee was no narrower in its class origins than its counterparts in many other towns. In any case, elite origins did not automatically preclude raising volunteer labour: Kitchener, whose first Recreation Committee was packed with local notables, ran a program that successfully mobilized volunteer labour.[24] What was distinctive about the Recreation Committee in the smaller industrial town was that it included no representatives at all from women's groups.

Their absence suggests that the likely explanation for the shortage of volunteers lay in the fact that about a third of the local industries employed women. Many women who, in an agricultural community or a larger city, might have been playground and nursery school volunteers or part-time paid staff, in this community were already thoroughly employed. In addition, the town's major industries were not high-wage, unionized firms, and so the husbands' and fathers' wages would have been, in general, relatively low. Finally, because of its small economic base, the town lacked the municipal budget to make up the labour

shortage with part-time paid staff. The fate of this public recreation program indicated that, at least in the early years of the movement, public
recreation could be threatened as much by lack of volunteer labour as
by incompetent recreation directors.[25] As married women's labour force
participation expanded over the 1950s, the volunteer resources of public recreation would show the effects.

The Woman Citizen: Private Leadership for Public Purposes

The central institution for volunteers was the Ontario Recreation Association. The origins of the ORA are to be found in the series of annual
provincial recreation conferences that were first organized in 1946 by
John Pearson and Brantford recreation enthusiasts to 'develop leadership.'[26] These conferences drew interested parties from all manner of
private charitable agencies and activity groups, as well as public recreationists from the provincial recreation authority and, in increasing
numbers, the brand new municipal recreation departments and their
volunteer workers. From these conferences grew the ORA; it was
planned in 1948 and was officially formed in 1949. Representatives from
all the various bodies became members of the ORA; the organization
included both professionals and 'lay people.'

The ORA's membership was not exclusively, or even predominantly,
female. Its 1951 list showed women represented 28 per cent of the total
members. But public recreation directors and assistant directors
counted for one in four of the total membership, and this group of public employees was 88 per cent men. The remaining 'private' sector members included volunteers, private agency workers, and industrial
recreation leaders. The membership list does not readily permit distinguishing among the different groups, some of which, like YMCA secre-
taries, were all men. Nevertheless, women were 32 per cent of this
private component of the ORA.[27] Women were certainly more numerous among the 'private' people than among the government professionals. This fact contributed to the gender associations of the public–
private distinction in recreation.

The ORA was an important institution for mediating the tensions
associated with public–private relationships. Not only did it bring
together the private agency workers with public recreation people, it
also gave public recreation advocates a forum for training private citizens as volunteers. Included in the training were efforts by recreation
directors to persuade their unpaid associates to leave behind some of
private recreation's charitable traditions. By training volunteer leaders,

the professionals hoped to steer them away from the illiberal cultural authoritarianism of some private recreation charities and to ensure that public recreation's distinctively responsive and participatory characteristics would be maintained. Volunteers experienced in welfare work, who thought of recreation mainly as moral reform for the misguided, could not be fired, which occasioned a lament from one director.[28] The ORA provided a place where the energies of such volunteers could be redirected.

Proper training for recreation commissioners and other administrative volunteers would also help the unpaid workers grasp the social integration aims of public recreation. Volunteers who became involved through their enthusiasm for specific activities sometimes did not readily appreciate the importance of providing other kinds of programming.[29] Seeking support from a recreation department for their own interests, they had to be convinced that serving 'all the people' sometimes meant that their own activity might not have first priority. Going to an ORA convention exposed them to the wider range of interests and the broader ideals of the movement. It also gave administrative volunteers the opportunity to see that all communities shared some common organizational problems.[30] In these ways, the ORA helped shift from the shoulders of individual recreation directors the burden of training volunteers, of educating private citizens in the perspective of public recreation's larger responsibilities.

The ORA's leaders also made the organization a venue for 'selling lay people on the importance of citizens' informed support for recreation.'[31] Articulating the ideals of citizen participation helped to get volunteers deeply involved in recreation and to keep them enthusiastic for as long as possible. At the ORA sessions and in the pages of its magazine, mundane committee tasks were inspirationally portrayed as exercises in democracy and cultural transformation. The annual conferences gave volunteers enjoyable opportunities to meet with like-minded folk and renew old acquaintances. The ORA's publications honoured otherwise nameless toilers, and spurred them on with encouraging examples. In these ways, the association supported volunteers and thus helped sustain the supply of private citizens willing to donate unpaid labour towards furthering a public program.

The CPB recognized the ORA's value in developing good participation by private individuals and agencies in public recreation. According to CPB director Ken Young, the Branch looked to the ORA to be 'the focus of a strong popular development in municipal recreation.' He also described the ORA as 'a good sounding board for public opinion regarding Municipal Recreation.' Not surprisingly, then, the CPB was the ORA's main source of funds. In 1954 the ORA's revenue from membership fees was about $555, while its grant from the province was $2,500. Also, until 1954 the CPB provided a staff member to the ORA to act as conference secretary. Government help at first was suspect: at the 1948 sessions, CPB staff felt like 'skunks at a wedding.' In 1950 the acceptance of the first grant of $1,000 was accompanied by the president's assertion, in the spirit of private enterprise, so to speak, that 'it was not our wish or desire to be dependent on Government grants.' By 1959, the association's self-generated revenue still being low, some members wondered how it might manage to pay for a full-time professional director.[32] Finally, in the mid 1960s the promise of more financial help from the government was a key factor in leading the ORA to decide to reorganize itself as the Ontario Municipal Recreation Association, a body that exclusively represented public agencies.[33]

This change in the ORA's relationship with government was not a one-sided conspiracy of the state to gain control of a popular movement. One influential member, a woman who had been active since 1950 in municipal politics, told the assembly in her 1955 conference evaluation that 'the director and staff members of the Community Programmes Branch were present, standing ready to help and giving signal assistance in a most unobtrusive way ... [They] pay more than lip service to the truth that recreation must have its roots in the local set-up ... A liaison like this is a pillar to good democratic government. Would it be de trop to observe that more relationships of this kind between the government and the citizens at large, might be more effective in preserving our democratic heritage, than merely deploring the incursion of the wolf Bureaucracy?'[34] As this passage suggests, the ORA was self-consciously engaged in constructing connections between 'citizens at large' and 'the government,' between the public and the private. In this relationship, the private was both subordinate and linked to women's work.

The public–private relationship was an unequal partnership: the ORA was 'the public relations arm of recreation.'[35] However necessary public relations may be, it is a service function rather than a line function. That is, public relations departments do not make a product; they help sell a product made by others. In the recreation movement, the product was made by the paid staff and the government agencies. The ORA could lobby government on recreation matters, but not decide them. It could set standards, but not enforce them. It practised its public relations mainly on its own members, by providing them with 'the opportunity to learn and acquaint themselves with the philosophy of recreation and the best and most approved methods, facilities and policies of recreation in Canada and beyond.' Its members were defined, within its ambit, as 'learners,' a status that, in liberal political theory, is subordinate to 'choosers.' As Samuel Bowles and Herbert Gintis have pointed out, liberal political theory has been applied to describe women, children, native peoples, or any 'dependent' group as learners, who by definition do not make policy.[36] 'Real' citizens, defined by participation in the work force, by property ownership, and by military service, do not have to take seriously the voices of such 'non-citizens,' even though the full citizen may rely for support and services on these supposed dependents.

The ORA's public relations functions matched the work women did on recreation commissions. The ORA had only a minimal budget and did not own any property. (The president had to borrow a Gestetner duplicator to print the ORA's bulletin.) The association's limited funds and its support function mirrored the housewife's normative dependent/service role, and this helps explain why women, who were largely excluded from being recreation director and from the higher ranks of administration in many towns, were relatively numerous and prominent as leaders in the ORA. Opportunities for female leadership were also relatively great within the ORA because recreation directors did not seek to be candidates for ORA executive positions.[37] The result was that it was the institutional base of the movement's leading women volunteers, and gave them access to a platform that was unequalled in other organizations in the recreation movement.

In 1953 one of the movement's leading academic authorities described ORA leaders Mrs Alma Flanagan and Miss Vera Falls as 'the outstanding volunteer workers in the province.'[38] Mrs Flanagan, the wife of a factory supervisor, was the ORA president in 1950–1. Described approvingly by a recreation director as the ORA's first really 'aggressive' leader, she began the association's monthly *Bulletin*. An insurance underwriter, Miss Vera Falls (later Mrs Burleigh), served as president in 1952 and again in 1954, and edited the expanded publication, named *Ora*, from 1955 to 1961. Both women, in their work on the publication, drew special attention to the accomplishments of women and to program questions concerning the sort of program to be provided for women and girls.[39] Their influence on the publication was particularly important, given that it was a key public relations tool.

Influence is a genuine form of power, but influence alone may not determine events. As the outcomes of volunteer influence described in this chapter and in Chapter 5 suggest, the labour of volunteer workers conferred on them insufficient influence to counter the agency of those who controlled property and law. Like the domestic labour of women, volunteer labour in recreation did not necessarily confer authority; it was just necessary. Many volunteers were needed to provide the labour that these minimally funded programs depended on to function. Like the sewing and saving and making do of the housewife in order to stretch a working-class breadwinner's meagre wage, the labour of citizens supported government-funded programs. The virtue made out of this necessity was that volunteer labour built a sense of community. Just as the domestic work of women is said to make a house a home, so the work of women as volunteers was to result not just in program activities but also in 'community.'

Finally, both their work as volunteers and their domestic labour blurred the distinction between leisure and labour. Public recreation was founded on people being willing 'to work to play' (or, more often, work so their children could play).[40] This socially useful spare-time work entailed for volunteers an increase in duty-bound activities and imposed labour. Pleasurable though the duties may have been at times, they nevertheless constrained the sort of individual freedom that the commercial varieties of recreation respected. Whereas most adult men and some waged women workers were able to purchase their means of play in the market place, recreation volunteers, like women in unpaid domestic labour, worked so that opportunities for play could be obtained without cash and could produce non-monetary benefits.

While not all volunteers in public recreation were women, the role of volunteer was women's place in recreation. They were the private leaders in a public program, and the public–private relationship thus constructed could be understood in two ways. One resonated with masculine models of citizenship: the partner in policy-making, the public-spirited administrator, the participating citizen.[41] The other, embodied in the ORA, expressed the values of women's volunteer work, based in the model of male-dominant marriage. Workers in the private sphere were the source of public recreation's community feeling. They gave their unpaid labour to produce needed services outside the money economy. And their labour, while honoured, did not translate into authority. The volunteer work of women perpetuated their status as helpers instead of making them leaders. This was the kind of indirect citizenship predicted by Pateman's critique of liberalism. This second-class-citizen status was sometimes resisted, but it was also powerfully reinforced by the preferences of recreation directors, male-led recreation commissions, and municipal governments.[42] Women volunteers in public recreation had been promised some kind of equality, but most appear to have known 'their place.' Community work was not an alternative to the domesticity whose exaggerated promise Betty Friedan attacked in 1963 in *The Feminine Mystique.* It was a part of it. A measure of the power of that mystique was that women who tried to transcend home life through community activism found that, even in this 'wider' sphere, they were still somehow wives, always somehow mothers.

7

From Movement to Municipal Service, 1955–1961

Once heralded as innovators in community life, by 1960 recreation organizers had acquired a reputation for conservatism, an image of being 'rather burly and unenterprising ... conformists ... safe, dull, gray and stodgy.' Lamented by the recreationist who reported it, this image regrettably had a genuine basis in the narrow range of activities ultimately sponsored by most municipal recreation departments. In the closing years of the 1950s, recreation in most municipalities had come to mean 'hockey, wrestling, or rock and roll,' that is, activities for young people, mainly physical, and mainly for boys. Against the best efforts of one of the agencies of the welfare state, the larger cultural preoccupation with youth that Adams describes had triumphed.[1] In 1961, according to CPB staff, 'the idea of recreation as a necessary part of life [for everyone had] yet to be sold to the public in Ontario.'[2] Included in the idea of recreation had been an ideal of democratic community, with social bonds forged through shared enjoyment and active citizenship founded in shared decision making. In this view, women would have been not only mothers, but also individuals. The failure to 'sell' this package, the failure to interpret recreation's values in this broader sense, was something other than a failure to promote keep-fit classes or hobby crafts. What languished in the late 1950s was the attempt by public recreationists to construct an innovative articulation of public and private, in which freedom and community were equally combined.

While the public recreation movement had succeeded in mobilizing the energies of volunteers for nearly a decade following the war, by the mid 1950s the potential for private leadership had approached its limit. As the Brantford case and the general pattern of women's volunteer work showed, the scope of citizen participation – one of the movement's key ideals – was constrained by private relationships, the largely taken-for-granted hierarchies of husband and wife, of owner and worker. As well, the willingness of public recreation directors to leave leadership in private hands was compromised: threats to the job security of directors and the survival of recreation programs prompted recourse to more directive forms of authority that were deemed suitably masculine. In the late 1950s these trends in the relationship of private energies and public programs showed up in two ways: through the decline of the ORA and in the search by the CPB for new ways to elicit direction from 'private' sources. The branch's liberal democratic commitments required that 'government' be led by 'the people'; faced with the decline of the ORA, which was the CPB's 'sounding board for public opinion,' the branch's liberalism shaped its vision of alternative approaches to 'the people.' Its considerations focused on 'popular demand,' a concept that symbolized the transition of public recreation from a movement of cooperating groups to a service offered to individual consumers.

'The People' Vanish

The year 1954 marked a watershed for the ORA. In that year the movement's optimistic spirit was clouded by the termination of the national physical fitness program that had been one of the sparks for public recreation in Ontario. Provincial government budget reductions also threatened the CPB's support for the ORA. Since Tett's departure in late 1952, the CPB, under instructions from the Department of Education, had been examining its expenses and minimizing its promotional programs, which included assessing the value of its grants to the ORA.[3] The outcome of this evaluation was that the ORA kept its funding but in 1954 lost the services of the CPB staff member who had been seconded to the ORA annual conference.

This was a small loss, to be sure, but other losses accumulated. Membership in 1954 was down to 56 per cent of its 1950 level. The conference in 1954 was called 'Recreation – Its Future?' The annual meeting saw a scripted discussion about money and membership issues, in which a designated audience member was to say: 'I agree with the concern expressed about O.R.A.'s future ...' Apparently, the ORA executive wanted to ensure that members knew the movement was in danger. In 1954 the ORA's Youth Division had to accept that it could not really function because its members had no funds for travel.[4] In mid 1955 the lay movement lost a vital leader when an American university hired social work professor Alan Klein, whose 'striking personality,' belief in citizen participation, and vision of recreation's social usefulness had energized the ORA since 1948.[5]

The shrinking membership in 1954 may have been a province-wide manifestation of a phenomenon whose effects have already been noted in Brantford, namely, the sudden sharp fascination with television that gripped Canada between 1953 and 1955. That two-year period saw an increase in television ownership nationwide, from 10 per cent of households to 40 per cent. Paul Rutherford suggests that the initial behaviour of new owners of television sets was to watch a lot of programming more or less indiscriminately. He also argues that, in the long run, television watching was a substitute only for other passive recreations and not a replacement for more active pastimes such as community work. However, between 1953 and 1955, television was having its initial entrancing effect on an unusually large number of families. In 1955, one of the recreation movement's rural leaders claimed that television watching was keeping people at home. Of course, some volunteers, critical of television's content, may have seen the new medium's expansion as a reason to redouble efforts to provide alternative recreations. Others tried to use TV as part of public recreation. For example, in Marathon, Ontario, boys and girls danced to shows like *American Bandstand* at the recreation centre. Apparently, however, some recreation volunteers did assume, rashly, that the fight against tedium and dangerous idleness was over and joined their families in front of the new toy.[6]

In addition to volunteers who were lost to television, some were undoubtedly drawn into paid employment. Married women were increasingly working for pay in the 1950s, and married women were overwhelmingly the majority among the women volunteers in Brantford and Simcoe County, and probably also elsewhere. New consumption needs, including the need for a television, dovetailed with an increased demand for labour in 'female' occupations. Consequently, participation of married women in the labour force nearly doubled between 1951 and 1961, rising from 11.2 per cent to 20.8 per cent. As Patricia Connelly has shown, data from 1954 and 1961 suggest that the majority of the married women entering the labour force came from relatively low-income families. However, married women from other economic strata were also choosing to work for pay, with slightly more than one-third of the sample in Connelly's 1961 data coming from higher-income families.[7] Thus, the whole social range from which the recreation movement drew volunteers was touched by the increasing participation in the labour force by married women.

Finally, it seems likely that by the late 1950s several generations of recreation volunteers had withdrawn from the movement, exhausted by the
scope of its demands. At least one woman volunteer was relieved, on leaving the ORA, to be able to re-establish a normal 'housekeeping routine.'[8] To one of ORA's professional members in 1959, the overworking
of volunteers, occasionally a matter for concern earlier in the 1950s,
seemed actually to threaten the progress of the recreation movement. 'I
don't think O.R.A. can go on forever without adequate staffing, draining
volunteers dry until they feel they have no more to give, fading out of the
picture to make way for a new batch and the whole process begins all
over again. Such a process lacks continuity, discourages volunteers and
prevents any kind of orderly progress and growth.'[9] He recommended
that the ORA somehow find money to hire a professional director.

Weighing against that suggestion was the feeling that the ORA would
not develop private leadership if professional recreation directors
assumed too great a role in its operation. In 1955 the ORA's professional
members questioned whether they were perhaps becoming 'too authoritative' within the organization and, whether their status as paid experts
allowed them inadvertently to take on 'too strong and prominent a place
in the O.R.A. administrative body.' The designated representative of
RDFO to ORA that year urged his fellow directors to avoid actions that
'might give the appearance, ever, of attempting to control [ORA] policy.' In warning against professional domination, he was responding, no
doubt, to concerns expressed earlier in 1955 by Vera Falls Burleigh in
her evaluation of the tenth annual provincial recreation conference. She
had noted, in a debate on the ORA's constitution, the lay person's 'failure to enter the discussion on equal terms with the professional person
[was] most regrettable.' The lay people, she observed, were articulate
and comfortable in smaller discussion groups, but 'reticent' in the plenary sessions devoted to the constitution.[10] This pattern of participation
illustrates the informal power of the mainly male professional group, a
power that was theirs to wield or not as they chose.

Conscious that exercising this power might undermine volunteer participation, the recreation directors resolved to constrain their own
agency. But where the professionals felt strongly on an issue, this resolve
might waver. Certainly, some recreation directors played a powerful role
in the later reorganization of the ORA. In the early 1960s the ORA
finally hired a recreation director as its head.[11] Even in the late 1950s,
the strong presence of the public recreation directors in the ORA had
compromised its status as representing 'private leadership.'

The other problem with taking the ORA as representative of 'the people's' views was that the association's members included both private agency representatives and people associated with municipal recreation. The integration of these two groups within the ORA was never achieved. In the late 1950s and early 1960s the question of the appropriate relationship between public and private recreation was tediously familiar and still unresolved. According to one observer, the ORA became increasingly 'nebulous,' stalled 'on a plateau' as others said.[12] It was a time for critical assessment and reflection on what might be the way forward. One social work professor, experienced in both public and private agencies, urged the ORA's members to look beyond the internal debates about private and public agencies to see what commercial recreation offered. He deplored the ORA's exclusive focus on 'organized' programs and 'active' rather than 'passive' recreations.[13] In effect, he asked them, as 'modern' recreation theorist Ott Romney might have done, to broaden their definition of recreation by taking the commercial world into account.

But while this expert counselled a move onto commercial recreation's terrain, other elements in the ORA showed a continuing loyalty to the charitable dimension of private recreation. In the late 1950s the ORA was instrumental in expanding recreation services to groups of people ill-served by the market. In 1956 the organization made its first contribution to the work of the Ontario Association for Retarded Children by helping to extend community recreation services to 'these our fellow citizens.'[14] In the late 1950s and early 1960s, recreationists lobbied successfully to have Indian reservations treated as municipalities for the purposes of recreation grants, so that these mainly rural communities, with little access to commercial entertainments, could claim the recreation funding available only through the channel of municipal government.[15] Such projects reflected the continuing commitment of some ORA members to the idea of recreation as a social welfare tool, and the private agency members in the ORA continued to aver that community recreation was something larger than merely municipal or publicly funded recreation. At the same time, other recreation workers (typically those linked to municipal programs) denied vehemently any association with charity.[16] With neither side's convictions altered, the public–private debate persisted, and made the ORA a fundamentally divided body.

The domination of the ORA by professionals, its decrease in size, and its internal divisions together diminished its usefulness as a sounding board for public policy. It was increasingly apparent that the ORA was not, in the words of one professional member, a 'grass-roots movement' but 'an assembly of devoted, interested community leaders.' In other words, the ORA was identifiably an interest group, consisting of the 'recreation-minded' and not the public in the broad sense of 'all potential participants in recreation programs.'[17] As the ORA became just another interest group, like the existing private, welfare-oriented recreation agencies, its significance for the CPB declined. The views of the ORA, though still valued by the branch, lost some of their lustre as the voice of 'the people.'

Giving in to 'Normal'

Faced with the decline of the ORA, the CPB, whose legitimacy as a liberal democratic government agency required that it respond to the people, began to rethink what it called 'the role of government.' On one hand, the private leadership they had relied on could no longer credibly be described as representing 'citizens in general.' But on the other hand, the ORA shared the CPB's reform goals (social integration and citizen participation), and so had served well for a time as a vehicle for promoting those purposes. With the ORA's decline, the CPB sought a new way of establishing channels of communication to the broader public.

In 1955 an initial effort to address this problem was a program to educate municipal recreation committees on the larger values of recreation. But by 1958 the CPB director acknowledged that 'short courses,' however useful in some respects, could not foster in all committee members the enthusiasm for the balanced programs some of the staff within the CPB continued to find lacking. They complained that some towns, instead of developing a genuinely balanced program of recreation, were taking an easier route. For example, by calling the square-dancing classes for seniors a 'community social recreation program,' some towns hoped to present a convincingly balanced look on their grant applications. In one northern town, infrequently visited by CPB staff, the recreation committee existed only on the grants forms; in reality, the earlier recreation agencies carried on their work independently, claiming funding for public recreation through a puppet authority. While few municipalities so clearly flouted the community organization aims of public recreation, many were reluctant or unable to provide as many volunteer leaders as the CPB field staff wanted. Instead, the CPB continued to receive requests for government-paid activity leaders.[18] In short, some communities were avoiding work that, from the CPB's point of view, was essential to achieve public recreation's goals.

The CPB staff had views on what the proper structure of municipal recreation programs should be, but they did not want to be intervening continually in local affairs, nor, with limited resources, would they have been able to so. This tension between their aspirations to a certain level of service and a principled view that recreation should be community-instead of government-led, prompted CPB staff members to ponder such paradoxical questions as 'How do we ... enable others to do [what we know is needed]?' and 'How can we provide opportunities for people and groups to be self-directing?'[19] In these questions, the wish that recreation might be a domain of self-reliance was voiced in a context of doubts that volunteer leaders would spontaneously undertake to provide on their own a satisfactory program. How could the CPB respond to accusations of government control directed at them, and at the Department of Education generally, in the late 1950s? Could 'enabling' as a style of leadership ensure that the social inclusiveness standard of recreation professionals would be met?[20] Their concerns about the deficiencies of volunteers presented CPB staff with a dilemma: how could they preserve the liberal proprieties and yet build the social basis for democracy?

Some of the CPB staff remained convinced of the old OAEB vision, and thus of their right as part of government to educate the people. At the 1956 staff conference, the director's opening statement affirmed that 'the legal basis of our service [is] ... "upon request," but we can give it a more dynamic and purposeful interpretation by emphasizing stimulation.' Some staff members clearly welcomed the implied permission to construct needs. At the following year's conference, in the session reserved for staff questions, one individual asked whether the branch had to assume 'that if there is no "request" for service from a community there is no need?' The reply was a reassurance that if the field representative identified a 'valid' need, a Branch adviser could be assigned to visit the municipality and 'initiate' a request. Given any kind of public demand, the branch could then 'stimulate' and 'interpret' recreation needs, so that volunteer energies would flow into desirable channels.[21]

But other CPB staffers recognized the contradiction inherent in government agents initiating requests for government services (do those requests represent public demand or not?). The result was occasional sharp differences among the CPB staff. For example, in a 1957 discussion of 'the role of a provincial government as an "enabler,"' three staff

groups each articulated a different image of their work. Two of the
models suggested were comparatively non-directive: leisure counselling
or public administration consulting. The third group, however, offered
an image that looked back to the illiberal traditions of private charity. Its
members said that the CPB's job was 'teaching.' 'What the government
does essentially is to "teach people what the government knows,
through valid research, is good for them." Research in other fields (e.g.
mental health) has led to preventive and remedial measures against
social evils. Constructive use of leisure time is also useful as a remedial
measure against some dangerous social evils.'[22]

This perspective elicited 'a good deal of opposition' from the other
two groups. The advocates of the teaching model defended 'teaching'
as something less authoritarian than 'telling.' Besides, they added, the
government's knowledge of 'what is good for the people' is based on
'exhaustive research,' and therefore, they implied, that knowledge was
not subjectively particular but was representative of universal values.
'Good' activities, if they were thus defined by research, could be legitimately imposed. Nevertheless, even in making an appeal to expertise,
the third group offended against one of the basic commitments of their
colleagues: that civil service professionals did not *direct*, but, unlike private agencies, responded to public demand. The force of the reaction
elicited by the teaching image suggests the discomfort that the others
felt with their own, less clearly acknowledged, prescriptive agendas. As
those who called themselves 'counsellors' admitted, they could not say
'how far the job of an "enabler" entail[ed] being a judge.'

The following year, 1958, saw an attempt to escape the 'enabling'
dilemma by a new method of program evaluation. Aware that a phrase
in the regulations – 'subject to approval by the Minister' – had raised
allegations of government control in the past, the director, in 1957, had
assigned a committee of three field representatives the task of making
the criteria of evaluation less vague and thus less open to the charge of
bureaucratic arbitrariness. At the following year's conference a new
method of evaluation was presented, according to which a program was
to be judged on its adequacy in five types of recreation for various age
groups.[23]

To the recreation typology used in the early 1950s – physical, social,
cultural, and educational – a new element, audience recreation, was
added in 1958. Cultural was renamed 'creative' and educational was
now 'intellectual.' These shifts showed that the standards of the professionals had begun to accommodate certain popular tastes. The category

of 'passive recreation,' which had been dismissed in earlier discussions, was now included as audience recreation, and the terms cultural and educational had been replaced by less 'highbrow' ones. But these signs of responsiveness were to be matched by a measure that promised to give the CPB a new regulatory mechanism. The committee proposed that, for each type of recreation, a norm for the rate of participation in relation to population be developed on the basis of observed rates in established 'successful' programs. For example, if, in towns with recreation programs deemed as a whole to be successful, 16 per cent of the population aged eighteen to twenty-four attended the Recreation Department's social recreation events, then that rate of participation would become the norm against which the quality of the programs in other towns for that age group would be judged.

According to its designers, this method of evaluation would not offend liberal sensitivities about government control. With a rhetorical flourish of which Romney or Tett would have been proud, they labelled the evaluation method with a populist paraphrase of the offending regulation. It was, they said, a way of measuring 'approval by the people.' They expressed the conviction that greater numbers of people attended recreation programs if high standards were achieved in leadership, facilities, and administration. In response to an anxious suggestion from a fellow staff member that people might prefer 'bad' programs, one of the standard's designers asserted: 'The people in the large class have chosen this recreation because it is what they enjoy most. Who are we to judge their choice?' His pure faith in the people's taste was diluted, however, by a fellow committee member's strangely Darwinian observation that, in order to develop the participation norms, the CPB would observe 'the most highly evolved communities in the province.' In this way, the CPB's professionals could still shape the evaluation by their own standards, while claiming a basis of authority in both 'the people's choice' and the inferential methods of social science.

The proposal left room for the professionals in Toronto to judge what constituted success in public recreation, but it also required that they accept more asymmetry in programming than the balance criterion alone would have permitted. If one section of the population was consistently neglected by recreation services, as some felt women (as individuals) and girls were, then the new evaluation criterion would merely enshrine this state of affairs as a norm. The implications for services to women and girls were made clear in the discussion at the 1958 staff meeting. One field representative asked that participation rates be divided by sex, and the design committee agreed that this could be done. The exchange reveals that these recreationists knew that including both sexes in calculations of participation for some kinds of recreation would produce apparently low rates of popular support for what were, in fact, very popular programs for boys.

As one of the more cynical staff members observed, the new method of evaluation was likely to appeal to the Department of Education. It was consistent with the advice Chief Director J.G. Althouse had given five years earlier to consolidate existing programs and to avoid 'pioneering,' especially in projects 'aimed at a small minority of participation.'[24] Like the marketing surveys whose methods the proposal adopted, it took the contours of popular taste as given and, unlike today's niche-conscious consumer research, also assumed homogeneity. If towns with good programs served a certain range of interests, then potentially all towns could and should serve those same interests. This was not the imposition of the norms of social idealists but it was a normalizing measure nonetheless. The reification of 'the people's choice' followed a logic that was at once electoral, commercial, and culturally conservative. Public money would not be spent to serve 'all the people' and to validate any and all expressed leisure preferences, but to serve 'the most people' who were engaged in activities that followed existing tastes.

What this meant was that groups who had not yet managed to secure the facilities and programs they preferred would be considered to represent a lesser recreation interest. Success in securing recreation services did not, however, necessarily correspond directly to the degree of community interest. For instance, where arenas and playgrounds were in competition in municipal budgets, the men's clubs that promoted arenas had several advantages over the women's clubs that most often supported the playgrounds. First, women were rarely represented on the property and facilities committees of the administrative bodies dealing with recreation. Secondly, they had to contend with what some male recreation directors said was a common view of playgrounds as being of 'low status,' an allusion to the association of playgrounds with services to the poor. Finally, the fundraising methods and the pool of potential donors of women's groups were less lucrative than those of the men's groups. In one small central Ontario town where there were two women's organizations strongly interested in recreation, the donations by men's groups exceeded the women's by a substantial margin. The total donations by the two women's groups were $480, whereas those of the two men's groups amounted to $1,380. In another town, the Lions

Club's bingo games to raise funds for a combined rink and arena were hugely successful because they were able to offer substantial cash prizes right from the beginning, thanks to seed money donated by a prosperous business-owner member, a type more common in men's groups than in women's.[25] Thus, where a men's club might be able to commit thousands of dollars annually for a rink or an arena, a comparable women's group might only be able to offer a few hundred dollars through collections from housekeeping money and revenue from bake sales. In such circumstances, men's clubs could offer municipal councils strong inducements to support their sports facilities projects. The resulting pattern of development in recreation services was as much a product of men's and women's relative economic power as it was of popular demand. Consequently, the CPB's proposed evaluation method, in the name of responsiveness to 'the people,' endorsed existing inequities.

Whether this method of evaluation was actually put rigorously to use is unclear. Events in the next few years strained the CPB's resources and probably precluded the research necessary to determine the necessary statistical standards. The significance of this method of evaluation is that it represented attempts by professionals employed by the state to formulate a policy tool that would accommodate contradictory principles. They wanted validation by public demand, but they also wanted to see the development of inclusive programs. In their view, empirical observations indicated popular preferences, but by choosing 'advanced' communities they could include a standard for quality. The result was a tool whose salient virtue was its appearance of objectivity – of neutrality on questions of leisure values. It was consistent with both the technocratic and populist variants of liberal democratic public administration.

Kids and Buildings

The debate within the CPB on the government's role indicates the gap that existed between the goals of these leisure reformers and the actual recreation services that had emerged in municipalities across the province since 1945. While the CPB sought to educate volunteers and recreation directors in a broad view of recreation's values, most municipalities continued to define recreation as activities for children and youth. Consequently, the growing areas of public recreation were services for these age groups, including facilities such as swimming pools. Brantford and Simcoe County were not alone in having arrived, by the route of popular demand, at a recreation service that targeted mainly the young. While few departments offered adult education programs, many offered well-attended day camps, youth dances, girls' and boys' clubs, minor sports, swimming lessons, and playgrounds. Even within the CPB, the central importance of recreation education specifically for children was the starting point of a 1959 staff report on the role of government.[26]

Many of the children's programs that dominated recreation trends required physical facilities. It was not surprising, therefore, that once building materials again became available after initial post-war shortages, many municipalities concentrated on constructing facilities. Accounts of municipal recreation departments during the 1950s often put swimming pools, arenas, and community centres at the forefront. By the end of the 1950s, many municipalities had combined their recreation office with the facilities-oriented parks department, or were planning to do so, in spite of some concerns among recreation directors that such amalgamations threatened to divert resources from program development.[27]

The preoccupation with facilities contributed to the erosion of citizen participation in the recreation movement. Even though facilities were built in response to public demand, their management required little public participation. Taking care of buildings also took up much of recreation directors' time, time that might otherwise have been spent interpreting recreation and helping establish links among community groups. According to one former recreation director, later a recreation professor, short-handed recreation departments sometimes found that taking care of facilities, planning budgets, and leading activities used up all their energies, leaving nothing for the 'time-consuming, demanding' leadership method of 'working intensively with volunteers.' In addition, the quality of service even well-directed volunteers could give was not up to the standards of many professionals. Managing facilities produced more predictable results. Moreover, it resembled a man's 'real' work more than did community organization, even though being what one sceptical director called a 'glorified janitor' had little to do with recreation's social reform goals.[28]

The CPB was critical of the public's focus on recreation facilities, but this issue was only one of the problems the CPB struggled with in the late 1950s. In 1959 and 1960, as the baby boom crescendoed, the Department of Education was swamped with demands for more school buildings. As early as 1958 the staff had begun to complain of a lack of support from the department. In the CPB, salaries were stagnating: in 1959, branch director Ken Young told his superior at the Department of

Education that, at present salary levels, recruiting and retaining staff had become difficult. Later, one leading staff member would recall an increasing realization among the CPB staff that the recreation movement's 'goals were still far from being achieved.' Sadly, the director began to suffer serious ill-health, which, for a time, complicated working relationships within the CPB and would lead ultimately to his death in 1961.[29]

Deprived of their admired leader, the staff also suffered in 1960–1 a serious blow to the prestige of the CPB's 'mission.' Recreation had come to be taken for granted in many communities as just another municipal service, and as a result its claim to leadership in leisure reform had already become vulnerable by the late 1950s. In 1959 a particular challenge came in the area of physical fitness. Prompted by a speech by the Duke of Edinburgh, a new push for federal fitness legislation arose in medical and amateur sport circles.[30] Although the initiative clearly touched on the recreationists' terrain, they were specifically excluded from the Ontario government's 1960 Study Committee on Physical Fitness. The committee nodded to the recreationists' belief that fitness was more than just physical activities, but insisted on limiting their inquiries to physical matters. Rather than working with recreationists, it chose to make doctors its chief experts. And rather than deploring the restriction of fitness activities to children and youth, the Study Committee argued that these groups were the most susceptible to being helped.[31] In 1961 the federal Fitness and Amateur Sport Act was passed, and with this event, initiatives for reform in one of public recreation's main areas of activity passed to a sparkling new government agency at the more prestigious national level. Explicitly health-oriented, the new national agency made no bones about its intention to improve Canadians.

While physical fitness experts could, and did, set about undertaking projects for mass testing and ranking of young Canadians and prescribing physical education curricula, the liberalism of recreationists had required a less directive approach. The notion that public programs should respond to public demand had indicated a degree of trust in pleasure, a belief that what gave people enjoyment was good for them and for society. They had combined this positive attitude towards leisure with a related confidence in the prospects for social integration. 'The people,' when given the opportunity to share leisure pursuits and to work together on social provision for leisure, would move towards an appreciation of community, through which they would grow as individuals and contribute their best as citizens. This confident assumption was rooted in the best tradition of social group work, its respect for the democratic possibilities in community organization.

But the liberal democratic ideal of responding to popular demand, while at least cognizant of cultural diversity as a positive good, tended to subvert the social integration project that the public recreationists had pursued. Struggle as they might to attend to popular demand, recreationists were unable to elicit requests for services from 'all the people.' From 1945 onwards, the popular demand that recreationists encountered had been shaped, as we saw in Chapter 1, by existing philanthropic recreation discourses: when offered state support for recreation, the people had responded in a vocabulary established in previous years by leisure reformers, by group workers, and, most recently, by army recreation officers. In municipal priorities, economic resources had privileged the demand expressed by men's service clubs. Further, public recreationists had found that requests for services came in patterns that reproduced the labour-linked social organization of leisure time. When it came to providing services to women as individuals and to girls, simply responding to popular demand was not an effective strategy for leisure reform.

There was something open-hearted and humanist in the belief of some public recreationists that popular demand could be the guide for government services. But the structuring of that demand by forces beyond recreationists' control meant that the voice of 'the people' nowhere spoke unedited. When the CPB staff turned to the use of aggregate statistical survey data, they were accepting a formally liberal but fundamentally undemocratic relation of state and society. Citizens would not suffer the imposition of a list of government-approved recreations. But neither would the state step in on the side of the underserved to support a universal entitlement. The market-inspired model of providing services to the maximum number of consumers, however efficient, accepted the limited contours of demand as they lay. Whatever differences in entitlement such arrangements allowed – and those based in gender were surely not the only ones – these inequities were preserved by the respect for freedom, narrowly defined.

Conclusion

Gender, Leisure, and Democracy in the Liberal Welfare State

The social politics of the 1960s had some of its roots in the ideals the activists of the 1960s shared with the liberal democrats of the late 1940s and early 1950s. Both took seriously the political relations of daily life, the 'small' matters of making decisions on the shop floor or in the grocery store. Like political philosopher Antonio Gramsci, both thought the means to a good society lay in 'relating the smallest activity to the greatest end.'[1] Both believed their organizing techniques would serve democracy. But the New Left of the 1960s (including the socialist feminists) paid attention to the structural conflicts of interest and experience that divided the citizenry, and declared themselves on the side of the oppressed. They identified some of the older agents of community organization, such as the Canadian Welfare Council, as ossified bureaucratic props of the status quo.[2] In some respects, by 1961 that charge could also fairly have been laid against Ontario's public recreation program. But the public recreationists had not begun as bureaucrats. At least some of them believed that their work had always been and continued to be in the service of empowering ordinary people. When the CPB hired a young community development worker in the late 1960s, he was surprised to find that his colleagues already understood his goals. They had been striving towards them for twenty years.[3]

However, public recreation in Ontario between 1945 and 1961, although it had survived, had also failed. Providing recreation had been accepted as a legitimate function of the state: there were public recreation jobs and public recreation buildings throughout the province. But the remaking of relationships between the state and civil society, one of the movement's political goals, was less clearly successful. After initial hopeful signs, the plan of fostering democratic citizens met with diminishing success. On a tempo that varied from place to place, volunteer participation that had swelled went on to stabilize or shrink. In the case of Brantford, the scope of the contributions by volunteers to the organization of recreation narrowed; the ORA's decline suggests that elsewhere, too, the volunteers' role in shaping policy (as opposed to running programs) contracted in the mid to late 1950s. As for fostering integrated communities, the other main political goal, presumably no one expected recreation to accomplish miracles. Nevertheless, with respect to gender, it is difficult even to see progress. Both recreation's participants and its volunteer leaders continued in the late 1950s, as they had in the 1940s, to pursue their activities and to exercise authority mainly in gender-divided, stratified groups. Services that were aimed at women came to address them chiefly as mothers, rather than as independent citizens. The social benefits of better citizen participation and more integrated communities were, of course, difficult to judge compared with the more countable services of recreation departments, such as the number of day camp places, the hours of rink time, or the range of activities on supervised playgrounds. However desirable such public amenities came to be, by the end of the 1950s their connection to a broader political agenda was remote. Public recreation had become a service run by a bureaucracy rather than a movement.

Public recreation's transformation over the period of this study from a movement to a municipal service took place in a social world where both labour and leisure were organized by gender. Most women married, and most married women worked without pay in their homes. The implications of this arrangement for leisure were that most women had less personal disposable income than men of their age and social position and, especially for their childrearing years, had fewer hours of time that were clearly non-work. Men's and women's different resources of time and money, which varied along other lines of social standing as well as on gender lines, also had implications for the potential of individuals as community leaders. In general, the new state agencies encountered between women and men different expectations and interests, abilities and energies. Neither the 'citizen' nor the 'activity enthusiast' was a gender-neutral individual.

As Carole Pateman's analysis of liberalism would suggest, an individual's experience of public recreation, like other aspects of the welfare state, depended significantly on his or her gender.[4] With respect to leadership, the credibility and the community clout of individuals depended on their association with organizations and the fit of their interests and ideas with those of other people who were deemed alike because of common social identities (such as mother, father, professional woman, breadwinner, or businessman). In seeking recreation's leaders, volunteer or paid, the provincial civil service condensed into the criterion 'acceptability to the community' a series of assumptions about who was entitled to exercise authority. Because the authority of the leaders of public recreation was difficult to establish, recreation commissions and provincial civil servants – cautiously – preferred men in leadership roles. The recreation directors themselves successfully sought state-backed credentials that enhanced the masculine authority of their occupation. Women, as volunteers and as paid workers, were helpers, advisers, and assistants; they were economical as employees and abundantly available for recreation's many routine tasks, although less so after the mid 1950s. Along with working-class men and young people, women exercised – with some notable exceptions – mainly 'the powers of the weak' instead of an effective, equal voice in decision-making forums.

There is considerable evidence that an individual's chance of using public recreation services depended on that person's gender. I have not undertaken in this study the immense task of counting the participants in categories of sex (or, for that matter, age, race, and class) in the activities in all of Ontario's municipal recreation programs at the beginning and end of this period. Much more research will be needed before an adequately rich empirical picture of the non-commercial leisure pursuits of men and women, boys and girls, can be drawn for Ontario in the 1950s. But through the aperture offered by the observations of recreationists, the reports of volunteers, and a limited survey of newspapers, an image of a gender division of leisure appears clearly. Recreation professionals and volunteer leaders observed that girls were less well served than boys. The activities most frequently attended by adult women – arts, crafts, and folk dancing – were often less well endowed with facilities and funding than were hockey and softball. Both the shortage for many women of clearly defined 'non-work' time and the relatively greater resources in many communities of men's service clubs contributed to these imbalances. Insofar as, in the spirit of liberalism, public recreation leaders working in the CPB or in municipal recreation departments merely responded to the wishes of their clientele, these agents of the state tended to provide for those groups that had the most leisure time and for the most active recreation organizations already in place. The former were boys and young men, and the latter were often amateur sports groups. The liberal state thus reproduced the gender structures of family life and civil society.

Moreover, recreation departments, as new state agencies, relied for their legitimacy on actively reflecting existing social hierarchies. When public recreation's professionals ultimately selected popular demand as the sole democratic criterion for recreation programming, they gave way, in the name of liberal values, to the ideology of the competitive market place. They accepted as a guide for legitimate governance the figure of the consumer who 'votes with his dollar.' In thus grounding their authority, they endorsed the metaphorical link between market-place choice and popular rule. When the latter was understood to be like the former, the citizen had only the choice of returning the government or not, of buying or not buying. Agency was whittled down to the choice of whether or not to participate, the means of influence that A.O. Hirschman calls 'exit.' The other kind of action Hirschman discusses – a mix of protest and organized pressure he calls 'voice' – thrives only when institutions work actively to encourage it in the expectation that, when the means to express criticism are ready to hand, they will be used and institutions will improve.[5] The ideal of Alinskyite citizen participation had valorized 'voice'; by contrast, the public-demand model shunted to the margins those, like Brantford's Bert Morgen, who exercised that collective, consciously political mode of power. Even though the recreation movement had its roots in a democratic vision of collective agency and universal entitlements to leisure, its leaders ended up accepting a market-mimicking liberal individualism. Accepting this conception of the polity meant that recreationists framed 'the voice of the people' as something heard most authentically in the accumulated small sounds of single ballots being cast or individual admission tickets being torn.

The limited agency allowed by this view of democracy was – and is – to some extent effective. In public recreation, programs were sometimes shaped by the accumulation of individual decisions to volunteer or to withhold free labour. Nevertheless, the range of this sort of agency was set by the exertion of formal, organized, legal power: the powers of the strong. We may recall that, by disbanding their community committee in 1949, women and men in downtown Brantford clearly expressed their views on the Recreation Commission's handling of their request for playgrounds. However, this 'exit' was followed up by Stephanie Burliuk's return the following year to press the demand in the Community Committees Council. Her exercise of 'voice,' supported by a powerful recreation director, was essential for the satisfaction (such as it was) of the downtown neighbourhood's needs. The limited extent of their victory can be laid at the feet of the property-minded businessmen of the Recreation Commission, whose legally constituted authority gave them the final say. As this case suggests, the exercise of power requires, for women as for any socially subordinate group, consciously defined agendas, deliberately organized solidarities, and strategically planned alliances in addition to the multiplication of quiet, individual choices to help or not to help.

Social group workers had imagined citizen participation in terms of organized, collective politics, but a more individualist, more strictly private political subjectivity emerged in the late 1950s as the counterpart to the new recreation bureaucracy. Both the causes and the consequences of this bureaucratization confirmed the power of existing social hierarchies. During the time of recreation's incorporation into the welfare state, the gender division of labour and leisure gave men (and especially white, Anglo-Celtic, middle-class men) more than it did to women of most social groups, the work-based skills, the interest, and the sense of entitlement and authority required to determine the character of public recreation. Admittedly, liberal-minded attention to public demand and the dependence of recreation on volunteers gave many women the opportunity to 'cast their vote,' as it were, on the results of male leaders' projects. But the power exercised in this mode tended, as does consumer choice in the market place, to endorse services and leadership that reflected the status quo and to affirm the arrangements that meshed best with the existing gendering of work and play. Thus, as it came to rely on 'private' direction in the commercial sense, bureaucratized public recreation offered a reduced challenge to existing relations of social power. Its liberalism confirmed the gender prejudices some recreationists had hoped to challenge.

Similarly, in this story a bureaucracy came into being because of liberal values, not in spite of them. As liberals, public recreationists had had to step away from earlier confident moralities. Social idealism or 'solidarism' had allowed early-twentieth-century leisure reformers to take as a given their right (and their responsibility) to show socially marginal 'others' how best to use their time. The temperance movement had had similar convictions, and without compunction had sought to use government power to impose sobriety on Canadians. But by the 1940s, such moral certainties had lost much of their legitimating power. Good will and good character had suspicious associations with ineffectively moralistic responses to the Depression. The supposed roots of altruism in neurotic desires had been exposed by the Freudians. The tyrannies of the Soviet Union had yet to be fully revealed, but Western governments were beginning to define the values they defended as opposite to those implied by the violations of civil liberties in the USSR. In this context, only empirical research that appeared to reveal 'the people's' needs was acceptable as the basis of public spending on social provision. This research and the social planning it supported was the job of paid professionals, whose expert service was not supposed to be either wholly altruistic or entirely based in moral vision. Professionals were expected to have these 'higher' qualities, to be sure, but what gave them their authority as agents of the state was their expertise. For citizens, freedom from subjection to the values of the powerful was supposed to be underwritten by social science. Rational, objective knowledge, not subjective morality, would underpin a public social service. Rationality would be the basis of rule – a classically liberal conviction – but because it put real power into the hands of a group whose public accountability was limited, the commitment to liberal values helped produce a new agent of potentially unfettered governing power.

This paradox did not go unnoticed in the 1950s. In a suburban recreation committee newsletter in 1951, we find the wryly clearsighted observation that 'A free country is one in which there is no particular individual to blame for the existing tyranny.'[6] The removal of professionals from politics, which was deliberately engineered in the case of public recreation directors, made calling them to account difficult. In 1958, Orson Welles's film *A Touch of Evil* expressed in a metaphorical form some of the anxiety that bureaucracy had been attracting in North American popular culture. The film is about a police detective whose passion for justice, unmatched by a willingness to accept proper limits on his power, led to a career of fabricating evidence, and ultimately to murder. In a room loomingly full of filing cabinets, bureaucracy's classic symbol, his crime is discovered. A lean and handsome Mexican police officer confronts the corrupt detective, challenging him to accept the constraints of the rule of law. But the corpulent villain, played by Welles, is more than a simple moral target. He turns out to have been right about the guilt of the man he had most recently framed, and perhaps he had been right about others in the past. He *had* earned the love and respect of some of the story's more honest figures, but, like the West in the cold war, and (closer to home) like the cold warriors in Canada's labour movement, he had used illiberal means to fight his supposedly good fight. As Jackson Lears observes, political life had come in the 1950s to be framed as tragically complex, and paradox dogged the administrative work even of idealistic reformers such as the CPB staff. To reject the world of necessary evils was to invite being labelled as 'immature.'[7] In this context, it was difficult to challenge common-sense constraints such as those that limited women's chances in life. These were among the 'existing tyrannies' of a 'free society.'

Throughout the post-war period, paradoxes within liberal democratic ideology were forcing awkward questions to the cultural surface. For gender discourse, Betty Friedan's *The Feminine Mystique* was one sign of the process. It was a liberal text, grounded in a commitment to equal opportunity and, in particular, equal chances for everyone to reach maturity in individual psychological development. Friedan argues that the women of her day had been offered a paradoxical model of maturity. Full development as a woman entailed arrested growth as a citizen. Mental health in one aspect of individuality meant mental deficiency, even sickness, in another. How was this paradox to be resolved? Like the public recreationists, Friedan proposed a social liberal model of mental health. She held that private life should not be sealed off from work and politics. To feel wholly alive, she argued, women had to be full citizens, to participate in these larger worlds.[8]

While Friedan framed this project as a matter of individual choice, the recreationists planned programs that they believed would bridge the public and private worlds and challenge classical liberalism's separation of domesticity and citizenship. They tried to bring the energy of large political enterprises into the apparently 'small' matters of arranging children's play groups and meeting neighbours. In state-sponsored recreation committees and clubs, they imagined they could create a space for a citizen subjectivity. Like the literary, social, and associational life that formed the basis in the eighteenth century for Western Europe's middle-class liberal democracies, the institutions of public recreation were meant to link the protected private world of personal interests to a public life, and ultimately (although indirectly) to the state.[9] Even at 'Family Fun Nights,' the practices of discussing and interpreting, recognizing commonalities and resolving disagreements would transform participants into citizens. To many, the social world of leisure might be nothing more than a sphere of passive consumption and, as such, the proper realm of women. However, Friedan and other critics of mass society saw the world of consumption, thus defined, as inimical to citizenship.[10] The public recreationists did, too. In addition, however, they also saw a means to develop in a positive way the political potential of leisure.

Leisure seemed to the recreationists to be an arena where people who felt shut out of democracy (such as Friedan's suburban housewife) could play a part in managing public institutions. In this aspect of their goals, recreationists were attempting to correct the disabling effects of state expansion and, in so doing, to alter common-sense ideas about state–society relations. As Jürgen Habermas argued in 1961, the penetration by welfare states of the private sphere (property relations, family life, labour markets, leisure pursuits, etc.) had put in question whether the exclusion of government from that sphere could any longer serve as a means of protecting political freedom. In the classical liberalism that had thus defined the political role of private life, the people were understood as private individuals, empowered against the state by their own resources of kin and wealth.[11] Implicitly, too, 'the people' were adult men. In Canada, since the early twentieth century, the regulation, taxation, and services of the welfare state had eroded this simple autonomy and the easy logic by which women had been defined as non-citizens.

But there was still the possibility that state power could be held accountable and made serviceable by a public of 'organized private people' not of private individuals.[12] The political purposes that had been served by the classic civil liberties – freedom of the press, assembly, and speech – could be accomplished in a welfare state only by positive versions. A liberal welfare state had actively to guarantee that society be organized to represent its plural and sometimes competing interests. There was no longer just one 'people' linked by a common culture, if there ever had been one. The civil society addressed by the welfare state contained multiple interest groups, one of which might be women as a category of citizens in public life. In this new liberal vision, this social multiplicity, when organized so as to foster critical discussion, would be the means by which a welfare state, staffed with potentially authoritarian bureaucrats, might avoid becoming oppressive.[13] The passion for neighbourhood committees that flourished in social work circles in the 1940s, a passion of which public recreation was a part, was precisely an attempt to construct organizations that might be effective guarantors of both freedom and democratic responsiveness in a welfare state.

And yet in this project the recreationists failed. They remained too committed to what Habermas calls 'the fiction of the *one* public.'[14] Some of private welfare workers' norms and assumptions, formed in earlier decades, continued to shape new social programs. The middle-class bias that had framed the settlement house movement's understanding of taste remained in both the expressed needs of the volunteers and in some aspects of the CPB. The normalizing statistical devices of social research became a new way of affirming a single standard of recreational value. Much of the planning for recreation had assumed that both needs and volunteer resources would derive from an homogenous family form, in which the time and energy of adult women were directed solely to caring for children and husband. Middle-class volunteers were advantaged in the conflicts of municipal politics, and nothing in the public recreation movement's assumptions required that this sort of advantage be met with an organized countervailing power. Even in the politics of playgrounds, 'the community' was not able always to find a 'general interest' that could serve as a basis for agreement and for universal, egalitarian treatment of citizens. Leisure had turned out not to be something that actually united all the people. Both volunteers and recreationists embraced professional direction – bureaucracy – as the resolution to the conflicts their social world inevitably produced. Particularities of taste and of leisure responsibilities thus remained little altered by the public recreation departments and their private partners. The social relations of power continued to constitute a divided, stratified public, whose lower ranks had neither the entitlements nor the authority of its upper layers. The public, even at play, remained gendered.

We look back at the 1950s now through four decades of history. The new social movements of the 1960s and 1970s shaped much of the politics in the intervening past, and these movements began as protests against the perceived conservatism and conformity of the 1950s. The fiction of the 'one public' has been an essential target for the New Left and feminisms, and for identity politics in general. Aiming to challenge the hegemony of the 'one public,' community organizations and even some political parties have devised organizational practices specifically designed to draw upon diversity. Coalitions are one such practice, and another is a range of caucuses, such as women's caucuses within unions and left organizations, and working-class or lesbian caucuses within women's movement groups. All of these are attempts to create democratic institutions that recognize and respond to varied, rather than homogenous bases of citizenship. The hope they serve is that no one will feel indifferent to or necessarily excluded from participation in political life. They are a form of popular 'constitutional' innovation, responding to the question philosopher James Tully argues is a 'political centre of gravity' of our time, that is, whether a constitution can recognize and accommodate cultural diversity.[15] In community politics, as on the larger constitutional stage, feminism and other social movements have put paid to bland, universalist assumptions about the bases of unity among 'the people.' The consequence has been a real improvement in the ways the connections between political institutions and social relations have come to be understood. Perhaps we are now far enough away from the 1950s to see that the legacy of that decade was more than just a fruitful revulsion against its assumptions about 'normal' life. Recent progressive political innovations also had roots in the period. There was something of the New Left in the public recreationists' dream of citizen participation, social well-being, and personal freedoms. And like today's activists for social change, they laboured for an inclusive democracy.

Appendix 1:

Note on Geographical Scope

The inclusive claims about Ontario in this study are based on a sample of municipalities. Seventy-six of these came from the municipality files in the B1 series of the Recreation in Ontario research fonds. This group accounts for 26 per cent of the total number of files that included material from the period 1945 to 1965. These seventy-six files were randomly selected by choosing every fifth name from the finding aid and by eliminating those where the material in the file was all post-1965. The list was then supplemented where it was necessary to ensure that all regions of the province were represented.

In addition to this base sample, two municipalities, Brantford and Simcoe County, received special attention. There are also two notable absences. One is the old City of Toronto: public recreation in the province's largest city encountered a unique environment, one where provision for recreation was incomparably more diverse and abundant than elsewhere in the province, both commercially and through various private welfare agencies. In Toronto, then, public recreation after the Second World War drew on unique assets and faced unique challenges. An anomaly in comparison with the rest of the province, the Toronto story lies largely outside the scope of this book, although several parts of present-day Toronto are covered, such as Leaside, East York, and Swansea. The other missing piece in this story of an Ontario phenomenon is a perspective on northern Ontario's company towns. In these towns, local government was formed in atypical conditions; to describe the distinctive relationship of the welfare state and civil society prevailing in company towns is a project different from the one I have undertaken here. Northern Ontario is represented in this volume by its larger regional centres, rather than by its company towns.

Some similarities may be observed between the larger centres of the north and Brantford, one of the two municipalities. A mid-sized industrial, administrative, and commercial centre, Brantford reflected urban Ontario's ethnic diversity and economic mix. This city is important to the history of public recreation because it was the site of the first venture on the post-war model of recreation organization. Moreover, its first professional recreation director, John Pearson, was an active and influential leader in the recreation movement. Fortunately, Brantford retained and successfully organized its municipal records, including those of its recreation commission.

The other municipality I was able to study closely is Simcoe County. With the county seat, Barrie, as its largest town, this county was overwhelmingly rural in the 1950s. Neither the poorest nor the most prosperous of Ontario's farming districts, it was distinctive for its vigorous rural associational life. One of these associations, the County Recreation Service, established in the late 1940s, was unique in the province as a county-based public recreation body. Unfortunately, many of its routine operating records have been lost. However, from the remaining reports, newspaper coverage, and historical papers written by participants in its early days, I obtained some understanding of rural recreation matters. One of its affiliated organizations, the Simcoe Arts and Crafts Association, has left abundant records and is featured in Chapter 6. Both Brantford and Simcoe County frequently provided detailed illustrations of general themes.

Appendix 2:

Note on Sources

A substantial proportion of the documents used in this study are held by the Archives of Ontario in a record group called Recreation in Ontario: Historical Resources Collection, which is located within the records of the Ministry of Tourism and Information. This research collection was originally compiled by Gail Pogue, Bryce Taylor, and others in the early 1970s to provide a basis for their historical study, published in two parts in 1972 and 1973 as supplements to the periodical *Recreation Review*. In 1985, Lloyd Minshall, Steven Johnston, and Jill Dunkley, in a project sponsored by York University's Leisure and Life Quality Institute, organized and catalogued the material. I appreciate immensely the work done by all those who helped create this resource; I hope that my interpretation of the history of public recreation in Ontario will reward their past labours by helping to stimulate discussion in the field.

I regret that restrictions imposed by Ontario's Freedom of Information and Protection of Privacy Act have required that I leave anonymous all but a few individuals who contributed to recreation in this province. Excepting civil servants ranked at branch director and higher and recreation directors and government consultants whose unique public contributions, once described, would make them clearly identifiable, individuals have been given pseudonyms or have been described simply by their occupation or function in recreation.

As well as requiring that I make individuals anonymous, the personal research agreement I entered into under the act prohibited me from contacting personally individuals whose names I obtained through the records. Consequently, access to this record group both facilitated and inhibited research. I was fortunate to be able to use interviews conducted by Gail Pogue and her associates in the early 1970s, but where those interviews missed or merely suggested points that I thought were important, I was unable to follow up or verify with the persons interviewed my understanding of what was implied by certain statements. I have used instead other documentary sources to follow up on such matters, but I regret not having been able to give those people who are still living the chance to express to me directly their views. One exception came about after I gave a conference paper on some of this material and historian David Millar offered to put me in contact with a friend, who turned out to be the woman named in Chapter 5 as Helen Wilson. I very much appreciate having been able to interview her.

Notes

SDMRO   Society of Directors of Municipal Recreation of Ontario
UAEB   Universities' Adult Education Board

Introduction: Politics and Playgrounds

1 'Liberty and Revolution,' in Stephen Eric Bronner, ed., *Twentieth Century Political Theory: A Reader* (New York: Routledge 1997), 29
2 Valverde, 'Building Anti-Delinquent Communities,' 21, 41n16
3 Eric Hobsbawm, *Age of Extremes: The Short Twentieth Century, 1914–1991* (London: Michael Joseph 1995), chapters 4 and 7; Corry, *Democratic Government and Politics*, 1–8, 432–40; Jaspers, *The Future of Mankind*, 291–9
4 Alan Wolfe, *Whose Keeper?* (Berkeley: University of California Press 1989), 112–13; Marshall, *Citizenship and Social Class*; Dewey, 'The Search for the Great Community,' 620–43
5 AO, RO, ser.C3, 37, file 1128, summary and evaluation of the tenth annual ORA conference, 1955
6 Charlotte Whitton to R.B. Bennett, 14 August 1946, cited in Owram, *The Government Generation*, 328; 'Government by Technicians Is Whitton's Fear,' *BrEx*, 20 February 1952, 20; Angus L. Macdonald, 'The Boundary Line That Unites [1949],' in *Speeches of Angus L. Macdonald* (Toronto: Longmans, Green and Company 1960), 174; Dawson, *Democratic Government in Canada*, 12–13; Corry, *Democratic Government and Politics*, 291–2, 299. I thank Jane Arscott for drawing my attention to the post-war textbooks by Dawson and Corry as examples in wider circles of the same democratic language I had found in the documents of the public recreation movement.
7 Corry, *Democratic Government and Politics*, 418–20. See also Jaspers, *The Future of Mankind*, 292, for the relevance of the size of a jurisdiction to the possibility of democracy.
8 *Reveille for Radicals*; Horwitt, *Let Them Call Me Rebel*
9 On professionalization and the limiting of popular involvement in social democratic politics in the late 1950s, see Michael Cross, *The Decline and Fall of a Good Idea: CCF-NDP Manifestoes, 1932–1969* (Toronto: New Hogtown Press 1974), 14–15; on the cooperative movement, see MacPherson, *Building and Protecting the Co-operative Movement*; on adult education, see Ron Faris, *The Passionate Educators* (Toronto: Peter Martin Associates 1995), 154; and on bureaucratization in the labour movement, see Craig Heron, 'Male Wage-earners and the State in Canada,' in Michael Earle, ed., *Workers and the State in Twentieth Century Nova Scotia* (Fredericton: Acadiensis 1989), 252–3; Bryan D. Palmer, *Working Class Experience: Rethinking the History of Canadian Labour, 1800–1991* (Toronto: McClelland and Stewart 1992), 284; and Shirley Tillot-

son, '"When Our Membership Awakens": Welfare Work and Canadian Union Activism, 1950–1965,' *Labour/Le Travail* 40 (1997), 137–70. Community organization expert Murray Ross explains the common intellectual roots that linked recreation, adult education, and the CCF in *The Y.M.C.A. in Canada*, 335–7.

10 John Porter, *The Vertical Mosaic* (Toronto: University of Toronto Press 1965), 26–7, 558

11 The distinction between 'relations' and 'discourse' here is akin to but not identical to the relation between 'practice' and 'ideology.' Discourse refers to more than just words or ideas; it includes the conceptual terms implicit in social practices of various kinds. But, however large the scope of discourse, there remain the mute structures, such as gender differences in labour force participation rates, to which discourse gives meaning. These raw, and by themselves meaningless (or even invisible) facts of existence remain essential to a number of the explanations offered in this book. For these, I use the terms relations or structures. This distinction is essential to avoiding the kind of fuzziness that Berkowitz suggests is a feature of the gender analysis Linda Gordon has applied to welfare history; see Edward D. Berkowitz, 'Social Security or Insecurity,' *Reviews in American History* 24 (1996), 128–9.

12 My approach closely resembles those taken by Skocpol in *Protecting Soldiers and Mothers* and Gordon in *Pitied but Not Entitled*. Like Gordon (p. 13), I do not want my focus on gender to imply that class, racial, or ethnic politics were insignificant influences in the policy processes and community politics I describe. Although I focus on gender, I attend in some degree to the interplay of gender relations and discourse with their class and ethnic equivalents.

13 Ferguson, *The Feminist Case against Bureaucracy*; Mackinnon, 'Feminism, Marxism, Method, and the State: An Agenda for Theory'

14 Examples of the left libertarian critique may be found in Herbert Marcuse, *One Dimensional Man* (Boston: Beacon Press 1964), and Foucault, 'The Subject and Power.'

15 Some examples of this large literature are: McIntosh, 'The State and the Oppression of Women'; Veronica Strong-Boag, '"Wages for Housework": Mothers' Allowances and the Beginnings of Social Security in Canada,' *Journal of Canadian Studies* 14, no. 1 (1979), 24–34; Andrew, 'Women and the Welfare State'; Jane Lewis, ed., *Women's Welfare, Women's Rights* (London: Croom Helm 1983); Jane Ursel, *Private Lives, Public Policy: 100 Years of State Intervention in the Family* (Toronto: Women's Press 1992); Jennifer G. Schirmer, *The Limits of Reform: Women, Capital, and Welfare* (Cambridge, Mass.: Schenkman Publishing 1982).

16 For a contribution to the history of sexuality that implies modern sexual

ideas are freer and less restrictive, see Michael Bliss, 'Pure Words on Avoided Subjects: Pre-Freudian Sexual Ideas in Canada,' Canadian Historical Association, *Historical Papers*, 1970, 90–108; for a discussion of the construction of a normative domestic heterosexuality in the 1950s, see Adams, *The Trouble with Normal*; for a critical reading of early 1980s gay leather bar culture as representing a certain homophobia, see Seymour Kleinberg, 'The New Masculinity of Gay Men, and Beyond,' in Michael Kaufman, ed., *Beyond Patriarchy* (Toronto: Oxford University Press 1987).

17 Pateman, 'The Patriarchal Welfare State,' and 'The Fraternal Social Contract'

18 NA, MG 28, I 10, 162, file 'Recreation, Public–Private Relationships, 1947–57,' Murray G. Ross, 'The Relationship between Public and Private Services in the Recreation Field,' paper given at the Canadian Conference on Social Work, 11 June 1948; 79, file 591, 'Study of Public Private Relationships in Social Welfare – Materials – Reports,' Bessie Touzel, 'Some Factors Affecting Public Private Relations in Social Work,' reprint of a paper given at the Canadian Conference of Social Work, 20 June 1952; NA, Audio Visual Records, *Who Is My Neighbour?*, film produced by the Canadian Welfare Council, ca 1950

19 The best survey of public welfare programs remains Guest, *The Emergence of Social Security in Canada.*

20 Little, 'The Blurring of Boundaries'; Shirley Tillotson, 'Class and Community in Canadian Welfare Work, 1933–1960,' *Journal of Canadian Studies* 32, no. 1 (1997), 74–5

21 Valverde, 'Mixing Public and Private'; *Quinquennial Census of Charitable and Benevolent Institutions, 1940* (Ottawa: Dominion Bureau of Statistics 1941), 34

22 NA, MG 28, I 10, 13, file 'CWC Division – Community Organization, 1933–34, Radio Broadcasts,' typescripts of speeches by Charlotte Whitton, Tom Moore, and R.B. Bennett

23 '2800 Workers at Welfare Rally,' *Vancouver Sun*, 28 October 1935, 13

24 Marsh, *Report on Social Security in Canada*, 199

25 Quoted in Marshall, *Aux origines*, 136–7

26 *The Real World of Democracy* (Oxford: Oxford University Press 1960)

27 Susan Prentice, 'Workers, Mothers, Reds: Toronto's Post-War Day Care Fight,' *Studies in Political Economy* 30 (1989), 127–8

28 Corry, *Democratic Government and Politics*, v, 418–40; Canadian Youth Commission, *Youth and Recreation*, ix; NA, RG 29, 829, file 214-4-5, S.B. Carey, executive secretary, NCPF, to president, Canadian Line Materials, 19 December 1946; memorandum from Doris W. Plewes, assistant director, to S.B. Carey,

executive secretary, 18 Dec. 1946; AO, RO, ser.C3, 36, file 1119, 'Our Way of Life 1951,' ORA *Bulletin* 7 (1951), 2

29 On the use of gendered binary oppositions in political language, see Scott, *Gender and the Politics of History*, 45–6, 55, and Sherry Ortner and Harriet B. Whitehead, eds., *Sexual Meanings: The Cultural Construction of Gender and Sexuality* (Cambridge: Cambridge University Press, 1981), 7.

30 Cronin, *The Politics of State Expansion*, 43–4, and Linda Gordon, 'Social Insurance and Public Assistance,' *American Historical Review* 97, no. 1 (1992), 19–53

31 See my 'Class and Community in Canadian Welfare Work, 1935–1960,' for a discussion of how these gender associations shaped the relationship between organized labour and social work.

32 Marshall, *Aux origines*, 131–57, 180–2

33 McFarland, *The Development of Public Recreation in Canada*, 18–39, 48–51

34 Marshall shows that in the case of family allowances and compulsory schooling, children's rights to equal opportunity were adduced to justify the surveillance and assessment the performance of adults as parents; see Marshall, *Aux origines*, 141, 150.

35 Pedersen, 'The Young Women's Christian Association in Canada'; Christina Simmons, 'Helping the Poorer Sisters: The Women of the Jost Mission, Halifax, 1905–1945,' in Veronica Strong-Boag and Anita Clair Fellman, eds., *Rethinking Canada: The Promise of Women's History* (Toronto: Copp Clark Pitman 1986), 164–5; J.P. Massicotte and C. Lessard, 'L'Église et le loisir au Québec au XXe siècle,' *Canadian Journal of the History of Sport* 13, no. 2 (1982), 45–55; David Howell and Peter Lindsay, 'Social Gospel and the Young Boy Problem, 1895–1925,' and Jean Barman, 'Sports and the Development of Character,' both in Mott, ed., *Sports in Canada*

36 Burke, *Seeking the Highest Good*

37 Shore, *The Science of Social Redemption*

38 Phyllis Barbara Schrodt, 'A History of Pro-Rec: The British Columbia Provincial Recreation Programme, 1934–1953,' PhD thesis, University of Alberta, 1979; Canadian Youth Commission, *Youth and Recreation*, 77–8. James Struthers has cast doubt on the priority that securing recipients' material welfare has had in Ontario's income support programs; see his 'How Much Is Enough? Creating a Social Minimum in Ontario,' *Canadian Historical Review* 72 (1991), 39–83. Undoubtedly, the same gap between professed purposes and de facto priorities existed in recreation programs for the unemployed, but aside from Ross's comments in *The Y.M.C.A. in Canada* and the recreation thesis cited here, the work of recreation agencies in Canada during the 1930s has received little historical analysis.

39 Robert C. Reinders, 'Toynbee Hall and the American Settlement Move-

ment,' *Social Service Review* 56, no. 1 (1982), 45–50; Ruth Hutchinson
Crocker, *Social Work and Social Order* (Chicago: University of Illinois Press
1992)

40 Dewey, 'The Search for the Great Community,' 622

41 The paragraph that follows is based on Reid, *From Character Building to Social
Treatment*, chapters 4–5; Konopka, 'History of Social Group Work,' in
Konopka, *Social Group Work*, 1–17; Margot Breton, 'Learning from Social
Group Work Traditions,' *Social Work with Groups* 13, no. 3 (1990), 21–34; Kir-
schner, *The Paradox of Professionalism*, 41; Ehrenreich, *The Altruistic Imagina-
tion*, 82; R.L. Schnell, '"A Children's Bureau for Canada": The Origins of the
Canadian Council on Child Welfare, 1913–1921,' in Moscovitch and Albert,
eds., *The 'Benevolent' State*, 106

42 'Drew Sees Youth Plan [as] Means to Combat Reds,' *Globe and Mail*, 10 April
1948

43 A good summary of the literature on this aspect of the history of public education may be found in Carolyn Strange and Tina Loo, *Making Good* (Toronto: University of Toronto Press 1997).

44 See note 35

45 AO, RO, ser.B1, 19, file 634, memorandum from district representative to
field supervisor, 8 Nov. 1955

46 On social work, including recreation services, designed to assimilate immigrants, see Franca Iacovetta, 'Making "New Canadians": Social Workers,
Women, and the Reshaping of Immigrant Families,' in Mariana Valverde
and Franca Iacovetta, eds., *Gender Conflicts* (Toronto: University of Toronto
Press 1992). On an effort in the realm of high culture to foster national identity, see Maria Tippett's *Making Culture: English-Canadian Institutions and the
Arts before the Massey Commission* (Toronto: University of Toronto Press 1990),
168–74.

47 Valverde, 'Building Anti-Delinquent Communities'; Adams, *The Trouble with
Normal*; Keshen, 'Wartime Jitters over Juveniles'

48 Valverde, 'Mixing Public and Private'; Little, 'The Blurring of Boundaries';
Andrew Jones and Leonard Rutman, *In the Children's Aid: J.J. Kelso and Child
Welfare in Ontario* (Toronto: University of Toronto Press 1981); James Struth-
ers, 'Regulating the Elderly: Old Age Pensions and the Formation of a Pen-
sion Bureaucracy in Ontario, 1929–45,' *Journal of the Canadian Historical
Association* (1992), 242–4

49 Valverde and Weir, 'The Struggles of the Immoral,' 32

50 Presented as innovative by Pogue and Taylor in their *History of Provincial Government Services of the Youth and Recreation Branch*, this precept was based in
John Dewey's progressive education theory and formed part of the ideals of

early-twentieth-century informal education and settlement house work. See, for example, adult educator Eduard Lindeman, quoted in Reid, *From Character Building to Social Treatment*, 100; Ross, *The Y.M.C.A. in Canada*, 466; and Mary Joplin Clarke, 'Report of the Standing Committee on Neighbourhood Work [1917],' in Paul Rutherford, ed., *Saving the Canadian City* (Toronto: University of Toronto Press 1974), 185.

51 Keane, *Democracy and Civil Society*, 4. For a valuable study of community politics in a rural Ontario community, see Barrett, *Paradise*. The depiction of community politics in this book is shaped by several choices about geographical scope; these are outlined in Appendix 1.

52 The naming of individuals in this book follows a practice determined by the terms of Ontario's Freedom of Information and Protection of Privacy Act, under which I was granted access to many of the records I used in my research; see Appendix 2 for an explanation of the practices I used for assigning pseudonyms to some people and in other ways rendering others anonymous.

1: Defining Recreation and Expressing Needs in a 'Free Society'

1 BRR, Bellview community committee file, flyers

2 Lundberg, Komarovsky, and McInerny, *Leisure: A Suburban Study*, v; AO, RG 29, 2008, file R433P; Cook, *Organizing the Community's Resources*, 4; Neumeyer and Neumeyer, *Leisure and Recreation*, 64, 81–2; AO, RO, ser.A9, 14, file 369, Taylor Statten, 'Twenty-five Years of Camping,' paper given at YMCA Institute on Character Education, 17 April 1931; ser.B1, 18, file 556, letter to J.K. Tett from a former RCAF associate, 10 Aug. 1945; Nova Scotia Archives and Records Management, Minutes of the Halifax Welfare Council, Recreation Division, 1934–45, MG 20, 413, file 1, comments by Dr Prince, 7 Jan. 1935; C.H. Mercer, 'Athletics at Dalhousie,' in *The Playgrounds, Halifax, N.S.* (Halifax: Nova Scotia Pictorial [ca 1934]), 4–5; NA, RG 29, 2009, file R433/1100-1/50, review of recreation in Canadian prisons since the colonial era, 1961

3 NA, MG 28, I 10, 164, file 10-5-1-6, interim report of the executive director, 6 Nov. 1931, quoted in Memorandum re: History of the Recreation Division of the Canadian Welfare Council, 2

4 Written by Americans, this work of synthesis is held in the collections of the two Canadian universities that offered recreation degree programs in the 1930s and early 1940s, McGill and the University of Toronto, the latter having offered the program through the Margaret Eaton School in the 1930s. These copies of the book were certainly acquired before 1958, when the Neumeyers published a new edition. In the absence of comparable Cana-

dian texts on this subject in the 1930s, and given the positive review the book received in the *New York Times* (14 June 1936), it seems likely that this work would have been purchased by major Canadian university libraries soon after its publication. This textbook was part of a broader pattern of international influence by American scholars on Canadian welfare circles, as is evident in the correspondence of the Canadian Council on Child and Family Welfare in the inter-war years, and it seems reasonable to suppose that it represents generally accepted professional opinion on recreation and leisure theory in Canada in the 1930s.

5 Neumeyer and Neumeyer, *Leisure and Recreation*, 58. An earlier proponent of this view was G.B. Cutten, *The Threats of Leisure* (New Haven: Yale University Press 1926). The view of spare time as dangerous can also be found in NA, MG 28, I 10, 8, file 42, proceedings of the Roundtable Conference on Leisure Time Activities, convened by the Division on Leisure Time and Educative Activities of the Canadian Council on Child and Family Welfare, 2 Oct. 1933; AO, RO, ser.A9, 17, file 461, interview transcript, 1–2; BRO, City of Brantford scrapbooks, 30 Jan. 1943–30 Oct. 1945, 129, 'Playgrounds Here to Have Good Leaders,' report of interview with Helen Dauncey of the National Recreation Association, New York City, *BrEx*, June 1945.

6 Cook, *Organizing*, 3; Neumeyer and Neumeyer, *Leisure and Recreation*, 13–14, 21; AO, RO, ser.A9, 17, file 461, interview transcript, 1–2

7 Neumeyer and Neumeyer, *Leisure and Recreation*, 63; Jesse Herriott, editor, *Canadian Physical Education Bulletin* 1, no. 1 (Oct. 1933), quoted in Gurney, *The CAHPER Story*, 117

8 Cook, *Organizing*, 5

9 Ibid., 4; Neumeyer and Neumeyer, *Leisure and Recreation*, 61; NA, RG 29, 1338, minutes of the NCPF, paper given by Jerry Mathisen on the B.C. Physical Fitness Program, from meeting of 23–4 May 1944; 2008, file R433P, Eric Muncaster, reprint from *Child and Family Welfare*, May 1934; the Dominion-Provincial Youth Training Plan, quoted in Canadian Youth Commission, *Youth and Recreation*, 77

10 NA, RG 29, 2008, file R433, draft for article for publication in *Health and Welfare Global Report*, 1954. Defining recreation as the opposite of work on a scale of tedium to creativity is a durable thread in recreation theory. This definition is clearly implied in the 1947 recommendations of a committee sponsored by the Canadian Association for Adult Education; see NA, MG 28, I 10, 162, file 'Recreation, Community Centre Work.' In 1988, Robert G. Hollands noted the continued acceptance of a 'degrading work/creative leisure' dichotomy in recent leisure theory; see Hollands, 'Leisure, Work and Working-Class Cultures,' 25.

11 Neumeyer and Neumeyer, *Leisure and Recreation*, 35–6. Carolyn Strange describes the formation in the 1920s of the ideas and practices that articulated the connections between the waged work of 'working girls' and their leisure-time pursuits; see *Toronto's Girl Problem*, 176–203.

12 Ibid.; NA, RG 29, 2008, file R433P, Eric Muncaster, *Bulletin No. 7 – The Special Needs of Men and Boys* (Ottawa 1933), 5–7

13 NA, RG 29, 2008, file R433P, Eric Muncaster, *Bulletin No. 8 – Recreation Services for Women and Girls* (Ottawa 1933), 2–3, 7

14 On moral reformers' preoccupation with leisure and sexuality earlier in the twentieth century, see Peiss, *Cheap Amusements* and Strange, *Toronto's Girl Problem*; on concerns about sexual morality in the 1930s, see John D'Emilio and Estelle Friedman, *Intimate Matters* (New York: Harper and Row 1988); Molly Haskell, *From Reverence to Rape* (New York: Holt Rinehart and Winston 1974); Lillian Faderman, *Odd Girls and Twilight Lovers* (New York: Penguin 1991).

15 Mary Louise Adams argues for the centrality in the 1950s of youth as the object of moral reform, including recreation services, in *The Trouble with Normal*, 96. In the provision of recreation services, she also notes, as I do, that there was concern among Toronto social planners in the 1950s that youth agencies were not readily responsive to the expressed needs of girls.

16 Pogue and Taylor, *History, Part I*, 5, 16–17; BAO, RO, City of Brantford scrapbooks, 30 Jan. 1943–30 Oct. 1945, 129, 'Playgrounds Here to Have Good Leaders,' report of interview with Helen Dauncey of the National Recreation Association, New York City, *BrEx*, June 1945; 31 Oct. 1945–31 Dec. 1945, 8, 'Commission Still Awaiting Word of Recreation Grants,' *BrEx*, ca 20 Nov. 1945; NA, RG 29, 1363, file 6, 'Danish Athlete Helps Others to Gain Health,' 1945; AO, RO, ser.B1, 18, file 507, 'Outline of a Physical Fitness and Recreational Programme for the Municipality of ...,' 1946; 20, file 706, candidate for a recreation director appointment to director of recreation branch, 25 May 1948; ser.A9, interview transcripts, 16, file 404, 1–4; file 452, 1–2; file 401, 2–3; NA, RG 29, 844, file 224-1-226, proceedings of the War Services Conference, 22 Jan. 1945, 18; representative of Hamilton Council of Adult Education Agencies to Ontario minister of labour, 15 Sept. 1943

17 NA, RG 29, 844, file 224-1-226, proceedings of the War Services Conference, 22 Jan. 1945, 18; AO, RO, ser.A9, 16, file 428, interview transcript, 3–4; Barry Broadfoot, *Six War Years, 1939–1945: Memories of Canadians at Home and Abroad* (Toronto: General Publishing 1974), 93–4; *BrEx*, 7 Oct. 1944, 26, news story on Community Wartime Recreation Council, NA, MG 28, I 10, 162, file 'Recreation, Public-Private, Relationships, 1947–1957,' Alan F. Klein, 'A Description of the Patterns of Organization Existing in Community Recreation,' 14 Nov. 1951, 5

18 For a progressive educator's psychoanalytically influenced repudiation of
    morality, convention, respectability, and religion, see A.S. Neill, 'Summer-
    hill,' in T.F. Coade, ed., *Manhood in the Making* (London: P. Davies 1939).
    For the revulsion against King and, in particular, against his sexual hypoc-
    risy, see C.P. Stacey's *A Very Double Life* (Toronto: Macmillan 1975), 41–6, 102.
    Although Stacey was only able to research King's private life after the King
    diaries became accessible, his perspective on King's personality was at least
    in part an expression of the hearty dislike the soldiers of Stacey's generation
    felt for King; see Stacey, 30.

19 Adams describes this committee's work in *The Trouble with Normal*, 156–7. Evi-
    dence in support of the label 'Victorian leftovers' may be found in the 1952
    edition of *The Canadian Parliamentary Guide* (Ottawa). Although it does not
    list the members of committees, it does inform us that there were *no* Sena-
    tors younger than age fifty-four. All had been born during Queen Victoria's
    reign, and the vast majority were over sixty-five. The committee's chairman,
    former New Brunswick politician J. Hayes Doone, was sixty-four in 1952. The
    voice of the Victorians still spoke in the 1950s, just as the voice of the 1940s is
    still audible in the 1990s. But in both cases, the voices that express those past
    eras are recognizably of another age.

20 *CC* 19 (March 1949), 14

21 The expressions in quotations are from the subtitle of *Off the Job Living*.

22 This paragraph and the one following are based on a Romney essay whose
    wide circulation is clear from the following citation: AO, RO, ser.C3, 36, file
    1119, G. Ott Romney, 'The Field of Recreation,' reprinted from *The Group*
    (publication of the American Association of Group Workers), ca 1950, 1–4,
    courtesy of the Physical Fitness Division, Department of National Health and
    Welfare. See also 37, file 1120, 'Record of Proceedings of the Ontario Recre-
    ation Conference Held at Oshawa, Ontario, April 9, 10, 11, 1948.'

23 The film was called *When All the People Play*. It was made by the National Film
    Board for the Physical Fitness Division of National Health and Welfare, and
    featured (though not exclusively) Annapolis Royal, NS, and Hugh Noble,
    the YMCA-educated director of that province's Physical Fitness Branch of
    the Department of Education.

24 C.K. Brightbill, 'Recreation,' reprint of an address to the ORA, in *CC* 21
    (May 1949), 9, 11. Similarly expansionary views were expressed by the then-
    president of the ORA, E.H. Devitt, in 'The Recreation Movement in Ontario
    (A Layman's Point-of-View),' *CC* 19 (March 1949).

25 NA, Audio Visual Section, 'When All the People Play' (ca 1948); AO, RO,
    ser.B1, 19, file 589, CPB district representative to CPB director, 15 Dec. 1950;
    ser.A9, 17, file 461, interview transcript, 12

26 Valverde and Weir, 'The Struggles of the Immoral,' 32

27 This may be inferred from the customary practice of paying girls and women lower wages, but there is also more direct evidence in Davies's *Leisure, Gender, and Poverty* that shows that British working-class husbands in the interwar years were entitled to a fixed sum of spending money out of their wage packet, whereas their wives had for themselves only what they could keep aside, if anything, from the housekeeping money.

28 I use here the stratification terminology from the original research, in which class was equated with status, defined by occupation of family head, sources of family income, and type of residential neighbourhood. See R. Clyde White, 'Social Class Differences in the Uses of Leisure,' *American Journal of Sociology* 61, no. 2 (1955), 146–7.

29 In the absence of detailed empirical studies of the leisure market in post-war Ontario, this assertion is based on the valuable study by Wethereall and Kmet, *Useful Pleasures: The Shaping of Leisure in Alberta, 1896–1945.* My general reading in the entertainment sections of 1950s Ontario newspapers and my conversations with seniors from Ontario confirm this broad picture, although the possibility of change during the 1950s in gendered patterns of commercial leisure consumption, both urban and rural, remains to be studied.

30 In addition to particular documents as noted, this paragraph draws on Peiss, *Cheap Amusements*, 12–33; Deem, *All Work and No Play?* 4–8; and Suzanne Morton, 'Men and Women in a Halifax Working-Class Neighbourhood in the 1920s,' PhD thesis, Dalhousie University, 1990, chapters 5–7. A great deal remains to be known about changes over the twentieth century in the leisure pursuits of married women and older single wage-earning women.

31 Christopher Dummitt, 'Better Left Unsaid: Power, Discourse, and Masculine Domesticity in Post-War Halifax, 1945–1960,' MA thesis, Dalhousie University, 1997, chapter 5; Strange, *Toronto's Girl Problem*; Ruth Millett, 'Wise Working Wife Takes Long View,' *BrEx*, 3 July 1951, 8; NA, RG 29, 2008, file R433P, Eric Muncaster, *Bulletin No. 8. – Recreation Services for Women and Girls*, 6; 'A Recreation Ladies' Auxiliary,' *CC* 56 (April 1952), 15

32 The transcript of this radio show was printed as part of 'Record of Proceedings of the Ontario Recreation Conference held at Oshawa, Ontario on April 9, 10, 11, 1948,' 24–7, in AO, RO, ser.C3, 37, file 1120.

33 On solidarism, see P.T. Rooke and R.L. Schnell, *No Bleeding Heart: Charlotte Whitton, a Feminist on the Right* (Vancouver: UBC Press 1987), 113–14.

34 'Prisons or straitjackets,' a variation of the expression 'playgrounds, not prisons,' appears in a discussion in the House of Commons on 7 March 1949 on the federal physical fitness program. Its champion was the Regina CCF MP,

J.O. Probe, and his speech illustrates perfectly the conception of recreation as a therapeutic means to solidarist ends. See also AO, RO, ser.A9, 16, file 437, interview transcript, 1; NA, MG 28, I 10, 8, file 42, 'Recreation Leadership Training Course Report,' Montreal Council of Social Agencies, 1929; NA, RG 29, 2009, file R433/100-1/50, review of recreation in prisons since the colonial era, 1961; Carolyn Strange, 'From Modern Babylon to a City upon a Hill: The Toronto Social Survey Commission of 1915 and the Search for Sexual Order in the City,' in Roger Hall, et al., eds., *Patterns of the Past: Interpreting Ontario's History* (Toronto: Ontario Historical Studies Series 1988), 267–9; NA, RG 29, 2008, file R433, Kenneth W. Kindelsperger, 'The Relationship of Recreation, Physical Education and Group Work,' *Recreation*, Jan. 1952, 421.

35 Kate Millett, *Sexual Politics* (New York: Ballantine 1969), 324–6. The list of traits is from 'Table I: Traits Assignable to Male (Instrumental) or Female (Expressive) Roles,' in Orville G. Brim, Jr, 'Family Structure and Sex Role Learning by Children: A Further Analysis of Helen Koch's Data,' quoted in Millett, 325.

36 Wini Breines, 'The 1950s: Gender and Some Social Science,' *Sociological Inquiry* 56, no. 1 (1986), 69–92; Dennis Wrong, 'The Oversocialized Conception of Man in Modern Sociology,' *American Sociological Review* 26, no. 2 (1961), 183–93; Strong-Boag, 'Home Dreams,' 477–8

37 Robert Rutherdale, 'Fatherhood and the Social Construction of Memory: Breadwinning and Male Parenting on a Job Frontier, 1945–66,' in J. Parr and M. Rosenfeld, eds., *Gender and History in Canada* (Toronto: Copp Clark 1996), 357–75

38 McFarland, *Development*, 38; NA, MG 28, I 10, 8, file 42, Charlotte Whitton to Captain Bowie, 26 May 1931; BRO, City of Brantford scrapbook, 30 Jan. 1943–30 Oct. 1945, 55, 'Will Set Up Playgrounds Commission,' *BrEx*, Jan. 1944; AO, RO, ser.B1, 20, file 693, newsclipping, 23 May 1945; 19, file 595, secretary-treasurer of the local recreational club to J.K. Tett, director of physical fitness and recreation, Department of Education, 7 Oct. 1947; 18, file 513, MRC president to J.K. Tett, 18 May 1949; NA, MG 28, I 10, 115, file 840, John Farina, secretary of Canadian Welfare Council Recreation Division, to Mrs Karel Buzek, National Council of Women Recreation Committee, 20 July 1956; Kathleen Dwyer, 'I am a Playground Supervisor,' *CC* 55 (April 1951), 12; 'Brantford Township May Soon Have a Parks Board,' *BrEx*, 3 May 1951, 27; BRR, CCC, minutes, 12 April 1950, 3

39 For examples of the link between recreation and delinquency prevention in the minds of community groups, see AO, RO, ser.B1, 18, file 515, grant application, 1945; 19, file 594, manager of a printing firm to the director of physi-

cal fitness, Department of Education, 5 Jan. 1946; 18, file 507, 'Outline of a
Physical Fitness and Recreational Programme for the Municipality of Arn-
prior,' 1946; NA, RG 29, 844, file 224-1-225, Chas. H. Bennett, Lions Club
International, to Mr Senior, Department of Pensions and National Health,
20 Nov. 1943; Pogue and Taylor, *History, Part I,* quoting a resolution by the
Township of Stanford, Niagara Falls, 8.

40 AO, RO, ser.B1, 19, file 634, organizing committee to Canadian Amateur
Athletic Association, 24 July 1945; NA, RG 29, 1338, NCPF, minutes, 5–9
April 1945, 6; 'Cure for Hoodlumism?' *Financial Post,* 5 Feb. 1949, 12

41 See also NA, RG 29, 843, file 224-1-75, 'Trends in Municipal Recreation,' by
Ernest Lee, national director of physical fitness, paper given to the Canadian
Federation of Mayors and Municipalities at Saskatoon, Aug. 1950, 1, in which
he states that the 'lack of organized recreation tends to create and encourage such individual and social pathology'; 843, file 224-1-64, 'Brief to the
National Council on Physical Fitness, by Howard Conquergood on Behalf of
the Canadian Congress of Labour'; *Globe and Mail,* 10 April 1948, 8.

42 Robert Tyre, *The Cross and the Square: The Kinsmen Story, 1920–1970* (Association of Kinsmen Clubs 1970), 24; AO, RO, ser.C3, 36, file 1119, ORA, Youth
Division report, 1950; ser.B1, 20, file 646, grant application, 1946; 19, file 575,
letter of inquiry to J.K. Tett, 11 May 1946; ser.B1, 22, file 788, annual report
of the Simcoe County Recreation Committee, 1958, 2; BRR, RC, minutes,
Program and personnel report, Jan. 1947; CCC, minutes, Sept. 1947, re Paris
Teen-Town, 2; *CC,* Jan.–Feb. 1956: 15–16; NA, RG 29, 844, file 224-1-244, promotional pamphlet for *Young Canada* by Kiwanis Club of St Boniface, Man.;
AO, RO, ser.B1, grant applications, 18, file 515, 1945; 19, file 634, 1945; 20,
file 679, 1946; 20, file 646, 1946; BRO, City of Brantford scrapbooks 30 Jan.
1943–30 Oct. 1945, 144, 'Seek Ontario Support for Civic Auditorium,' *BrEx,*
1945; NA, RG 29, 844, file 224-1-225, Chas. H. Bennett, Lions Club International, to Mr Senior, Department of Pensions and National Health, 20 Nov.
1943, indicating that the Ontario and Quebec section of the Lions Club had
undertaken collectively to organize to prevent delinquency. For the description of recreation as 'fighting foreign 'isms,' see AO, RO, ser.B1, 20, file 656,
letter from the recreation director to a neighbourhood club, included in
1950 annual report.

43 AO, RO, ser.C3, 36, file 1119, Alan F. Klein, 'The Voice of Recreation'
(1951), 5; ser.B1, 18, file 537, 'Teen Towns,' *Recreation Bulletin,* Dec. 1946; file
507, grant application, 1948; 20, file 743, Social recreation advisor to district
representative, 15 Feb. 1954; BRR, RC, minutes, 9 Oct. 1947; Strange, *Toronto's Girl Problem,* 181–3; Adams, *The Trouble with Normal,* 73–7

44 BRR, RC, minutes, 15 March 1945; CCC, minutes, 11 Aug. 1948, 2; Norma

Houghton, 'Recreational Activities for Girls and Women,' *Journal of the Canadian Association for Health, Physical Education and Recreation* 20, no. 5 (Jan. 1955), 18–20; AO, RO, ser.B1, 19, file 634, grant application, 1954; 19, file 575, J.K. Tett to Miss M.M., Oct. 1946; J.K. Tett to Mr A.C., 29 Sept. 1948; memorandum from CPB district representative to J.K. Tett, and memorandum from J.K. Tett to CPB field representative, 28 March 1951; ser.A9, 15, file 381, newsclippings, 'The Sports Mill [column],' 22 and 24 Sept. 1948

45 NA, RG 29, 1338, NCPF, minutes, 28–30 Nov. 1945, 'Address by Brooke Claxton,' 7; AO, RO, ser.A9, 15, file 379, clipping, 'Budget Problems Beset Councillors as Tax Rate Struck Monday Night,' 14 May 1953; Pogue and Taylor, *History, Part I*, 96; NA, MG 28, I 10, 162, 'A Description,' 15–16

46 NA, MG 28 I 10, 162, Klein, 'A Description'; AO, RO, ser.B1, 18, file 513, president of Community Athletic and Recreation Council to J.K. Tett, 15 Sept. 1948; ser.C3, 38, file 1137, *Report of the 7th Provincial Recreation Conference*, digest of T.W. Thompson, parks and facilities adviser, CPB, 'Soft Soap and Good Manners,' 25; BRO, City of Brantford, scrapbook, 144, 'Seek Ontario Support for Civic Auditorium,' *BrEx*, – 1945

47 Pogue and Taylor, *History, Part II*, 7; AO, RO, ser.B1, 20, file 690, CPB district representative to CPB field supervisor, 25 Nov. 1955; 18, file 513, grant applications, 1947–8; ser.B3. 23, file 850, 'A Balanced Community Programme,' handbook published by the North Bay office of the CPB, 3; Pogue and Taylor, *History, Part I*, 95

48 AO, RO, ser.B1, grant applications, 20, file 646, 1946; 18, file 498, 1944–8; ser.A9, 16, file 401, interview transcript, 17; BRR, RC, minutes, report of the first recreation excursion to Toronto, March 1950; community committees files, Parsons Park, *Eagle Place Community News*, 9 Sept. 1950, back page; CCC, minutes, 5 Sept. 1951; 'Women Take High Honors for Work in Crafts Fair,' *BrEx*, 3 April 1951, 8; SCA, SCACA, memberships, 1954–62; Historical information and speeches, transcript of Kate Aitken Tamblyn broadcast, 14 Mar. 1951, 2–4; Simcoe Area Tweedsmuir History of the Women's Institutes, biographical note on Mrs Harry (Mabel) Ottaway

49 AO, RO, ser.C3, 37, file 1120, 'The Juniper Family's Spare Time,' in 'Record of Proceedings of the Ontario Recreation Conference Held at Oshawa, Ontario, April 9, 10, 11, 1948'; 36, file 1119, presidential speech; 'Rod & Gun Clubs as Family Recreation,' *O.R.A. Bulletin* 5 (Jan. 1951), 5–6; NA, RG 29, 1338, NCPF minutes, 18 Oct. 1946, 17. For the concept of women's interest in 'relational recreation,' see Henderson, et al., *A Leisure of One's Own.*

50 'Club Plans Party for Husbands,' *BrEx*, 2 April 1951, 8; 'Bell Rebekah Lodge sponsored a 16-table Euchre in the Canadian Daughter's Hall,' in ibid.; AO, RO, ser.B1, 19, file 601, fundraising, community dancing and euchre, 31 Jan.

1946; BRR, CCC, minutes, 7 July 1948, 2; AO, RO, ser.B1, 20, file 646, grant applications, 1948–9

51 BRR, community committees files, executive lists for North Ward, Iroquois, Bellview, and Arrowdale, 1953–61; Ruth Millett, 'Wise Working Wife Takes Long View,' *BrEx*, 3 July 1951, 8; 'A Recreation Ladies' Auxiliary,' *CC* 56 (April 1952), 15; NA, RG 29, 843, file 224-1-64, Howard Conquergood, brief to the National Council on Physical Fitness on behalf of the Canadian Congress of Labour, 3; SCA, SCACA, minutes, 28 Feb. 1948, 1; AO, RO, ser.B1, 19, file 591, includes a letter from a female secretary of a farm forum group to the provincial recreation branch, seeking a social recreation leader for a Federation of Agriculture recreation night, 19 Jan. 1946; 'Fathers' Night at Fairview,' *BrEx*, 9 Jan. 1952, 6

52 AO, RO, ser.B1, 20, file 646, grant applications, 1948–9; BRR, community committees files, Parsons Park, 'Ladies' Last Year?,' in *Eagle Place Community News*, Sept. 1950; AO, RG 2, ser.S-2, 3, grant applications 1949; NA, MG 28, I 10, 162, Klein, 'A Description,' 14 Nov. 1951, 9, 15; AO, RO, ser.B3, 26, file 925, work log of Community Programs Branch Facilities advisor, entry for 22 Oct. 1956; ser.B1, 21, file 755, CPB field supervisor to district representative, 20 Oct. 1953; ser.A9, 15, file 382, 'Centre Director's Resignation Accepted by Commission,' *Windsor Daily Star*, 27 Oct 1954, 5; 'Centre Director Resigns, Takes Huntsville Post,' *Chatham Daily News*, 23 Aug. 1955, 9; ser.A9, 16, file 404, interview transcript, 5; Pogue and Taylor, *History, Part I*, citing resolution sent to the National Council on Physical Fitness by the Township of Stanford, Ontario, 8; ser.C3, 33, file 1069, E.H. Storey, 'A Report ... Regarding the Repeal of the National Physical Fitness Act,' in the 1955 Annual Report of the Recreation Directors' Federation of Ontario

53 SCA, SCACA, minutes, clipping on Handicraft Open House, March 1946; SCACA, correspondence, Louise Colley to Bunty Muff, 15 Feb. 1962; BRR, RC, Minutes, 'Report of the First Recreation Excursion to Toronto,' March 1950; NA, Audio Visual Section, *Fitness Is a Family Affair*, footage of women in woodworking shop

54 NA, RG 29, 843, file 224-1-117 (where there is mention of the Provincial Women's Softball Association of Ontario); photo cutline on picture of woman bowler who 'registered a perfect 450 ... The 12-strike event is a rarity and among women almost unique,' *BrEx*, 4 Jan. 1952, 11; 'Brant's "Scrambled Egg" Attracts Toronto Scribe,' re women's membership in the Brantford Curling Club, *BrEx*, 9 Jan. 1952, 14; 'New Girls' Team in Intermediate Basketball Loop,' *BrEx*, 14; AO, RO, ser.B1, 19, file 634, program for Gala Winter Carnival showing preponderance of girls and women in figure skating and speed-skating races for adult women; Jean Pennick, personal communication

55 AO, RO, ser.C3, 36, file 1119, *O.R.A. Bulletin*, Nov. 1951, 6; Norma Hough-
    ton, 'Recreational Activities for Girls and Women,' Canadian Association for
    Health, Physical Education and Recreation, *Journal* 20, no. 5 (Jan. 1955), 19;
    AO, RO, ser.C3, file 1075, *S.D.M.R.O. Bulletin*, March 1960, 17–18; ser.B1, 19,
    file 534, grant applications 1954–5; *CC* 54 (Feb. 1952), inside front cover

2: Making a Democratic Bureaucracy, 1945–1949

1 Shore, *The Science of Social Redemption*; Burke, *Seeking the Highest Good*
2 AO, RO, ser.B3, 24, file 872, John K. Tett, 'Recreation in Ontario,' reprinted
    from *Saskatchewan Recreation* and *Canadian School Journal*, ca 1950
3 Canada, House of Commons, *Special Committee on Social Security, Minutes of
    Proceedings and Evidence*, 1943, 32, 34; Pogue and Taylor, *History, Part I*, 5; Can-
    ada, House of Commons, *Debates*, 24 June 1946, 2796–7
4 A typical definition of 'total fitness' appears in NA, RG 29, 1338, NCPF, min-
    utes, April 1945, 8.
5 Ibid., 1363, file 6, 'Danish Athlete Helps Others to Gain Health,' clipping
    from an Ottawa newspaper, ca 1945; 1338, NCPF, minutes, 23 May 1944, 1;
    AO, RO, ser.A9, 16, file 448, interview transcript, 20
6 AO, RO, ser.B1, 20, file 693, superintendent of Children's Aid Society to
    chief director of Education, 11 May 1945; NA, RG 29, file 829, file 214-4-5,
    A.A. Burridge, 'Annual Report 1944–45 – Ontario,' 2; AO, RG 2, ser.S-1, 2,
    policy files, 1946–51, president of Lewis Craft Supplies Limited to Colonel
    George Drew, 18 May 1945
7 Owram, *The Government Generation*, 319; Canada, House of Commons,
    Debates, 15 April 1949; Smith, 'First Person Plural,' 1–14; AO, RO, ser.A9,
    interview transcripts, 16, file 440, 1–2; file 448, 19; 17 file 461, 3; ser.B1, 20,
    file 662, Hamilton Council of Adult Education Agencies to Charles Daley,
    Ontario Minister of Labour, 15 Sept. 1943; Pogue and Taylor, *History, Part I*,
    16–7, and *Part II*, 3; Ontario Regulations, 1945, nos. 76–77 (*Ontario Gazette*, 20
    Oct. 1945, 1835–7); AO, RG 2, ser.S-7, 1, UAEB, minutes, 1945–7
8 AO, RO, ser.B1, 18, file 507, letter from a barrister to John J. [sic] Tett, 18
    July 1945; file 536, letter from a local Lions Club to the Department of Edu-
    cation, 11 July 1945; 19, file 634, organizing committee to Tett, 21 Aug. 1945,
    with letter from the committee to the Canadian Amateur Athletic Associa-
    tion, 24 July 1945; file 601, director of physical fitness and recreation to sec-
    retary treasurer of a MRC, 8 April 1946; file 575, secretary of a private athletic
    commission to director of recreational activity, 11 May 1946; BRO, City of
    Brantford scrapbooks, 31 Oct. 1945–31 Dec. 1945, 8, 'Commission Still Await-
    ing Word of Recreation Grants,' *BrEx*, ca 20 Nov. 1945; NA, MG 28, I 10, 162,

file 'Recreation, Public-Private Relationships, 1947–1957,' Klein, 'A Description of the Patterns of Organization Existing in Community Recreation,' 14 Nov. 1951, 5

9 Insert announcing the appointment of J.K. Tett as director of the CPB, *CC* 32 (April 1950); AO, RO, ser.A9, interview transcripts, 16, file 428, 6; 16, file 440, 4; 16, file 448, 17; ser.B1, 20, file 706, director of physical fitness and recreation to secretary of private athletic commission, 2 Jan. 1946; RG 2, ser.S-1, 2, Policy files, 1946–51, 'Memorandum for the Honourable George H. Drew, Premier of Ontario and Minister of Education ... on Physical Fitness and Recreation in the Province of Ontario from April 1st to July 20, 1945' (emphasis added)

10 AO, RO, ser.B1, 18, file 536, letter from a local Lions Club to the Department of Education, 11 July 1945; 19, file 634, Tett to private athletic commission, 24 Aug. 1945; 20, file 706, Tett to town clerk, 10 May 1947; ser.A9, interview transcripts, 16, file 428, 6; file 440, 4; file 448, 17; Pogue and Taylor, *History, Part II*, 22

11 BRO, City of Brantford scrapbooks, 31 Oct. 1945–31 Dec. 1945, 8, 'Commission Still Awaiting Word of Recreation Grants,' *BrEx*, ca 20 Nov. 1945

12 AO, RO, ser.A9, interview transcripts, 16, file 430, 3; 17, file 466, 10; Pedersen, 'The Young Women's Christian Association,' 292 ff; Ontario Regulations, 1945, no. 77; Pogue and Taylor, *History, Part II*, 16; MG 28, I 10, 162, Klein, 'A Description,' 6; AO, RO, ser.A9, 17, file 466, interview transcript, 10

13 AO, RO, ser.B3, 24, file 872, John K. Tett, 'Recreation in Ontario'; ser.B1, 19, file 634, director of physical fitness and recreation to the secretary treasurer of a MRC, 8 April 1946; file 601, director of physical fitness and recreation to the recreation director, 26 April 1946; J.K. Tett to G.C. Robinson, quoted in Pogue and Taylor, *History, Part I*, 23; Ontario Regulations, 1945, no. 77

14 The organization began under the name Universities' Adult Education Board of Ontario, but in Sept. 1946 it became the Ontario Adult Education Board. For convenience, I have adopted the later name. AO, RG 2, ser.S-7, 1, UAEB, minutes, 20 Sept. 1946, 1.

15 Ontario Regulations, 1945, no. 76; for Dunlop's position, see Smith, 'First Person Plural,' 14, note 3; about the director, see *Kingston City Directory* (Might Publishing), 1939, 1941; AO, RO, ser.B3, 23, file 847, 'A Report on Community Programmes in the Province of Ontario' (1948), 1

16 AO, RO, ser.A9, interview transcripts, 16, file 413, 1–2, 11–12, 15, 18; file 440, 8

17 AO, RG 2, ser.S-7, 1, UAEB, minutes, 27 Oct. 1945, 3; 15 Dec. 1945, 10; 9 Feb. 1946, 9; 16 March 1946, 6; OAEB, minutes, 20 Sept. 1946, 2; ser.S-1, 1, CPB Report for 1953; 'Appointment of Assistant Director,' *CC* 33 (May 1950); AO,

RO, ser.A9, interview transcripts, 16, file 440, 1; 16, file 431, 1; *London City Directory* (Vernon), 1937–49; *Ottawa City Directory* (Might Publishing), 1924, 1929, 1934, 1939, 1945

18 AO, RG 2, ser.S-7, 1, UAEB, minutes, 27 Oct. 1945, 3

19 Ibid., ser.B3, 23, file 847, 'A Report on Community Programmes in the Province of Ontario' (1948), 23; E.C. Cross, 'The First Year – and Looking Forward,' *CC* 13 (Sept. 1948), 1–4

20 Ontario Regulations, 1945, no. 76, s.5(a); AO, RO, ser.B3, 23, file 847, 'A Report on Community Programmes in the Province of Ontario' (1948), 31. Pogue and Taylor, *History, Part I*, 19. For a critical view of an adult education method that sees no intrinsic value in popular cultural pursuits, but that uses them as stepping stones for the 'improvement' of taste, see J.A. Simpson, 'Education for Leisure,' *Journal of Education*, Feb.–April 1967, 9.

21 NA, MG 28, I 10, 8, file 42, Anne Hodgkins, 'Suggestions for a Business Girls Club' (1931)

22 AO, RO, ser.A9, 16, file 440, 10–11

23 Ontario Regulations, 1945, no. 76, s.6(c); AO, RG 2, ser.S-7, 1, UAEB, minutes, 15 Dec. 1945; proposed budget and minutes, 4 May 1946, 5; AO, RO, ser.A9, interview transcripts, 16, file 413, 4; 16, file 440; 17, file 468, 15; BRR, CCC, minutes 17 Nov. 1948, 1

24 AO, RO, ser.B1, 19, file 634, recreation director to director of physical fitness and recreation, 13 Sept. 1946; RG 2, ser.S-7, 1, OAEB, minutes, 20 Sept. 1946; UAEB, minutes, 16 March 1946, 525

25 AO, RO, ser.B1, 20, file 679, volunteer recreation organizer to director of physical fitness and recreation, 11 April 1946; 18, file 507, High school teacher to director of physical fitness and recreation, 19 March 1946; ser.A9, 16, file 448, interview transcript, 17; RG 2, ser.S-1, 6, file 'Music Correspondence, 1945–1947'; file 'Handcrafts Reports, 1946'; NA, MG 28, I 10, 162, 'A Description,' 3

26 AO, RO, ser.B3, 24, file 872, 'Report to the Ontario Adult Education Board,' 26 Nov. 1947; RG 2, ser.S-1, 2, policy files, 1946–51, memorandum from director of Physical Education Branch to director of Community Programmes Section, supervisor of Rural Community Programmes, and director of physical fitness and recreation, 26 Nov. 1947; policy files, 1946–51, general memorandum from J.K. Tett, 13 Oct. 1948; ser.S-7, 1, OAEB, minutes, 29 March 1947, 2; 'In Memoriam, Ewart C. Cross,' insert in *CC* 30 (Feb. 1950)

27 AO, RO, ser.A9, 16, file 413, interview transcript, 6

28 Ibid., ser.B3, 24, file 872, report to the Ontario Adult Education Board, 26 Nov. 1947

29 AO, RG 2, ser.S-1, 2, policy files 1946–51, memorandum from director of physical fitness and recreation to chief director of education, 8 Dec. 1947; 6, file Barrie Conference of Recreation Directors, 1947,' summary of Romney's talk (described as 'perhaps the most significant message to the conference'); J.K. Tett to G. Ott Romney, 12 Nov. 1947; RO, ser.A9, interview transcripts, 16, file 439, 20; file 448, 16; file 439, 12; Pogue and Taylor, *History, Part II*, 22

30 AO, RO, ser.B3, 23, file 847, 'A Report on Community Programmes in the Province of Ontario' (1948), 4; ser.B1, 18, file 507, Tett to secretary treasurer of recreation committee, 13 Feb. 1948; file 513, president of recreation committee to Tett, 9 Sept. 1947; 18 May 1949; 20, file 706, Tett to town clerk, 10 May 1947; 16 July 1947; Assistant district representative to director of physical fitness and recreation, 26 May 1948; secretary-treasurer of recreation committee to Tett, 13 July 1949; file 655, Tett to member of recreation committee, 12 Aug. 1949; 20, file 650, village secretary to Tett, 20 March 1948; Tett to district representative, 28 Sept. 1948; box 18, file 526, district representative to Tett, Sept. 1947; file 537, district representative to Tett, 8 Dec. 1949

31 Ibid., ser.B1, 20, file 693, correspondence between district representative, Tett, and recreation director, 12 May–3 Oct. 1949; 18, file 634, recreation director to Tett, 8 Oct. 1947; box 19, file 595, secretary-treasurer of recreational club to Tett, 7 Oct. 1947; 18, file 526, Kiwanis Club to Tett, Jan. 1948; Tett to district representative, 17 Nov. 1948; 19, file 575, Tett to a sports columnist, 29 Sept. 1948; 20, file 646, sports director for National Cellulose to Tett, 3 Dec. 1948; ser.A9, 16, file 456, Interview transcript, 16; Pogue and Taylor, *History, Part II*, 22

32 AO, RO, ser.B1, 20, file 646, Tett to sports director for National Cellulose, 14 Dec. 1948; 19, file 634, Tett to recreation director, 26 April 1946

33 NA, MG 28, I 10, 162, Klein, 'A Description,' 4; Ontario Regulations, 1949, no. 21, esp. s.1(1)(k)

34 AO, RG 2, ser.S-1, 2, deputy minister of education to Tett, 12 Aug. 1949; 'In Memoriam: Ewart C. Cross,' insert in *CC* 30 (Feb. 1950); AO, RO, ser.A9, 16, file 413, interview transcript, 6

35 Pogue and Taylor, *History*, does not offer an explanation, and K.L. Young's and J.K. Tett's recollections on this matter are not available: Young died in 1961, and for some reason the Recreation in Ontario fonds at the AO does not contain an interview with Tett. Two interviewees who recalled Tett's role made some critical comments, and then asked the interviewer to turn off her tape recorder before they said anything more about Tett. Another individual, who admired Tett, spoke of his having been 'significantly denigrated by the current [1971] Department.' See AO, RO, ser.A9, interview transcripts, 16, file 413, 11–12; file 428, 4–5; file 431, 19; file 440, 10; file 456, 16.

36 The OAEB's 'comprehensive plan' revealed its sympathies with the opinion expressed by, for example, the recreation researchers for the Canadian Youth Commission, who deplored the 'haphazard' development of recreation in the past and declared that 'modern efficiency demands nothing less than planning for the total community.' See Canadian Youth Commission, *Youth and Recreation*, 50.

3: Regulation and the Gendering of a New Profession, 1949–1954

1 *The Grounding of Modern Feminism* (New Haven: Yale University Press 1987), chapter 7

2 Stivers, *Gender Images in Public Administration*; Kinnear, *In Subordination*

3 AO, RG 2, ser.S-1, 2, Policy files, 1946–51, chief director of education to minister of education, 4 May 1945; AO, RO, ser.B1, 18, file 536, director of physical fitness and recreation to member of MRC, 9 Oct. 1945; 20, file 706, director of physical fitness and recreation to town clerk, 10 May 1947

4 Canada had two degree programs in physical education for women in the inter-war years, one at McGill University, and the other at Margaret Eaton College, which was later absorbed into a new co-educational program created at the University of Toronto in the 1940s. These were described to me by Dorothy Walker, a graduate of the Margaret Eaton College an and employee in the 1940 and 1950s of the Physical Fitness Division of the Nova Scotian Department of Education. According to her, the graduates of these programs staffed YWCAs, company recreation programs, municipal recreation programs, and the sports and fitness programs at private schools for girls.

5 Theobald, *The Female in Public Recreation*, 6; NA, MG 28, I 198, Records of the Young Women's Christian Association of Canada, 77, Canadian YWCA staff directory, Nov. 1948; MG 28, I 95, Records of the Young Men's Christian Association of Canada, 247, YMCA year book and official roster for calendar year 1948

6 Struthers, '"Lord Give Us Men,"' 133; NA, MG 28, I 10, 164, file 10-5-1-6, 'Memorandum re: History of the Recreation Division of the Canadian Welfare Council,' excerpt from board minutes, 16 Jan. 1936, 11; Donald C. Reitzes and Dietrich C. Reitzes, *The Alinsky Legacy: Alive and Kicking* (Greenwich, Conn.: JAI Press 1987), which discusses Saul Alinsky's early career organizing recreation with delinquent boys; AO, RO, ser.B3, 24, file 872, 'Report of Miss –, Director of the Dale Community Centre,' 29 May 1940, which makes reference to the limited adequacy of female staff in working with boys and the need for male counsellors.

7 Pogue and Taylor, 'Directors of Recreation – Ontario 1948,' *History, Part I,* 64–5; *CC* 14 (Oct. 1948), 15–16; AO, RO, ser.A5, 11, file 316, CPB, Youth and Recreation Division, supervisor of field services, 'Ontario Municipal Directors and Assistant Directors of Recreation, Jan. 1963'

8 I assembled a sample of sixty-three biographies of men and women who worked as recreation directors and assistant recreation directors in Ontario between 1945 and 1961. The main sources from which this sample was compiled are: (1) the *Community Courier* (a monthly publication of the CPB, begun in 1948); (2) the *Bulletin* of the SDMRO; (3) annual reports of the Simcoe County Recreation Services; (4) the records of the Brantford Recreation Commission and the *Brantford Expositor,* (5) the municipalities files of the CPB (AO, RO, ser.B1); and (6) transcripts of interviews with recreationists (AO, RO, ser.A9) conducted in 1971 and 1973 by three different individuals, whose names may not be disclosed under my research agreement, but to whose work I am greatly indebted. The interviewees were chosen, with the help of a long-time CPB employee who was still with the Youth and Recreation Branch, as representative of various fields within recreation, as representative of all regions within Ontario, and as someone who made 'a significant contribution to the recreation movement in Ontario' (AO, RO, ser.A9, 17, file 480, 'Working File – Interviews'). The data for 1963 are from AO, RO, 'Ontario Municipal Directors and Assistant Directors of Recreation, Jan. 1963.'

9 For the ideal of non-intervention, see AO, RO, ser.B1, 20, file 646, CPB recreation adviser to sports director for National Cellulose, 14 Dec. 1948; for attitudes towards the organizational and financial difficulties of the recreation program in a medium-sized southern Ontario industrial town (population 6,000 in 1946), see file 679, 1946–51, especially district representative to CPB Director, 31 July 1951.

10 AO, RO, ser.A9, 16, file 456, interview transcript, 4; City of Brantford, scrapbooks, 31 Oct. 1945–31 Dec. 1945, 12, 'Civic Centre Question Seen as Asking Council to Provide Leadership,' *BrEx,* 30 Nov. 1945; Pogue and Taylor, *History, Part II,* 16; Canadian Youth Commission, *Youth and Recreation,* vii

11 Owram, *Born at the Right Time,* 65, 69, 117; AO, RO, ser.B1, 19, file 634, recreation director to CPB director, 29 May 1950; 18, file 507, grant applications, 1946–56; district representative to CPB Director, 6 Aug. 1956

12 NA, RG 29, 843, file 24-1-75, *13th Annual Conference of the Canadian Federation of Mayors and Municipalities: A Brief Report* (1950), resolution 17, 4

13 J.T. Bryden and Eric Hardy, 'Abolish the National Physical Fitness Undertaking?' *Effective Government* (open letter published by Citizens Research Institute of Canada), 16 Nov. 1951; NA, RG 29, 114, file 840, 'National Council on

Physical Fitness, 1947–1956,' director of Citizens Research Institute to executive assistant of Canadian Welfare Council, 2 March 1954; Macintosh, et al., *Sport and Politics in Canada*, 20; RG 29, 1338, National Council on Physical Fitness, minutes, 10–12 April 1951, 19

14 On Klein's efforts, see AO, RO, ser.A9, 16, file 439, interview transcript, 6–7; on program closures, see ser.B1, 20, file 646, district representative to CPB director, 11 Dec. 1950; 27 Aug. 1951; file 679, district representative to CPB director, 31 July 1951; ser.C3, 36, file 1119, *O.R.A. Bulletin* 7 (March. 1951), 4; 'Municipal Economy Misplaced States Recreation Counsellor,' *BE* 1 March 1951, 8; 'Recreation A Community Asset,' *BE*, 26 Oct. 1950, 15; 'Rec. Chairman Thanks Voters for Support,' *BE*, 14 Dec. 1950, 1; 'Municipal Economy Misplaced States Recreation Counsellor,' *BE*, 1 March 1951, 8.

15 AO, RO, ser.C3, 36, file 1119, *O.R.A. Bulletin* 7 (March 1951), 4; ser.B1, 18, file 537, district representative to CPB director, 29 Feb. 1952; BRR, RC, minutes, Executive Committee meeting, 11 June 1952; and publicity and public relations report, 30 Oct. 1952; SCA, Women's Institutes of Simcoe County, 'History of Simcoe North District,' in Simcoe Area District Tweedsmuir History, minutes, 29 May 1953; SCACA, minutes, 27 Feb. 1953; 3, 23 June 1953; SCC, minutes, 15 June 1953, 4; 'Report of Recreation Director to the County Council, Jan. 1954,' 106; AO, RO, ser.A9, 15, file 379, 'Budget Problems Beset Councillors as Tax Rate Struck Monday Night,' newspaper clipping, 14 May 1953

16 Ontario, Department of Education, *Report of the Minister*, 1949–53; AO, RO, ser.C3, 36, file 1119, Klein, 'Voice of Recreation,' 1–2, 5–6; for examples of criticism from taxpayers, see ser.C3, 36, file 1119, Ontario Recreation Association, Youth Division report, Ottawa group, 1950; 33, file 1074, 'Recreation in the Atomic Age,' address first given in Jan. 1952; ser.A9, interview transcripts, 16, file 427, 5–6; 17, file 470, 3

17 AO, RO, ser.A9, 16, file 450, interview transcript, 3–4; ser.C3, 33, file 1074, 'Report for Northwestern Zone,' *R.D.F.O. Bulletin*, April 1953. In 1955, statistics on a regionally representative selection of thirty-one medium-sized to large Ontario municipalities (ranging in size from Waterloo to Ottawa) showed 42 per cent of recreation directors had held their present job for three or fewer years, while fully 65 per cent had been in their current position for five years or less. RO, ser.B1, 22, file 799, field supervisor to recreation director, Jan. 1955; for the expression 'mortality rate' see ser.C3, 33, file 1081, 'S.D.M.R.O.: The First Ten Years, 1946–1956,' 4; ser.A9, 16, file 456, interview transcript, 19.

18 Ontario, Department of Education, *Report of the Minister*, 1949, 33; AO, RO, ser.A9, 16, file 49, interview transcript, 11–12. The exchange was as follows:

interviewer: 'But wasn't the early philosophy of the Community Programmes basically to promote a full programme, a comprehensive programme for recreation?' Response from former OAEB assistant director, later CPB district representative, field services supervisor, and branch director: 'It was a balanced programme.'

19 Ontario Regulations, 1949, no. 21, s.1(1)(k); AO, RO, ser.B3, 23, file 838, 'Community Recreation in Ontario,' *Family Herald and Weekly Star*, 5 April 1951

20 AO, RO, ser.B1, 19, file 592, form letter over signature of CPB director to MRC, 12 March 1951; ser.A9, 16, interview transcripts, 16, file 448, 3–4; file 439, 23; 17, file 461, 13–14; John Pearson, 'Working in Recreation,' *CC* 19 (March 1949), 3–4

21 AO, RO, ser.B1, 20, file 646, CPB director to town clerk, 24 Dec. 1952; 19, file 592, memorandum for file by CPB executive assistant; NA, MG 28, I 10, 162, Klein, 'A Description,' 10. The warning letter is included in many of the community files in RO, ser.B1.

22 AO, RO, ser.A9, interview transcripts, 16, file 436, 19; file 447, 9. District representatives were required to supply a completed assessment form for the grant applications of the municipalities in their areas. AO, RG 2, ser.S-1, 1, 'Branch Policy Memoranda 1948–1962,' memorandum from CPB director to branch staff, 27 Nov. 1950; RO, ser.B3, 24, file 873, staff conference report, Sept. 1957, 7.

23 AO, RO, ser.B1, 18, file 557, field supervisor to district representative, 22 Feb. 1956

24 Ibid., ser.B3, 23, file 857, 'A Report on Community Programmes in the Province of Ontario,' 1948, 7; 24, file 872, John K. Tett, 'Recreation in Ontario'; ser.A9, interview transcripts, 16, file 445, 14, 18; file 413, 10; AO, RO, ser.B1, 20, file 646, CPB recreation advisor to sports director for National Cellulose, 14 Dec. 1948

25 For an example of how such support was part of developing volunteer leaders, see AO, RO, ser.B3, 24, file 872, 'Policy (Leadership training): Development of Recreation,' 31 Jan. 1951, 1; ser.A9, 16, file 476, interview transcript, 9; ser.B1, 18, file 513, district representative to CPB recreation advisor, 3 June 1948.

26 AO, RO, ser.B1, 18, file 507, MRC to CPB, 21 Oct. 1948; file 571, member of Parliament to CPB director, 31 March 1950; 21, file 755, district representative to field supervisor, 14 Oct. 1953; 20, file 662, Physical Fitness and Recreation Branch to MRC member, 8 Dec. 1945; file 655, district representative to district representative, 15 July 1949; CPB director to MRC member, 12 Aug. 1949; 19, file 634, letter from recreation director soliciting a letter of

support from the CPB, 29 May 1950; RG 2, ser.S-1, 3, memorandum from CPB director to all district representatives, 11 Feb. 1949

27 AO, RO, ser.B1, 18, file 507, CPB to MRC, 4 Nov. 1949; 19, file 634, 'Application for Approval of Director of Recreation,' 25 Oct. 1955

28 Ibid., 19, file 575, esp. secretary of athletic commission to director of recreational activity [director of physical fitness and recreation], 11 May 1946; district representative to director of physical fitness and recreation, 26 Jan. 1949; CPB director to district representative, 28 March 1951. On the general problem of hiring sport directors as recreation directors, see NA, MG 28, I 10, 162, file 'Recreation, Public-Private Relationships, 1947–1957,' Klein, 'A Description,' 6. A specific example of such a director being unsatisfactory even to the Physical Fitness and Recreation Branch is in AO, RO, ser.B1, 19, file 601, director of physical fitness and recreation to secretary-treasurer of an MRC, 8 April 1946.

29 AO, RO, ser.B1, 20, file 706, town clerk to director of physical fitness and recreation, 19 May 1947; 9 July 1947

30 Ibid., ser.A3, 4, file 96, 'Three Year In-service Training Course – Second Year, People,' 3, which states: 'In 1949 we were in a depression – about 500,000 people in Canada were unemployed.' BRR, RC, minutes, programme and personnel report, 3 May 1948; minutes, 16 April 1953, 2; 'Unemployment to Be Studied,' BrEx, 7 Jan. 1952, 2; 'Jobless Situation Is Called National Scandal,' BrEx, 2 Feb. 1952

31 AO, RO, ser.A9, 16, file 448, interview transcript, 2; ser.B1, 19, file 634, MRC to director of physical fitness and recreation, 20 April 1946; 18, file 507, MRC to CPB, 28 Oct. 1949; ser.A9, 15, file 381, 'The Sports Mill,' newspaper clippings, 22, 24 Sept. 1948; b17, file 477, interview transcript, 1; BAO, RO, City of Brantford scrapbook, 30 Jan. 1943–30 Oct. 1945, clipping, 87, 'Program of Recreation Is Proposed'; Council minutes, roll 3, 619, 14 Feb. 1944. Untrained directors were probably also chosen on the basis of their connections to the political leaders of the community, although my research did not uncover direct evidence of this, only the suspicions on the part of private recreation agencies of the deleterious effect of 'politics' on service standards; see NA, MG 28, I 10, 8, file 42, memorandum from Howard Braucher, NRA, to leaders in community chests, 13 July 1931. AO, RO, ser.B1, 18, file 526, district representative to director of physical fitness and recreation, Sept. 1947; 20, file 688, 12 Jan. 1955; Smith 'First Person Plural,' 11; NA, MG 28, I 10, 162, Klein, 'A Description,' 17–18.

32 See AO, RO, ser.B1, 20, file 631, for the history of recreation organizing between 1945 and 1960; ser.C3, 36, file 1119, ORA proceedings, for a discussion on recreation legislation in 1950; ser.B1, 19, file 575, CPB director to

Lions Club president, refusing funding for projects not administered by an
MRC; Lions Club officer to the Department of Education, 11 July 1945,
and the reply by the director of physical fitness and recreation, 16 July
1945.

33 NA, MG 28, I 10, 162, file 'Recreation, Public-Private, Relationships 1947–
1957,' Murray G. Ross, 'Relationship Between Public and Private Services in
the Recreation Field,' paper given at the Canadian conference on Social
Work in Hamilton, 11 June 1948, 6; 164, file 10-5-1-6, 'Memorandum re: History of the Recreation Division of the Canadian Welfare Council,' excerpt
from Board Minutes of 5 March 1952; 'History of the Recreation Division of
the Canadian Welfare Council: Selected Highlights,' excerpt from Appendix
E, Minutes of the Recreation Division annual meeting for 1952; AO, RO,
ser.B1, 19, file 634, program for Gala Winter Carnival, 22 Feb. 1946

34 AO, RO, ser.A9, 15, file 832, 'Centre Director Resigns, Takes Huntsville
Post,' clipping, 23 Aug. 1955; ser.C3, 38, file 1137, report of the 7th Provincial Recreation Conference, 1952, including a digest of 'Soft Soap and Good
Manners,' and comments on the risk to programming of over-investment in
facilities; NA, MG 28, I 10, 162, Klein, 'A Description,' 15–16; C.K. Brightbill,
speech to ORA, reprinted in *CC* 21 (May 1949), 9; BRR, RC, minutes, 14 Oct.
1947, which contains a reference to conflict between parks administrators
and recreation directors; NA, Audio Visual Section, *When All the People Play*,
with a scene showing child being warned off the grass in a public park; AO,
RO, ser.B1, 18, file 557, field representative to field supervisor, 8 Sept. 1960;
A.G. Ley, 'Right between the Eyes,' *CC* 13 (Sept. 1948), 14–17; Isobel McLaggan, 'Community Organization for Recreation,' *Canadian Welfare*, 1 Dec.
1948, 32–3; NA, RG 29, 843, file 224-1-75, John Pearson, 'National Survey of
Recreation in Canadian Municipalities: Some Implications for Municipal
Government,' report to the 14th Annual conference of mayors and munici-
palities, June 1951, 3

35 AO, RO, ser.B1, 19, file 575, CPB director to field representative, 28 March
1951; 20, file 657, field representative to CPB director, 10 Jan. 1950; ser.A9,
interview transcripts, 16, file 427, 3–4; file 431, 22–3; file 446, 14; file 401, 3;
file 434, 1–2; b17, file 461, 10–14; file 466, 10; file 468, 15; RG 2, ser.S-1, 1,
CPB director to deputy minister, 26 Oct. 1956. On the similar effect on
regional program development of the CPB district representatives' different
qualities, see Pogue and Taylor, *History, Part II*, 24.

36 AO, RO, ser.A9, interview transcripts, 16, file 403, 1; file 421, 1; file 445, 2; file
452, 1–2; 17, file 477, 1; ser.B1, 18, file 513, MRC president to CPB director, 6
May 1947; 19, file 601, director of physical fitness and recreation to secretary
treasurer of MRC, 8 April 1946; annual report, 1949; file 634, grant applica-

tion, 1951, district representative's comments; field supervisor to district representative, 16 Nov. 1955

37 Ibid., ser.A9, interview transcripts, 16, file 439, 1; file 447, 9

38 Ibid., 16, file 447, 9; ser.B3, 24, file 872, John K. Tett, 'Recreation in Ontario'

39 Ibid., ser.B3, 21, file 878, CPB director, address to ORA, ca 1963, 2; ser.A3, b5, file 113, 1954; ser.A9, 16, file 439, interview transcript, 2; Pogue and Taylor, *History, Part II*, 9

40 That the course was semi-annual rather than annual as Pogue and Taylor assert was inferred from a 1950 report on the Fifth Provincial Training Course. With the earliest evidence of any provincially sponsored training course being Pogue and Taylor's report on a 1948 one, and with other evidence that the course was first proposed in 1947, it seems likely that there were two per year. See Pogue and Taylor, *History, Part II*, 9; AO, RG 2, ser.S-1, 6, 'Barrie Conference of Recreation Directors 1947,' transcript of speech by C.E. Hendry, 5; RO, ser.A3, 5, file 113, report of the fifth provincial training course of municipal recreation directors'; ser.C3, 33, file 1081, 'S.D.M.R.O.: The First Ten Years, 1946–1956,' 4; ser.A3, 5, file 113, 'Bulletin to MRCs,' 4 Dec. 1953; BRR, RC, minutes, executive committee meeting, 11 March 1953; AO, 'Bulletin to MRCs,' 4 Dec. 1953.

41 SCA, SCC, minutes, 31 Dec. 1947, 9; BRO, City of Brantford, scrapbooks, 30 Jan. 1943–30 Oct. 1945, 55, 'Will Set Up Playgrounds Commission,' Jan. 1944; AO, RO, ser.B1, 19, file 601, report on spring and summer activities, 1947; 20, file 657, form letter from Guelph Council of Social Agencies to Ontario MRCs, 14 May 1948; ser.A9, 16, file 418, interview transcript, 25

42 AO, RG 2, ser.S-1, 3, file 'Memoranda to *All* District Representatives, 1947–1949' 'Report of Conference of Recreational Directors, Oshawa, Jan. 27th to 31st, 1947,' report of Charles Hendry's speech; policy files, 1946–51, J.K. Tett to Charles Hendry, 11 Feb. 1947

43 *CC* 21 (May 1949), speech to the ORA, 8–11; *CC* 49 (Sept. 1951), 2

44 Struthers, '"Lord Give Us Men,"' 133–5; AO, RO, ser.B1, 20, file 662, job description for general secretary of the Dale Community Centre, 24 July 1950; Stivers, *Gender Images in Public Administration*, 117–91; Trolander, *Professionalism and Social Change*, 51; NA, MG 28, I 10, 77, file 564, 'Labour-General, 1952–62,' meeting between Gordon Cushing, R.E.G. Davis, D. Crawley, and Leslie Wismer; 'Girls Can't Win, Men Won't Listen,' *BrEx*, 20 May 1952, 10; Wilensky and Lebeaux, *Industrial Society and Social Welfare*, (New York: Free Press 1958), 323. My thanks to the anonymous reviewer of this manuscript who drew my attention to the discussion of social work and gender roles in this last work.

45 AO, RO, ser.A9, 17, file 469, interview transcript, 4; ser.A3, 5, file 113, hand-

written speakers' notes on strengths and weakness of the in-service course, 1954; SCA, Simcoe County Council, minutes, report of the recreation director to the County Council, January, 1952, 147–8; BRR, RC, minutes, 'Re: Programme Load of Assistant Directors,' 1952

46 The marital status of male recreation directors cannot be determined from lists of directors. However, a long-time volunteer leader who reflected on the responsibilities of the occupation in 1960 took for granted that recreation directors had wives, and that wives helped share the burdens of the job. See AO, RO, ser.A9, 13, file 355, editorial in *Ora* 11 (April 1960), 11–12. On the strains of a recreation director's schedule on his relationship with his wife, see 16, file 448, interview transcript, 5. On the long hours and their effect on the family life of a CPB representative, see 16, file 473, interview transcript, 5. Mrs Don Shay, 'So You're the Wife of a Recreation Director,' *CC* 122 (Dec. 1959).

47 The only woman in this group who was called Mrs was head of her own household since at least 1948. She may have been separated or divorced, rather than widowed.

48 Strong-Boag, 'Canada's Wage-Earning Wives'

49 Penina Migdal Glazer and Miriam Slater, *Unequal Colleagues: The Entrance of Women into the Professions, 1890–1940* (New Brunswick, NJ: Rutgers University Press 1986), 211–13; Kinnear, *In Subordination*, 164

50 AO, RO, ser.A9, 16, file 431, interview transcript, 22

51 Ibid., ser.B1, 20, file 693, district representative to CPB director, 19 May 1949; file 655, comments by district representative on candidate for recreation director position, 26 Feb. 1957

52 Ibid., ser.C4, 40, file 1226, national YWCA health and physical education secretary to woman recreation director, 30 Nov. 1954, reporting CPB official's support for a woman director's candidacy for a national recreation organization executive position; ser.B1, 22, file 817, field supervisor to district representative, 21 Oct. 1957; RG 2, ser.S-1, 2, Branch policy memoranda, 1948–62, CPB director to national YWCA health education secretary, Sept. 1950

53 The description of the provincial recreation authority's staff complement is based on the following sources: AO, RG 2, RO, ser.A9, interview transcripts; ser.S-1, 1, CPB report for 1953; 'Salaries, Estimates, and Inventories, 1951–1959,' salaries chart for 1955–6; staff list of head office of Community Programmes Section; 6, file 'OAEB, 1947–1948; ser.S-7, 1, OAEB minutes; RO, ser.A9, interview transcripts; ser.B3, 23, file 857, CPB staff conference reports, 1955–60; *CC* lists of district representatives, various dates. Individuals employed only briefly may not appear on any of the lists consulted.

54 AO, RO, ser.A9, 16, file 434, interview transcripts, 1–2; file 444, 2, 16; appointment notice, *CC* 17 (1949), 1

4: Constructing Community, Legitimating Authority, 1946–1958

1 Owram, *The Government Generation*; Burke, *Seeking the Highest Good*; Richard
   Allen, *The Social Passion* (Toronto: University of Toronto Press 1971); Struthers, '"Lord Give Us Men"'; Gale Wills, *A Marriage of Convenience* (Toronto:
   University of Toronto Press 1995). A key text expressing opposition to the
   interventionist state is Hayek, *The Road to Serfdom*. In Canada, Leonard
   Marsh's *Report on Social Security for Canada* (1943) represented a welfare-
   centred contribution to the planning side of the debate.
2 AO, RO, ser.B2, 23, file 838, 'Community Recreation in Ontario,' clipping
   Family Herald and Weekly Star, 5 April 1951; ser.B3, 23, file 857, *The Story of a
   Community* (published by the CPB, ca 1956), 5–7, 12
3 Several elements in this project of social transformation are discussed in Valverde, 'Building Anti-Delinquent Communities.'
4 NA, MG 28, I 10, 162, file 'Recreation, Public-Private Relationships, 1947–
   1957,' Klein, 'A Description,' 9–10; Murray G. Ross, 'Relationship between
   Public and Private Services in the Recreation Field,' paper given at Canadian
   Conference on Social Work, Hamilton, 11 June 1948; AO, RO, ser.A9, 14, file
   381, 'The Sports Mill,' clippings, the *Daily Standard Freeholder*, 22, 24 Sept.
   1948
5 AO, RO, ser.B1, 20, file 656, Guelph annual report for 1950 (unpaginated).
   The director of National Health and Welfare's Physical Fitness Division calls
   for recreation leaders across the country to undertake the responsibility of
   interpreting recreation: 'It is true that the needs of the people determine
   the recreational program to be offered; but it is the leaders of the people
   who must first make them aware of their needs.' NA, RG 29, 843, file 224-1-
   75, Ernest Lee, 'Trends in Municipal Recreation,' paper given to the Canadian Federation of Mayors and Municipalities at Saskatoon, Aug. 1950, 8.
6 AO, RO, ser.A9, interview transcripts, 16, file 433, 4; 17, file 461, 13–14;
   ser.B1, 20, file 655, chairman of MRC to CPB director, 22 March 1952; file
   646, sports director for National Cellulose to CPB director, 3 Dec. 1948
7 BRO, Minutes of the Brantford City Council, roll 3, 619, 14 Feb. 1944; City of
   Brantford scrapbooks, 14 Dec. 1945–31 March 1946, 327, report on recreation director speaking to Optimist Club, *BrEx*, ca 20 Nov. 1945; 30 Jan.
   1943–30 Oct. 1945, 134, 'Council of Social Agencies Moves to Halt Delinquency,' *BrEx*, 16 Aug. 1945; AO, RO, ser.A9, interview transcripts, 16, file
   416, 28; file 439, 16–17; panel discussion, *CC* 23 (July 1949), 12; SCA, SCC,
   minutes, 'Appendix, Simcoe County Recreation Committee,' 1948, 95, 97;
   'Appendix, Recreation Director Simcoe County,' 1952, 147; AO, RO, ser.B1,
   20, file 657, form letter from Guelph Council of Social Agencies, 14 May

1948. For the relationships between activity groups and recreation commissions, see A.G. Ley, 'Right between the Eyes,' *CC* 13 (Sept. 1948), 14–17. AO, RO, ser.B1, 20, file 655, auditor's report for recreation committee, 7 Feb. 1951; file 646, memorandum from district representative to CPB director, 18 Dec. 1952.

8 AO, RO, ser.C4, 41, file 1237, *The YMCA and Public Recreation: Report of a Commission of the National Council of the YMCA's of Canada* (1950), esp. 10, 38–41

9 BRO, City of Brantford scrapbooks, 31 Oct. 1945–31 Dec. 1945, 1, 'John Pearson New Director of Recreation,' clipping, *BrEx*, 2 Nov. 1945; AO, RO, ser.C3, 33, file 1074, 'A Message from your Convention Committee,' Nov. 1953; file 1069, 'Qualifications for Recreation Personnel' (unpaginated). See also ibid., 36, file 1119 for the ORA's 1951 'Report on Standards Committee,' which makes even greater demands of the director's personality.

10 'Failing to sell program and self to the public' was the expression used by the recreation commission that fired the tactless recreation director mentioned above.

11 AO, RO, ser.B1, 19, file 534, MRC to director of physical fitness and recreation, 20 April 1946. For another example of this kind of hiring rationale, see b18, file 507, MRC to CPB, 28 Oct. 1949.

12 Ibid., ser.A9, interview transcripts, 16, file 439, 18; file 448, 3, 18–19

13 BRO, City of Brantford scrapbooks, 1 Jan. 1946–7 June 1947, 5, 'Community Committee Is Formed,' 9 Jan. 1946; 7, 'Victoria Rink Ice Carnival Draws Crowd,' 26 Jan. 1946; AO, RO, ser.A9, interview transcripts, 16, file 439, 1; file 448, 20–1; ser.B1, b20, file 656, 'Recreation Time Is Opportunity Time' (discussion of Sunny Acres Neighbourhood Club); BRO, City of Brantford scrapbooks, 30 Jan. 1943–30 Oct. 1945, 131, 'Propose Concerts, Singing,' *BrEx*, 13 July 1945; 135, 'Community "Sing,"' *BrEx*, 24 Aug. 1945; 'Bathing Beauties, Folk Dancers Demonstrate County Recreation Program Annual Review Night,' *BE*, 28 May 1952, 5; BRR, CCC, minutes, 8 Dec. 1948, 2; 'Swimming Classes Get Under Way in County despite Cool Weather,' *BE*, 12 July 1951, 1; 'Night Class Registration Double This Year at Collegiate Institute,' *BE*, 23 Oct. 1950, sect. 2, 1; 'Old Barn Dance Winds Up Stayner Recreation Course,' *BE*, 11 June 1951, 9; SCA, printed minutes of SCC, 'Appendix, Recreation Director Simcoe County,' 1952, 149; BRR, CCC, minutes, 8 Dec. 1948, 3

14 NA, MG 28, I 10, 162, file 'Recreation, Public-Private, Relationships 1947–1957,' excerpts from proceedings of the Recreation Division's 1947 workshop on public and private responsibilities, 4

15 'Recreation Fair First of Kind in Province,' *BrEx*, 2 April 1951, 11; BRR, RC, minutes, 1950–1, report of the executive committee meeting, 5 March 1951; AO, RO, ser.A9, 16, file 448, interview transcript, 21

16 AO, RO, ser.A9, 16, file 427, interview transcript, 3–4. I infer the organiza-
    tional commitments of the director in Leaside from knowing who trained
    him and from his approbation of the recreation committee's initiative.

17 For a reference to a recreation survey as scientific, see *CC*, 18 (March 1949),
    1–3. SCA, SCACA, file 'Historical Information and Speeches,' founding
    member of SCACA to Jean, 4 Dec. 1970; BRO, City of Brantford scrapbooks,
    30 Jan. 1943–30 Oct. 1945, 119, 'Discuss Recreation,' *BrEx*, 20 April 1945;
    BRR, RC, minutes, 24 March 1959, 3; 31 Jan. 1957, 2; AO, RO, ser.A9, 16, file
    433, interview transcript, 7

18 AO, RO, ser.B1, 19, file 601, East York annual report, 1949

19 Ibid., ser.A9, interview transcripts, 17, file 461, 10; file 474, 3; ser.B1, 22, file
    817, CPB field supervisor to district representative, 21 Oct. 1957; 19, file 589,
    report of the district representative, 1949; ser.B3, 24, file 872, CPB, 'Policy on
    Leadership Training,' 31 Jan. 1951; RG 2, ser.S-1, 1, file 'Reports, 1953–56,'
    memorandum for chief director from CPB director re Lennox-Addington,
    Prince Edward and Adolphustown Townships, 17 Oct. 1956; 2, file 'Inter-
    views with Regional Supervisors on Policy, etc., 1954'; Pogue and Taylor, *His-
    tory, Part II*, 12

20 In this enterprise, recreation directors were performing within the liberal
    mould the ideological work Homi Bhabha prescribes for politically engaged
    socialist theorists in 'The Commitment to Theory,' in *The Location of Culture*
    (New York: Routledge 1994), 26–7. But in essentializing 'the people' they
    prompted wounded and perplexed responses to the complexity and instabil-
    ity of their political object, just as Bhabha's analysis would lead us to expect.

21 AO, RO, ser.B1, 21, file 740, brief submitted to North Bay City Council by the
    president of Nipissing Art Club, describing events between 1937 and 1962, 23
    Feb. 1962; president of Nipissing Art Club to CPB Director, 3 March 1962;
    SCA, SCACA Council, minutes of the provisional committee of the Simcoe
    County Arts and Crafts Group, 20 Oct. 1945, 2; AO, RO, ser.A9, 16, file 433,
    interview transcript, 7; ser.B1, 18, file 513, president of MRC to director of
    physical fitness and recreation, 15 Sept. 1948

22 AO, RO, ser.B1, 20, file 656, Guelph annual report for 1950, public relations
    section; file 537, CPB Director to chairman of an MRC, 7 Feb. 1951; 19, file
    634, MRC to Department of Education, 29 April 1953; file 601, annual report
    for East York, 1949; 19, file 634, memorandum from district representative to
    CPB, 5 Nov. 1951; 18, file 557, district representative to field supervisor, 9
    Sept. 1960; ser.A9, interview transcripts, 16, file 403, 5–6; file 404, 1–4, 9–10;
    file 414, 1–3; file 427, 1; file 441, 1; file 448, 1; file 449, 1; file 456, 1; 17, file
    461, 1; file 462, 2; BRR, RC, minutes 22 May 1946, 'Summer staff'

23 Thomas R. Laws, 'The New Clergyman,' in Ronald Gross and Paul Oster-

man, eds., *The New Professionals* (New York: Simon and Schuster 1972), 136;
AO, RO, ser.A9, 17, file 469, interview transcript, 5

24 AO, RO, ser.A9, 16, file 401, interview transcript, 13–14

25 Ibid., 17, file 474, 3

26 Ibid., file 461, 1–2, 19

27 Ibid., 16, file 415, 2

28 Ibid., file 431, 22

29 Adams, *The Trouble with Normal*, 97

30 In *Making Sex*, 28–9, 198–9, 241, Laqueur traces the persistent and variously
    remade articulation of activity and masculinity from Aristotle to Rousseau to
    Freud. Freud's contribution to this current in western gender discourse may
    be sampled in Sigmund Freud, 'Infant Sexuality,' *Three Essays on the Theory of
    Sexuality* (London: Imago 1949), 97n1.

31 *Ontario Regulations*, 1951, no. 521; NA, MG 28, I 10, Klein, 'A Description';
    AO, RO, ser.B1, 19, file 634, memorandum from district representative to
    field supervisor, 29 Jan. 1957; 20, file 679, district representative's report,
    1953; BRR, RC, minutes, by-law 3281, as amended by by-law 3463, and min-
    utes for 22 Feb. 1954, report of steering committees to plan the formation of
    the recreation association

32 'Recreation a Community Asset [editorial],' *BE*, 26 Oct. 1950, 15; 'Rec.
    Chairman Thanks Voters for Support,' *BE*, 14 Dec. 1950, 1; BRR, RC, min-
    utes, 15 June 1950, 1; minutes, Programme and Personnel Committee, 1 Feb.
    1950; AO, RO, ser.B1, 20, file 657, district representative to CPB director, 10
    Jan. 1950, 31 Jan. 1950

33 AO, RO, ser.A9, 17, file 461, interview transcript, 13–14; ser.B1, 21, file 740,
    President of Nipissing Art Club to CPB director, 3 March 1962

34 Ibid., ser.A9, 17, file 465, interview transcript, 1–2, 5–6

35 Ibid., ser.B1, 19 file 634, recreation director to CPB director, 29 May 1950;
    grant appliction, 1950; field representative to CPB director, 5 Nov. 1951; grant
    application, 1951; president of recreation committee to CPB director, 28 Feb.
    1953; field representative to CPB director, 12 March 1953, 29 April 1953; pres-
    ident of recreation committee to Department of Education, 20 April 1953

36 Ibid., ser.A9, 15, file 382, clipping, 'Centre Director's Resignation Accepted
    by Commission: [Ex-director] ... Reviews Program's Growth,' *Windsor Daily
    Star*, 27 Oct. 1954, 5; *Shepherd's Chatham City Directory*, 1946–7; *Vernon's
    Chatham City Directory*, 1954; NA, MG 28, I 95, records of the Young Men's
    Christian Association of Canada, year book and official roster, 1938, 162; AO,
    RO, ser.A9, 15, file 382, clippings, '[Recreation Director] Resigns, Takes Post
    in Ohio,' *Chatham Daily News*, 27 Oct. 1954; 'City Bids [Ex-director] Goodbye
    with Cheers, Presents,' 13 Nov. 1954, 1

37 AO, RO, ser.B1, 22, file 804, chairman of MRC to CPB, 18 Jan. 1949; memorandum from district representative, 6 Dec. 1948

38 Ibid., 20, file 655, memorandum from district representative to CPB Director, 19 Feb. 1952, 4 March 1952

39 Ibid., ser.A9, 15, file 382, clipping, 'Centre Director's Resignation Accepted by Commission,' *Windsor Daily Star*, 27 Oct. 1954, 5; ser.B1, 18, file 542, 'Events as They Took Place in Burlington; Also, Information Gained,' by district representative, 10 Dec. 1954; ser.C3, 33, file 1076, 'Our Recreation Director,' *S.D.M.R.O. Bulletin*, 1965

40 My capsule description of the class lines in men's attire is based on a examination of photographs in *Steel Labour* (Canadian edition) for 1948 and 1958; on a similar scrutiny of photographs in *Community Courier* of mixed gender and men's social groups (with special attention to those ones where members' occupations are identified); and on an examination of photographs of the recreation directors' in-service course meeting in 1951.

41 *Outline of a Theory of Practice* (Cambridge: Cambridge University Press 1977), 94

42 AO, RO, ser.C3, 36, file 1119, ORA Youth Division report, 1950; ser.A9, interview transcripts, b16, file 427, 5–6; file 448, 4; NA, RG 29, 2009, file R434/100, reprint of Isobel McLaggan, 'Community Organization for Recreation,' *Canadian Welfare*, 1 Dec. 1948

43 AO, RO, ser.B1, 20, file 679, district representative to CPB director, 1 Dec. 1949; ser.C4, 41, file 1237, National Council of the YMCAs of Canada, *The YMCA and Public Recreation*, Feb. 1950; SCA, SCACA, minutes, 23 Sept. 1948, 3; NA, RG 29, v843, file 224-1-75, John Pearson, 'National Survey of Recreation in Canadian Municipalities: Some Implications for Municipal Government,' paper presented to the 14th Annual Conference of Canadian Mayors and Municipalities; MG 28, I 10, 1622, file 'Recreation: Public-Private, Relationships, 1947–1957,' especially the paper given by Murray G. Ross at the Canadian Conference on Social Work, 11 June 1948; Pogue and Taylor, *History, Part II*, 16–17; E.C. Cross CPB director, 'The First Year – and Looking Forward,' *CC* 13 (Sept. 1948), 1–2

44 AO, RO, ser.A9, interview transcripts, 16, file 448, 12; and file 427, 5–6; Mrs Don Shay, 'So You're the Wife of a Recreation Director,' *CC* 122 (Dec. 1959), 4

45 Whyte, *The Organization Man*, 144–8. Celibacy here means only 'state of being unmarried,' though abstention from sexual relations seems likely as well. The term was chosen specifically to include widows and women who intended to marry, as well as never-married women who had chosen career over marriage and family.

46 Michael Silverstein describes his own discovery of the way a professional job can impart masculinity to a male individual through the authority that is conferred on him: 'The History of a Short, Unsuccessful Academic Career,' in Joseph Pleck and Jack Sawyer, eds., *Men and Masculinity* (Englewood Cliffs, NJ: Prentice-Hall 1974), 107–23.

47 AO, RO, ser.B1, 18, file 557, field supervisor to district representative, 6 May 1958

48 Ibid., ser.B2, 23, file 838, containing a clipping commenting on recreation director's low pay, long hours, and worthwhile work: 'Innisfil Notes. Agric. Federation Had a Good Year,' Nov. 1962. On devotion to service as essential to survival and success, see ser.C3, b37, file 1128, report of the tenth annual ORA conference, 'Summary and Evaluation,' 1. see also ser.C3, 33, file 1069, 'Qualifications for Recreation Personnel,' *R.D.F.O. Annual Report*, 1955. For an instance of how willingness to work long hours could be used rhetorically as evidence of moral superiority, both of paid and of unpaid workers, see ser.A9, 15, file 382, clipping, 'Centre Director's Resignation Accepted by Commission: [Ex-director] ... Reviews Program's Growth,' *Windsor Daily Star*, 27 Oct. 1954, 5. On the usefulness to professionals of the service ethic, see Wilding, *Professional Power and Social Welfare*, 77. AO, RO, ser.A9, 16, file 431, interview transcript, 22–3.

49 AO, RO, ser.A9, 16, file 448, interview transcript, 12. The ideal that recreation directors cheerfully serve the people was (and probably still is) so important that one recreation director asked that the interviewer not publish his very mild expression of contempt for community volunteers who offer ill-informed criticism of recreation directors. The recreation directors shared with other welfare professionals the desire to act always in a caring way towards the public, but in the face of criticism, recreation directors were not free from the disabling conviction that clients can be wrong about whether or not they have been helped. For an account of the genesis of this conviction and others, see John McKnight, 'Professionalized Service and Disabling Help,' esp. 83–9.

50 AO, RO, ser.A9, 13, file 355, 'The Challenge of Change,' speech reprinted with discussion summary in *Ora* 13 (Dec. 1962), 19; b15, file 382, clipping, 'Centre Director Resigns, Takes Huntsville Post,' *Chatham Daily News*, undated, 9

51 Ibid., 17, file 469, interview transcript, 4; ser.B1, 20, file 693, district representative to CPB director, 19 May 1949; file 693, recreation director to CPB director, 30 June 1950

52 Ibid., ser.C3, 33, file 1081, *S.D.M.R.O.: The First Ten Years, 1946–1956*, 2–4; file 1069, 'Membership Report,' 2, *R.D.F.O. Annual Report*, 1955; 'Membership

List,' *R.D.F.O. Annual Report*, 1956; '33%,' *R.D.F.O. Annual Report*, 1957; ser.B3, 21, file 878, CPB director, address to ORA, ca 1963, 2

53 Ibid., ser.C3, 33, file 1081, *S.D.M.R.O.: The First Ten Years*, 9

54 This and subsequent items are quoted from the code as it appears in AO, RO, ser.C3, 3, file 1074, *RDFO Membership Brochure*, inside front cover

55 Ibid., ser.A3, 5, file 113, 'The Professional Worker' (CPB document), 1957; ser.A9, 16, file 439, interview transcript, 4; ser.C3, 33, file 1081, *S.D.M.R.O.: The First Ten Years, 1946–1956*, 2, 9

56 Ibid., ser.C3, 37, file 1128, report of the eleventh annual ORA conference, Resolution no. 4, 53; Report of the tenth annual ORA conference, 'Summary and Evaluation,' 1–2; 33, file 1069, *R.D.F.O. Annual Report*, 1955, section 5a; RG 2, ser.S-1, 1, memorandum to deputy minister of education from CPB director, 26 Oct. 1956

57 AO, RO, ser.C3, 33, file 1069, report of membership chairman and copy of the draft act in *R.D.F.O. Annual Report*, 1957; Ontario Regulations, 1957, no. 57, sect. 5(1); BRR, RC, minutes, 15 July 1958, 1; Ontario, *Statutes*, 1958, cap. 132. sect. 2

58 AO, RO, ser.A9, 13, file 355, Ross C. Rathie, 'In the Profession ... Significant Advance,' *Ora*, 9 (Sept. 1958), 6; Ontario, *Statutes*, 1958, cap. 132, sect. 10(c); ser.C3, 33, file 1069, 'Constitution, section 2(c)(3),' *S.D.M.R.O. Annual Report*, 1959

59 Records of the Department of Justice (Ottawa), Recreation Directors' Federation of Ontario, 'Problems in the Control of Criminal Sexual Psychopaths,' brief to be presented to the Royal Commission on the Criminal Law Relating to Criminal Sexual Psychopaths (1956–8). My thanks to Rob Champagne for access to a copy of this document. A perception of working-class men as more likely than those from the middle class to abuse children may have been part of the basis for the view expressed in 1961 that, in amalgamated parks and recreation departments, care would have to be exercised to ensure that 'a higher calibre of maintenance employee [worked] in situations involving contact with children.' See AO, RO, ser.B1, 17, file 494, 'The Amalgamation of Recreation and Parks in Brantford,' 5. For the blacklisting, see AO, RG 2, ser.S-1, 3, CPB director to all district representatives, 11 Feb. 1949.

60 AO, RO, ser.B1, 20, file 655, application for approval of recreation director appointment, 26 Feb. 1957. For his race and the CPB's concerns about racism, see the memorandum from field Supervisor to district representative, 17 April 1957 and from CPB director to deputy minister of education, 27 April 1957, and for his qualifications, see field supervisor to field supervisor, 14 May 1957.

61 AO, RO, ser.A9, interview transcripts, 17, file 469, 11; 16, file 428, 2

62 Ibid., 16, file 421, 6–7

63 Ibid., file 403, 5–6

64 Ibid., file 450, 8; the same point is also expressed in file 448, 18, and file 437, 3–4.

65 Ibid., ser.B3, 24, file 872, 'Policy (Leadership Training),' CPB document, 31 Jan. 1951, 1. This document specifically concerns training volunteer leaders, but the passage quoted comes from the general section on 'characteristics of a "leader,"' which would seem to be understood to apply to any leader, paid or not.

66 Not having seen photographs of all of Ontario's recreation directors in the 1950s, I cannot be entirely sure that only one man of colour became a recreation director; however, the tensions surrounding this man's career and the absence of other men or women of colour in the group and individual photographs I have seen suggest strongly that he was the only one. My identification of his class background is based on his having a university degree; see AO, RO, ser.B1, 20, file 655, application for approval of recreation director appoinment, 26 Feb. 1957.

67 Ibid., ser.C3, 33, file 1069, report of the director of training, *S.D.M.R.O. Annual Report*, 1959, 28

68 Ibid., ser.A9, 16, file 439, interview transcript, 17–18

5: The Meanings of Citizen Participation: Brantford, 1945–1957

1 AO, RO, ser.C3, 36, file 1119, 'Our Way of Life 1951,' *ORA Bulletin* 7 (1951), 2. The history of this whole period of community organization and its ties to citizen participation in welfare provision has not yet been written. I have found evidence of the breadth and heterogeneity of the organizing spirit in, NA, MG 28, I 10, 49, file 439, Eurith Goold (National Council of the YWCA) to Elizabeth S.L. Govan (Canadian Welfare Council), 11 Dec. 1953; City of Vancouver Archives, United Way (Vancouver), Records of the United Way of the Lower Mainland, Social Planning Section files, A to N, 1940–50, 'Neighbourhood Council Developments, 1953–54'; Jacquelyn Gale Wills, 'Efficiency, Feminism, and Co-operative Democracy: Origins of the Toronto Social Planning Council, 1918–1957,' PhD thesis, University of Toronto 1989); Smith, 'First Person Plural'; Arthur Morgan, *The Small Community: Foundation of Democratic Life, What It Is and How to Achieve It* (New York: Harper & Brothers 1942), esp. 279–82. A recent scholarly study of community organization as part of housing reform in the post-war period is Kevin Brushett, '"People and Government Travelling Together": Community

Organization, the State and Post-War Reconstruction in Toronto, 1943–1953,' paper presented at the Canadian Historical Association, 5–8 June 1997.

2 Small towns and villages required less elaborate committee structures, and Toronto entered the post-war period with an elaborate non-participatory public recreation system already in place from the inter-war period. Consequently, the most ambitious experiments took place in mid-sized cities, as well as in one county (i.e., a rural munipality). As examples, for Hamilton, see AO, RO, ser.A9, 16, file 459, interview transcript, 9–11; for Guelph, see ser.B1, 20, file 657, T.A. Leishman to J.K. Tett, 10 Jan. 1950; for Toronto Township (Mississauga), ser.A9, 16, file 433, interview transcript, 4; for Simcoe County, see SCA, Recreation Department Records, Louise Colley, 'The Process of Change in the Structure and Functioning of a Rural Agency'; AO, RO, ser.A9, 16, file 416, interview transcript; Pogue and Taylor, *History, Part I*, 16–17; 'Drew Sees Youth Plan as Means to Combat Reds,' *Globe and Mail*, 10 April 1948.

3 The tendency of professional self-interest to produce bureaucracy is by now a set-piece of sociology. I do not deny this tendency, but wish to suggest here that it is complemented by the socially constructed agency of clients and by the dynamics of politics in municipal government. Critiques of the welfare professions may be found in Wilding, *Professional Power and Social Welfare*, and John McKnight, 'Professionalized Service and Disabling Help,' in Illich, et al., eds., *Disabling Professions*.

4 For an account of this perspective in the previous post-war period, see Naylor, *The New Democracy*.

5 AO, RO, ser.A9, 16, file 448, interview transcript, 1–2, 11; BRO, City of Brantford scrapbooks, 31 Oct. 1945–31 Dec. 1945, 1, 'John Pearson New Director of Recreation,' *BrEx*, 2 Nov. 1945; W. Kenneth Dunn, et al., comp., *[McGill University], Directory of Graduates, 1890–1965* (Montreal 1966)

6 BRR, RC, minutes, Pearson to Alinsky, 5 Jan. 1953; Donald C. Reitzes and Dietrich C. Reitzes, *The Alinsky Legacy: Alive and Kicking* (Greenwich, Conn.: JAI Press 1987), 1–8, quoted by Reitzes and Reitzes from *Current Biography*, 4 (1968), 8

7 BRO, City Council, minutes, microfilm roll 3, 14 Feb. 1944, 619; 24 April 1944, 670

8 *Reveille for Radicals*, 87–91, 219

9 Mr Pearson is no longer alive, and so my understanding of his views is based on documents and on the interview conducted with him in the 1970s. See AO, RO, ser.A9, 16, file 448, interview transcript, 2, 18, 21.

10 BRR, RC, minutes, annual report, 1948

11 MacPherson, *Building and Protecting the Co-operative Movement*, app. C; Robert
   Clark, *A Glimpse of the Past: A Centennial History of Brantford and Brant County*
   (Brantford: Brantford Historical Society 1966), 56–7; Naylor, *The New Democracy*, 217; Elizabeth Kelly, *Our Expectations: A History of Brantford's Labour Movement* (Brantford: Brantford Labour Council 1987), 99. For the terms of office
   of the mayors, see Ontario, Department of Municipal Affairs, *Municipal Directory*, 1948–60; for their occupations, see *Vernon's City Directory*. AO, RO,
   ser.A9, 16, file 448, interview transcript, 2; *Fortieth Annual Report of Labour
   Organization in Canada (1950–51 edition)* (Ottawa 1951), 10; *Ninth Census of
   Canada* (1951), 4, table 22.
12 AO, RO, ser.A9, 16, file 448, interview transcript, 3, 18–19; interview with
   former Brantford recreation department staff member, conducted by the
   author on 25 June 1992
13 AO, RO, ser.A9, 16, file 448, interview transcript, 18–19
14 Ibid., interview transcript, 3–4, 18–19; ser.B1, 18, file 537, first issue of *Recreation Service Bulletin*, ca Feb. 1946
15 BRR, CCC, minutes, 12 Jan. 1949, 1; CCC, minutes, 5 Sept. 1951, 1 (lists eighteen committees); AO, RO, ser.A9, 16, file 448, interview transcript, 3–4
   (gives figure of sixteen)
16 The range of common volunteer activities is evident throughout the records
   of the CCC and in the Recreation office's community committees files. A
   particularly detailed single source is the *Eagle Place Community News*, three
   issues of which (Sept. 1950, March 1951, and Sept. 1951) are located in the
   Parsons' Park file. The role of adult volunteers as program leaders in the evenings, who supplemented the paid daytime supervision, is noted in BRR, RC,
   minutes, John Pearson to the Ottawa Playgrounds Department director,
   21 Jan. 1953, and in the North Ward Community Committee file, minutes,
   9 April 1954; the community committees were also called on to maintain
   rink discipline by providing supervision at 'nominal cost' (RC, minutes,
   15 Jan. 1948, 1). A general statement on the volunteers' role in running craft
   courses can be found in CCC, minutes, report of the Community Centres
   committee, 5 Sept. 1951. The minutes of the CCC meeting for 7 July 1948
   describe that season's roster of street dances (four) and community concerts
   (eleven) organized by various member committees; they also indicate that
   the CCC's amateur talent contest, a parade float, and a refreshments conces-
   sion figured that year in Brantford Day festivities organized by local merchants. The CCCs were also active in Labour Day celebrations (CCC,
   minutes, 6 June 1951, 1). Women's groups tabulated the results of Brantford's first recreation survey (see RC, minutes 15 March 1945, 1–2). Volunteer labour for building equipment (a stage, a sandbox canopy, rinks, and

rink shacks) is noted in AO, RO, ser.B1, box 18, file 537, *Service*, no. 1, ca Feb. 1946; RC, minutes, 8 July 1948, 1; 15 Jan. 1959, 2; Westdale Community Centre community committee file, letter from committee chairman to Brantford RC, 21 Jan. 1957; CCC, minutes, 3 Jan. 1951, 3.

17 AO, RO, ser.B1, 18, file 537, editorial, *Recreation Service Bulletin*, no. 1; ser.A9, 16, file 448, interview transcript, 6

18 The committees represented by existing lists include neither the ones from the city's wealthier neighbourhoods, like Dufferin and Lansdowne, nor the one from the poorest downtown area. Fewer single women than single men were involved in these committees and the commission: nine women versus twenty men. On a percentage basis, the gap is smaller: the nine women represent 8 per cent of the women, while the twenty men were 10 per cent of the men. The percentage of non-Anglo-Celtic Brantford residents was derived from figures given in *Census of Canada*, 1951, vol. 1.

19 BRO, City of Brantford scrapbooks, 1 Jan. 1946–7 June 1947, 5, 'Community Committee is Formed,' *BrEx*, 9 Jan. 1946; 7, 'Victoria Ice Rink Carnival Draws Crowd,' *BrEx*, 26 Jan. 1946; 10, 'Ice Carnival Arranged for Spring Street (Holmedale),' *BrEx*, Jan. 1946; 13, 'Recreation Rink Carnival Planned,' *BrEx*, 12 Feb. 1946; 5, 'Community Committee is Formed,' *BrEx*, 9 Jan. 1946. The information on telephone service is based on the 1946 *Vernon Directory* street listing for Chestnut Street, a cross street that ran from the bottom to the top of the hill near the park. At the bottom of Chestnut, below Kerr Avenue, sixteen of twenty-three homes had no phone; above Kerr, all had phones.

20 BRR, community committees files, Arrowdale, 'Notes on the Community Committees,' Sept. 1952, by the counsellor of the Community Centres; counsellor; interview with former Brantford Recreation Department staff member, conducted by the author on 29 June 1992

21 This area was the Lansdowne-Holmedale-Dufferin area. Substantially middle class with a working-class fringe near adjacent factories, the multiplication and mutation of community committees in this area may have been the result of class tensions. The Dufferin committee succeeded the Holmedale committee, the name change signalling a shift in the committee's geographical centre towards the area's more middle-class part. In an intermediate phase, the committee was simply named the Spring Street Playground Committee. A former Recreation Department staff member recalls one working-class Holmedale committee member's opinion that the wealthier members looked down on him (interview conducted by author, 25 June 1992). The Lansdowne committee centred on a prosperous neighbourhood, near Dufferin. Unfortunately, the changes cannot be precisely dated nor fully explained because few early records of these particular committees survive.

The changes described here are inferred from BRR, community committees files, Dufferin (formerly Holmedale), Hallowe'en parade poster, and BRO, RC, annual report, 1955, 'Community Committees Dec. 1955.'

22 BRR, RC, minutes, 'Report of the Nominating Committee,' 1953

23 BRR, CCC, minutes, Sept. 1947, 1

24 In the title of the conclusion to *Heroes of Their Own Lives: The Politics and History of Family Violence, Boston, 1880–1960* (New York: Viking 1988), Gordon quotes this expression, which seems to have been given currency in feminist theory by Elizabeth Janeway when she used it for the title of her book (New York: Knopf 1980).

25 BRR, CCC, minutes, 22 Jan. 1947, 2; 9 June 1948, 1; 17 Nov. 1948, 3; annual report 1948; 'Report from a Meeting on Community Centre Plans, Oct. 3/50, City Hall,' 1; 'Report of the First Recreation Excursion to Toronto,' March 1950; AO, RO, ser.A9, interview transcripts, 16, file 448, 12; file 427, 3–4

26 The names of Brantford people active as volunteers in the recreation movement have been changed, in accordance with the practice I adopted for other municipalities where I had access to records in a provincial collection covered at the time of my research under the Ontario Freedom of Information and Protection of Privacy Act.

27 BRR, CCC, minutes, June 1948, 2; 7 July 1948, 3; minutes, 10 June 1948; 14 Oct. 1948, 3

28 Ibid., minutes, 31 Oct. 1948, 2; 11 Nov. 1948, 3; RC, minutes, 10 Feb. 1949, 1

29 Ibid., RC, minutes, untitled document summarizing the work of the Recreation Commission from 1945 to 1948, and minutes, 10 June 1948

30 Ibid., 8 June 1949, 3; 14 July 1949; CCC, minutes, minutes, 10 May 1950, 1; 6 Sept. 1950, 1

31 Ibid., CCC, 31 Oct. 1948, 2; 9 Feb. 1949, 2; RC, minutes, Resolutions and Recommendations from Community Committees' Conference, 10 June 1950

32 'C. Callan Heads Massey-Harris Credit Union,' *BrEx*, 23 Jan. 1952, 22; *BrEx*, 2 Feb. 1950, 6; AO, RO, ser.A9, 16, file 448, interview transcript, 21

33 BRR, RC, minutes, list of RC members and minutes, 12 Oct. 1950, 2

34 AO, RO, ser.A9, 18, file 537, copy of by-law 3281, 7 May 1951; BRR, RC, minutes, 12 Oct. 1950, 2; CCC, minutes, Report of the Community Centres Committee, 5 Sept. 1951; minutes, 28 March 1951

35 BRR, RC, minutes, 12 April 1951, 1–2

36 Ibid., CCC minutes, 9 March 1949, 2; CCC, minutes, 6 June 1951, 2

37 This organizational choice indicates an important feature of the recreation volunteers' understanding of their citizenship. Being a policy intervenor is part of what political theorists Samuel Bowles and Herbert Gintis call being

a 'chooser,' a status that they point out is, in liberal political theory, opposed to the status of 'learner,' a status that is held to be appropriate for women, children, native peoples, or any 'dependent' group, whose alleged incapacities make them temporarily or permanently unable to make decisions about their own or the collective good. When the CCC rejected an organizational structure that was symbolic of 'learner' status, it implicitly denied that its members were dependent. See *Democracy and Capitalism*, 121–7.

38 BRR, CCC, minutes, 3 Jan. 1951, 1–2

39 Ibid., RC, minutes, 11 Sept. 1952, 1–2. Notably, the City Council representative on the commission at this time was UAW union officer Charles Ward, and he seems to have been the only commissioner to suggest that not all the possibilities for purchasable land had yet been exhausted.

40 BRR, RC, minutes, Pearson to Alinsky, 5 Jan. 1953; 'The Area Director,' 2 April 1953; AO, RO, ser.A9, 17, file 478, interview transcript, 4

41 BRR, CCC, minutes, 17 Nov. 1948, 3; 'Report of Committee Set Up to Suggest Future Functions of This Council,' 13 Dec. 1950; RC, minutes, 'Report from a Meeting on Community Centre Plans, Oct. 3/50, City Hall,' 2; 'Report of the First Recreation Excursion to Toronto'

42 BRR, RC, minutes, 'Report of the First Recreation Excursion to Toronto'; AO, RO, ser.A9, 17, file 469, interview transcript, 2–3, 20. There are frequent minor inaccuracies in the transcripts of these interviews, and I have assumed the interviewee's spoken comment included the preposition 'in,' but even without it the content of the observation is unchanged.

43 BRR, CCC, minutes, 9 March 1953; 9 Sept. 1953, 2; 8 April 1953, 3

44 BRR, RC, minutes, 'Report from a Meeting on Community Centre Plans, Oct. 3/50, City Hall,' 1; CCC, minutes, 29 Sept. 1948, 1–2; Community Centres Committee, report, 5 Sept. 1951; RC, minutes, 'Community Centres – 1954'; interviews with a former Brantford Recreation Department staff member, conducted by the author in 13 July 1992 and on 25 June 1992

45 BRR, CCC, minutes, 7 Sept. 1948, 1; report of Community Centre Special Committee, Sept. 1948; 'Special Meeting of Community Committees to Discuss Plans for Fall and Winter Community Programmes,' 23 Sept. 1953

46 Movie-going in Canada declined after 1952, an indication that television-viewing had begun to shape leisure pursuits. According to national statistics on television ownership, the years from 1953 to 1955 showed the greatest three-year rate of increase in the period 1953–61, rising from 10 per cent of households to 40 per cent. (See Rutherford, *When Television Was Young*, 12, 49.) For the expression 'work to play,' see *CC* 16 (Dec. 1948), 14. BRR, community committees files, North Ward, minutes, 21 Sept. 1953.

47 BRR, RC, minutes, Report of the Nominating Committee (re: 1954 commissioners)

48 I was unable to date precisely the change of recreation director in 1956; however, the new director appears in this role in the City Council minutes for the first time on 12 Oct. 1956, and his predecessor's last appearance in the same minutes was 30 Jan. 1956; see BRO, City Council, minutes, roll 1, Oct. 1950–56 (mfm). The quotation is from AO, RO, ser.A9, 17, file 474, interview transcript, 3–4.

49 BRR, CCC, minutes, 9 Oct. 1953, 1; AO, RO, ser.A9, 17, file 474, interview transcript, 7

50 BRO, Brantford Recreation Commission, annual report, 1957, 'Director's Report,' item (2)

51 Peiss, *Cheap Amusements*, 12–33; Deem, *All Work and No Play?* 4–8; Meg Luxton, *More than a Labour of Love* (Toronto: Women's Press 1980), 19–21, 195–9; Ruth Millett, 'Women Aren't So Badly Off,' *BrEx*, 13 Sept. 1952

52 The importance of citizen participation in the welfare state was recognized by political scientist Leo Panitch when he included an article on the subject in an anthology on the political economy of the Canadian state. However, it appears that neither Panitch nor Martin Loney (the author of the article) knew of the 1945–55 efforts of social activists, some state-funded and some not, to foster citizen participation. Loney, 'A Political Economy of Citizen Participation,' 451.

53 A Canadian conservative writer whose view of community celebrates the relations of dominance and subordination that he believes follow from natural differences in ability between the sexes is William Gairdner. See, for example, his *The War against the Family: A Parent Speaks Out* (Toronto: Stoddart 1992), esp. 84–5.

6: The Feminine Mystique in Community Leadership: Women Volunteers in Public Recreation

1 Christina McCall Newman, 'What's So Funny about the Royal Commission on the Status of Women?' *Saturday Night* 84 (Jan. 1969), 21–4; Kate Aitken, 'Women Are Misfits in Politics,' *Maclean's* 71 (4 Jan. 1958), 6, 40; David MacDonald, 'Powerful Women's Lobby in Canada,' *Chatelaine*, June 1957, 58; Gillian A. Walker, *Family Violence and the Women's Movement* (Toronto: University of Toronto Press 1990), 118

2 AO, RO, ser.C3, 36, file 1119, ORA conference reports, Earle Zeigler, 'The Volunteer Workers – Their Faith.' For a discussion of one service club's ladies' auxiliary, first organized in 1942, see Robert Tyre, *The Cross and the*

Square: The Kinsmen Story, 1920–1970 (Toronto: Association of Kinsmen Clubs, 1970), 102.

3 AO, RO, ser.B1, 20, file 656, recreation director to Sunny Acres Neighbourhood Club, ca 1950; 18, file 513, MRC president to director of physical fitness and recreation, 15 Sept. 1948; 19, file 595, secretary-treasurer of MRC to director of physical fitness and recreation, 7 Oct. 1947; 'A Recreation Ladies' Auxiliary,' *CC* 56 (1950), 15

4 BRR, CCC, minutes, Community Centres Committee, report, 5 Sept. 1951; 31 Oct. 1951; CCC, minutes, 29 Sept. 1948, 1–2. In Brantford, male craft volunteers were in leatherwork, old-time fiddle-playing, art, and woodworking. The woodworking instructor refused to accept that all craft instructors should get a $3 flat rate, and successfully held out for $5 per night. On rates of pay in other communities, see AO, RO, ser.B1, grant applications, 18, file 507, 1947; file 513, 1947; file 537, 1950; 19, file 634, 1948; 20, file 646; 18, file 557, annual report, 1958.

5 BRR, RC, minutes, 1952–3, member lists; NA, MG 28, I 10, Klein, 'A Description,' 12

6 The observation to this effect made in Klein, 'A Description,' 13, is borne out by the lists of recreation committees on grant applications in ser. B1 (the municipalities files) in RO at the AO.

7 AO, RO, ser.B1, 18, file 513, president of Recreation Committee to director of physical fitness and recreation, 6 May 1947

8 Ibid., ser.B3, 24, file 872, 'Policy (Leadership training) and Development of Recreation,' 31 Jan. 1951, 1

9 Ibid., ser.C3, 36, file 1119, *ORA Bulletin*, Nov. 1951, 6

10 Ibid., ser.B1, 21, file 740, brief presented city council by art club, 23 Feb. 1962

11 The narrative is based on: ibid., 619, file 631, document describing the history of recreation organization in the community between 1945 and 1960; *CC* 18 (Feb. 1949), 1–3. For biographical information on the first director and his comments on the first council, see AO, RO, ser.A9, 16, file 434, 1–3; for biographical information on second recreation director, see ser.C3, 33, file 1075, *S.D.M.R.O. Bulletin*, March 1960, 8; and ser.A9, 16, file 421, interview transcript, 1; on the gender composition of the Home and School councils, see Terry Crowley, 'Parents in a Hurry: The Early Home and School Movement in Ontario,' *Histoire sociale/Social History* 19, no. 38 (1986), 323–42. To ensure anonymity, as required by Ontario's Freedom of Information and Protection of Privacy Act, for the individuals concerned in these events, I cannot report the source for the Home and School's pre-war activity: the title of the book would identify the municipality.

12 See Figure 4.1 for a list of leisure-time associations that illustrates this point.

13 NA, MG 28, I 10, Klein, 'A Description,' 13, 18

14 The town of Wiarton seems to have undergone a similar gender shift in this period; see Mrs J.W. Kastner, 'Wiarton Community Centre,' *Food for Thought*, Nov. 1944, 13–17, esp. 14 and 16. McFarland has documented the transfer of authority in early-twentieth-century programs for playgrounds from local councils of women to municipal councils. According to McFarland, the 'ladies were happy to place someone else in charge and play a supportive role.' McFarland, committed to 'broadly-based support' for playground development, suggests that other groups, such as men's service clubs, regrettably have not always followed this same route, but have attempted instead to maintain control over the facilities they established. See McFarland, *The Development*, chapter 2, esp. 38.

15 SCA, SCACA, minutes, 'A Meeting to Discuss the Formation of an Arts and Crafts Group,' 5 Oct. 1945, 1; 22 Oct. 1947, 2; newspaper clipping describing first public meeting, 17 Nov. 1945; account book 1954–62, membership lists; minutes of the provisional committee, 20 Oct. 1945, 1; Historical Information and Speeches, Nora Marshall, untitled typescript accompanied by a note describing the document as 'the *real* story' of the SCACA's origins; AO, RO, ser.B3, 30, file 1226, curriculum vitae for Louise Colley, 1955

16 SCA, SCACA, Historical Information and Speeches, Louise Colley, 'The Development of the Simcoe County Arts and Crafts Association,' ca 1952, 2; SCACA *Bulletin*, editor's report on the Quilt and Rug Fair, 1958; SCACA, minutes of a meeting to discuss the formation of an arts and crafts group, 5 Oct. 1945; attendance roster and minutes of provisional committee meeting, 3 Nov. 1945; slate of officers and minutes notebook of Quilt and Rug Fair Committee, member list, 1948–51; Women's Institutes of Simcoe County, Simcoe Area Tweedsmuir History, member biographies; AO, RO, ser.A9, 16, file 416, interview transcript, 18, 28. Names from SCACA minutes were identified in *Vernon's Directory of Barrie and Orillia*, 1942 and 1952. In the absence of directories for the county's smaller towns or farm families, no systematic picture of the membership's social status or class background can be compiled.

17 SCA, SCACA *Bulletin*, editor's reports on Quilt and Rug Fair, 2 Nov. 1953, 6 Nov. 1954, Dec. 1955, 14 Nov. 1956, 16 Oct. 1957, and 1958; 'Record 4,000 at Beeton Fall Fair Shows Growth over Past Years,' *BE*, 2 Oct. 1951; W.H. Cranston and Melwyn Breen, 'Simcoe County: Where History and Future Pay Off,' *Saturday Night*, 26 June 1951, 8–9, 16 (the Crafts Association and its most famous associate, Thor Hansen, are mentioned on page 8)

18 SCA, SCACA correspondence, bulletin editor to beginning editor of an art-

ists' association bulletin, 19 Oct. 1961; SCACA, minutes, 27 Feb. 1953; 3, 23 June 1953, 1; SCACA account book, 1954–62

19 AO, RO, ser.B3, 23, file 838, newspaper clippings, 'County Raps City over Cost Share,' *BE*, ca Jan. 1961; 'Innisfil Notes. Agric. Federation Had a Good Year,' *BE*, Nov. 1962; AO, RO, ser.A9, 16, file 416, interview transcript, 15–17, 22–3; SCA, SCACA, minutes, 14 June 1962, 1–2; Simcoe Area Women's Institute minutes of executive meeting, 21 March 1962; SCC, *Minutes*, 26 April 1962, 3 (reporting a complaint from a local women's institute regarding a proposed increase in swimming-class and day-camp prices)

20 SCA, SCC, minutes, 5 June 1962, 35–6; Appendix, 'Community and Recreation,' by Bernard St. Amant, chairman of the Recreation Board, 104; 'Special Recreation Report No. 1,' by Ken Gillespie, chairman of the Special Recreation Committee, 23 Nov. 1962, 105; AO, RO, ser.B3, 23, file 838, 'Floyd Griesbach: Recreation Director Takes Pakistan Post,' *BE*, 2 Oct. 1962; 'County Recreation Board Told of Season's Work,' *BE*, 4 Sept. 1962; ser.B3, 23, file 838, 'Innisfil Notes. Agric. Federation Had a Good Year,' *BE*, Nov. 1962; SCA, SCACA, minutes, 14 June 1962, 2; Simcoe Area Women's Institute, minutes of executive meeting, 10 Sept. 1962; AO, RO, ser.A9, 16, file 416, interview transcript, 23; SCA, Simcoe County Recreation Department Records, Louise Colley, 'The Process of Change in the Structure and Functioning of a Rural Agency,' 9–10

21 SCA, SCC, minutes, June 1963, 53; November 1963, 85; AO, RO, ser.A9, 16, file 416, interview transcript, 23

22 AO, RO, ser.C3, 36, file 1119, ORA conference reports, Earle Zeigler, 'The Volunteer Workers – Their Faith'

23 Ibid., ser.B1, 20, file 646, CPB director to town clerk, 24 Dec. 1952

24 Ibid., memorandum from CPB district representative to acting director, 9 Dec. 1948; grant application, 1946; file 693, photocopied clipping from the *Kitchener-Waterloo Record*, 23 May 1945; and file 693

25 Ibid., file 646, grant application, 1946; 19, file 589, report by CPB district representative, 1955; *Census of Canada*, 1941 indicates that women represented 29 per cent of the manufacturing labour force, and manufacturing jobs were 47.9 per cent of all jobs in this town; AO, RO, ser.A9, 15, file 380, newspaper clipping concerning the resignation of the recreation director originally hired in April 1946, dated 14 Nov. 1948. (The newspaper's name and article title have been omitted to ensure the privacy of the individuals concerned.)

26 Pogue and Taylor, *History, Part II*, 22

27 AO, RO, ser.C3, 36, file 1119, membership list, 1951

28 Ibid., ser.A9, 16, file 401, interview transcript, 2

29 Ibid., file 433, interview transcript, 7. An example of this sort of criticism

causing difficulties for another director may be found in ser.B1, 20, file 693, CPB field representative to CPB director, 12 May 1949.

30 Ibid., ser.A9, 16, file 433, interview transcript, 26

31 Ibid., file 439, 6–7. The transcript of this interview tape contains many errors. The passage quoted here reads differently in the transcript, and I have changed it in accordance with the context and my understanding of Klein's views. The transcript reads: 'selling the lay people on the importance a citizens formed support for recreation and that it was vital that the communities' got in back of the program because if they didn't it would just become a top down recreation thing like the cities were ordinarily doing and it wouldn't be a modern kind.'

32 AO, RG 2, ser.S-1, 1, file 'Memoranda to Chief Director and Deputy Minister,' CPB director to chief director and deputy minister, 21 June 1954; CPB director to chief director, 9 March 1954. The ORA's membership revenue was calculated on the basis of the known rates of dues and the number of individual members plus the numbers of municipalities that were members, whose dues ranged between $5 and $25. The actual distribution within that range being unknown, municipal dues revenue was calculated from an estimated median rate of $15. See also AO, RO, ser.C3, 37, file 1125, membership report, 1954; report of ORA executive secretary, 1954, 2; ser.A9, interview transcripts, 16, file 439, 19; file 433, 15; and file 407, 12; ser.C3, 36, file 1119, president's report, 19 May 1950, 2–3; *Ora* 10, no. 3 (June 1959), 8.

33 AO, RO, ser.A9, 16, file 407, interview transcript, 12

34 Ibid., ser.C3, 37, file 1128, summary and evaluation of the tenth annual ORA conference, 1955; ser.A9, 13, file 355, *Ora* 12, no. 3 (Sept. 1961), 2

35 This passage and the one quoted further on in the paragraph are from AO, RO, ser.C3, 36, file 1119, 'O.R.A. Functions,' 1951.

36 Bowles and Gintis, *Democracy and Capitalism*, 121–7

37 AO, RO, ser.C3, 33, file 1069, Society of Directors of Municipal Recreation, *Annual Report*, 1955, sect. 5a

38 Ibid., file 1074, Earle Zeigler, 'Recreation in the Atomic Age,' 9

39 Ibid., ser.A3, 5, file 113, report of the fifth provincial training course of municipal recreation directors, 2; ser.C3, 36, file 1119, presidential speech by Mrs Flanagan, 1950; 37, file 1125, report of the ORA publications committee, 1954; ser.A9, 16, file 456, interview transcript, 16; ser.C3, 37, file 1120, 'Twenty Years in Review,' by ORA executive secretary, 1966, 7; ser.C3, 36, file 1119, *O.R.A. Bulletin*, Nov. 1951, 6; ser.A3, 5, file 113, report of the fifth provincial training course of municipal recreation directors, 2; *ORA Bulletin* 5 (Jan. 1951), 6; *Ora* 8, no. 5 (Oct. 1957), editorial

40 *CC* 16 (Dec. 1948), 14

41 Jeff Bishop and Paul Hoggett, in *Organizing around Enthusiasms*, 127, make a similar observation about the gender associations of this way of understanding the public purposes that are served by private leadership.

42 Pateman, 'The Fraternal Social Contract'

7: From Movement to Municipal Service, 1955–1961

1 *Ora* 11, no. 3 (June 1960), 5; AO, RO, ser.C3, 24, file 873, CPB staff conference proceedings, 7–9; RO, annual reports of Brantford RC, 1955, director's report, 3; RO, ser.B1, 20, file 706, field supervisor's comments on grant application, 1956; ser.A9, 16, file 442, interview transcript, 16; NA, MG 28, I 10, 77, file 'Labour-General, 1952–62,' R.E.G. Davis to Peter Newman, 18 Nov. 1957. For an exception to the general rule, see AO, RO, ser.B1, 20, file 655, note on grant application from field supervisor to CPB director, 3 April 1957; Adams, *The Trouble with Normal*.

2 AO, RO, ser.B3, 24, file 873, CPB staff conference report, June 1961, 12. In 1962, the new branch head acknowledged that 'the future of recreation was slightly tarnished' (see Leishman, 'Recreation and Fitness,' 28).

3 AO, RG 2, ser.S-1, 1, file 'Branch Policy Memoranda, 1948–1962,' address by Dr J.G. Althouse to CPB staff conference, 11, 12 Dec. 1952; file 'Memoranda to Chief Director and Deputy Minister,' CPB director to chief director, 9 March 1954; CPB director to chief director and deputy minister, 21 June 1954

4 AO, RO, ser.C3, 36, file 1119, membership report, 1950; b37, file 1125, membership report, 1954; 1954 conference program; memorandum re 1954 annual meeting, 4; report of Youth Advisory Committee, 29 April 1954

5 Ibid., ser.A3, 5, file 113, Report of the Fifth Provincial Training Course of Municipal Recreation Directors, 1; *CC* 94 (Oct. 1955), 1–2; RO, ser.C3, 37, file 1120, 'Twenty Years in Review,' by ORA executive secretary, 1966, comment on Klein's popularity in ORA

6 Rutherford, *When Television Was Young*, 12, 49, 448; AO, RO, ser.B1, 19, file 589, report by CPB district representative, 1955. My thanks to Ray Desrosiers for telling me about the dances in Marathon. For recreation movement criticisms of television content see RO, ser.C3, 36, file 1119, 'This 'n' That from the Almanac,' *ORA Bulletin* 10 (June 1951).

7 Pat Armstrong and Hugh Armstrong, *The Double Ghetto: Canadian Women and Their Segregated Work*, rev. ed. (Toronto: McClelland and Stewart 1984), 169; Patricia Connelly, *Last Hired, First Fired: Women and the Canadian Work Force* (Toronto: Women's Press 1978), 70. The scope of middle-class women's waged work is described and the debates concerning such work discussed in Strong-Boag, 'Canada's Wage-Earning Wives.'

8 After she left ORA, she wrote to a friend that 'I am just beginning to realize the time I gave to O.R.A. Am actually returning to housekeeping routine.' See AO, RO, ser.C3, 37, file 1149, ORA correspondence file, 1954, 'Mrs Flanagan' to K.G., 1954.

9 *Ora* 10, no. 3 (June 1959), 8. For earlier expressions of concern about the overuse of volunteers, see AO, RO, ser.C3, 36, file 1119, report on discussion group for service clubs and fraternal organizations and Earle Zeigler, 'The Volunteer Workers – Their Faith.'

10 AO, RO, ser.C3, 37, file 1128, report of the tenth annual ORA conference, 'Summary and Evaluation,' 1–2; 33, file 1069, RDFO, *Annual Report*, 1955, sect, 5a. For the recollections of rank-and-file SDMRO members of a time when 'there were too many professionals taking leadership roles in the ORA,' see AO, RO, ser.A9, interview transcripts, 16, file 450, 14–15; 17, file 463, 13.

11 AO, RO, ser.A9, 16, file 439, interview transcript, 10

12 Ibid.; *Ora* 10, no. 3 (June 1959), 8. 'Plateau of achievement' was the expression Pogue and Taylor chose, quoting from the 1958 CPB staff conference proceedings, to describe the period 1955–9; see *History, Part II*, 42.

13 AO, RO, ser.C3, 38, file 1137, report of the 13th ORA conference, 1–2

14 Ibid., report of the 11th ORA conference, 53; b36, file 1119, fourth annual report of the ORA Recreation for the Retarded Committee, 2

15 Ibid., ser.B3, 23, file 857, 29 May 1960, 9; ser.A9, interview transcripts, 16, file 456, 16; file 407, 6–7. In the north, this money was accompanied by the help of non-native civil servants, which, in the sensible view of one northern recreation director, meant that it was an exercise in cultural imposition; see file 450, interview transcript, 4–5. How the money was used may have varied around the province. Programs conducted under this funding arrangement, which foundered on the federal-provincial jurisdictional issue after about five years (see file 442, interview transcript, 10–11), might be an accessible and fruitful area for research on various levels of government (native and non-native) and cultural policy in the early 1960s.

16 Ibid., ser.C3, 36, file 1119, point-form summary of report by ORA president, 1959; b38, file 1137, report of the 14th ORA conference, Miss Florence Philpott, 'Sharing the Wealth,' 20; NA, MG 28, I 10, 165, file 'Conference on Leisure, Synopsis, 1959–61,' Mrs Florence Zimmerman, 'Recreation Division Assessment Report,' 17

17 *Ora* 10, no. 3 (June 1959), 8. The expression, 'recreation-minded,' is quoted from BRR, RC, minutes, questionnaire to community committees, 2 Dec. 1952

18 AO, RO, ser.B3, 24, file 873, CPB staff conference reports, Sept. 1955, 2, 6, 9;

Sept. 1956, 9–11; June 1958, 5; ser.B1, 20, file 670, field representative to field supervisor, 13 Sept. 1961

19 Ibid., ser.B3, 24, file 873, CPB staff conference report, Sept. 1957, 7. The first question has been rearranged from its original form, to emphasise a pronoun referent. The original reads 'How do we do what is needed, or how enable others to do it?'

20 Pogue and Taylor, *History, Part II*, 36; AO, RO, ser.B3, 24, file 873, CPB staff conference report, June 1958, 5

21 AO, RO, ser.B3, 24, file 873, CPB staff conference reports, Sept. 1956, 1, 4; Sept. 1957, 14

22 This quotation and those following in this paragraph are all from ibid., Sept. 1957, 4–5

23 Ibid., 12; Pogue and Taylor, *History, Part II*, 36; AO, RG 2, ser.S-1, 2, policy Files, 1946–51, 'The People's Loss,' *Toronto Star*, 9 April 1946, editorial, with a reference to the 'dictatorial powers' given to the minister of education by the regulations of the earliest provincial recreation programs. The description of the new method and the discussion surrounding its introduction are based on and direct quotations are taken from AO, RO, ser.B3, 24, file 873, CPB staff conference report, June 1958, 7–10.

24 AO, RG 2, ser.S-1, 1, file 'Branch Policy Memoranda, 1948–1962,' address by Dr J.G. Althouse to CPB staff conference, 11–12 Dec. 1952

25 BRR, RC, minutes; AO, RO, ser.C3, 36, file 1119, *O.R.A. Bulletin*, Nov. 1951, 6; Mrs Norma Houghton, 'Recreational Activities for Girls and Women,' *Journal of the Canadian Association for Health, Physical Education and Recreation* 20, no. 5 (Jan. 1955), 18–20; AO, RO, ser.B1, 19, file 601, report on spring and summer activities, 1947; 18, file 537, 'The New Role of the Playground,' *Recreation Bulletin*; b20, file 655, budget statement for 1951 and auditor's report, 7 Feb. 1951; personal communication with former club member, A.W. Cooke

26 BRO, annual reports of Brantford RC, 1955, 'Director's Report,' 3. See also Chapter 6 concerning the 1962 Simcoe County by-law revision. BRR, community committees files, North Ward, president of Recreation Committee to recreation director, 5 Dec. 1960; RC, minutes, 27 May 1958, 2; NA, MG 28, I 10, 77, file 'Labour-General, 1952–62,' R.E.G. Davis to Peter Newman, 18 Nov. 1957; AO, RO, ser.B3, 24, file 873, CPB staff conference report, June 1959, 2; June 1958, 5; ser.B1, 18, file 557, community centre annual report, 1958; 19, file 634, grant application, 1956; 20, file 688, clerk comptroller to CPB facilities advisor, 12 Jan. 1955; 22, file 788, annual report, 1958, 2; ser.C3, 33, file 1075, *S.D.M.R.O. Bulletin*, March 1960, 17–18; ser.B3, 24, file 873, CPB staff conference report, June 1959, 1.

27 AO, RO, ser.B1, 20, file 662, 'History of Recreation, 1908–70'; 22, file 817, 'History of the Recreation and Parks Department, ... 1947–68'; 20, file 706, field representative's comments on grant application, 1958; 17, file 494, G.N. Strickland, 'The Amalgamation of Recreation and Parks in Brantford,' March 1961, 2; ser.A9, interview transcripts, 16, file 459, 9; file 427, 5–6; file 445, 14; BRR, RC, minutes, 28 Jan. 1958, 1

28 AO, RO, ser.A9, interview transcripts, 16, file 459, 9–10; file 410, 25; file 427, 9; 13, file 355, 'The Challenge of Change,' speech reprinted with discussion summary in *Ora* 13 (Dec. 1962), 19; Pogue and Taylor, *History, Part II*, 20–1; BRR, RC, minutes, 28 Jan. 1958, 1

29 AO, RO, ser.B1, 18, file 502, field supervisor to field representative, 29 Oct. 1954; 20, file 706, field representative's comments on grant application, 1958; ser.C3, 38, file 1137, CPB facilities advisor, 'Soft Soap ...,' address to ORA conference, 1952; ser.B3, 26, file 925, facilities advisor's work report for 1959; 24, file 873, CPB staff conference report, June 1958, 5; RG 2, ser.S-1, 1, file 'Salaries, Estimates, and Inventories 1951–1959,' CPB director to acting chief director of education, Dec.[?] 1958; CPB director to deputy minister of education, 17 March 1959; T.A. Leishman, 'Recreation and Fitness,' *CC* 131 (March 1962), 28; Pogue and Taylor, *History, Part II*, 22

30 Macintosh, et al., *Sport and Politics in Canada*, 10–11, 24–6

31 AO, RO, ser.B3, 24, file 873, CPB staff conference report, June 1960, 8

Conclusion: Gender, Leisure, and Democracy in the Liberal Welfare State

1 'Cocaine,' in *Pre-Prison Writings*, ed. Richard Bellamy, trans. Virginia Cox (Cambridge: Cambridge University Press 1994), 72

2 Loney, 'A Political Economy of Citizen Participation'

3 AO, RO, ser.A9, interview transcript, box 16, file 445, 18

4 Pateman, 'The Patriarchal Welfare State,' and 'The Fraternal Social Contract'

5 A.O. Hirschman, *Exit, Voice, and Loyalty: Responses to Decline in Firms, Organizations, and States* (Cambridge: Harvard University Press 1970), 3–5, 21–43; Bowles and Gintis, *Democracy and Capitalism*, 127

6 BRR, community committees files, Parsons Park newsletter, 'Gleanings' column, September 1951

7 'A Matter of Taste: Corporate Cultural Hegemony in a Mass-Consumption Society,' in Lary May, ed., *Recasting America: Culture and Politics in the Age of Cold War* (Chicago: University of Chicago Press 1989), 40

8 Of women in the grip of the feminine mystique, Friedan wrote that they 'never [made] a commitment of their own to society' and 'never [realized] their human potential.' To have 'humanity' meant to be 'a builder and

designer of the world,' and women who thought they could do so through being housewives had made a 'mistaken choice' as a result either of self-deception or deception by others. Psychological health required that women, like men, direct attention 'outward to other people and to problems of the world.' See *The Feminine Mystique* (New York: Norton 1963), 311–12, 319, 336.

9 Jürgen Habermas, *The Structural Transformation of the Public Sphere*, chapters 4–7

10 Strong-Boag, 'Home Dreams'

11 Habermas, *Structural Transformation*, 222–35

12 Ibid., 232

13 Ibid., 222–35

14 Ibid., 56

15 James Tully, *Strange Multiplicity: Constitutionalism in an Age of Diversity* (Cambridge: Cambridge University Press 1995), 15

Selected Bibliography

Adams, Mary Louise. *The Trouble with Normal: Postwar Youth and the Making of Heterosexuality.* Toronto: University of Toronto Press 1997

Alinsky, Saul D. *Reveille for Radicals.* Chicago: University of Chicago Press 1946

Andrew, Caroline. 'Women and the Welfare State.' *Canadian Journal of Political Science* 17, no. 4 (1984), 667–83

Barrett, Michèle. *Women's Oppression Today.* London: Verso 1980

Barrett, Stanley. *Paradise: Class, Commuters, and Ethnicity in Rural Ontario.* Toronto: University of Toronto Press 1995

Bishop, Jeff, and Paul Hoggett. *Organizing around Enthusiasms: Mutual Aid in Leisure.* London: Comedia Publishing Group 1986

Bowles, Samuel, and Herbert Gintis. *Democracy and Capitalism: Property, Community, and the Contradictions of Modern Social Thought.* New York: Basic Books 1987

Brantford City Council. Minutes, 1944–60. City of Brantford Records Office

Brantford Parks and Recreation Commission. Records. Brantford Parks and Recreation Department Office

Brantford Recreation Commission. Annual Reports, 1944–60. City of Brantford Records Office

Burke, Sara Z. *Seeking the Highest Good: Social Service and Gender at the University of Toronto, 1888–1937.* Toronto: University of Toronto Press 1996

Canada. Department of Justice. Briefs Presented to the Royal Commission on the Criminal Law Relating to Criminal Sexual Psychopaths. Recreation Directors' Federation of Ontario. 'Problems in the Control of Criminal Sexual Psychopaths.' ca 1957

– Department of National Health and Welfare. Records. National Archives of Canada

– House of Commons. *Debates,* 1942–55

– *Special Committee on Social Security, Minutes of Proceedings and Evidence.* 1943

Canadian Council on Social Development (Canadian Welfare Council). National Archives of Canada.

Canadian Youth Commission. *Youth and Recreation: New Plans for New Times.* Toronto: Ryerson Press 1946

Citizens' Research Institute of Canada. *Annual Report.* Toronto: Citizens' Research Institute of Canada 1947–53

City of Brantford. Department of Assessment. *Assessment Commissioners,* Annual Report. 1949

City of Brantford. Scrapbooks. City of Brantford Records Office

Clarke, John, and Chas Critcher. *The Devil Makes Work: Leisure in Capitalist Britain.* London: Macmillan 1985

Coalter, Fred, ed. *The Politics of Leisure.* London: Leisure Studies Association 1986

Cook, William R. *Organizing the Community's Resources for Use of Leisure Time.* Ottawa: Canadian Welfare Council. 1938. Reprint from *Child and Family Welfare,* March, 1938

Corrigan, Philip, and Derek Sayer, eds. 'Introduction' to *The Great Arch: English State Formation as Cultural Revolution.* London: Basil Blackwell 1986

Corry, J.A. *Democratic Government and Politics.* Toronto: University of Toronto Press 1946

Cronin, James E. *The Politics of State Expansion.* London: Routledge 1991

Davies, Andrew. *Leisure, Gender and Poverty.* Buckingham: Open University Press 1992

Dawson, R. MacGregor. *Democratic Government in Canada.* Toronto: Copp Clark 1949

Deem, Rosemary. *All Work and No Play? The Sociology of Women and Leisure.* Milton Keynes: Open University Press 1986

Denning, Michael, et al. 'Scholarly Controversy: Mass Culture.' *International Labor and Working-Class History* 37 (1990), 4–40

Dewey, John. 'The Search for the Great Community [1927].' In *The Philosophy of John Dewey: The Lived Experience,* ed. John J. McDermott. New York: Putnam's 1974

Donnelly, Peter. '"... A Grand Good Thing?" Politics and National Parks.' Paper presented at the 7th Commonwealth and International Conference on Sport, Physical Education, Dance, Recreation, and Health, Glasgow, Scotland, 18–23 July 1986

Ehrenreich, John. *The Altruistic Imagination: A History of Social Work and Social Policy in the United States.* Ithaca, NY: Cornell University Press 1985

Ferguson, Kathy E. *The Feminist Case against Bureaucracy.* Philadelphia: Temple University Press 1984

Fit for Tomorrow. Film made for the Department of National Welfare, Physical Fitness Division, ca1948. National Archives of Canada

Fitness Is a Family Affair. Film made for the Department of National Welfare, Physical Fitness Division, ca1948. National Archives of Canada

Fletcher, Sheila. *Women First: The Female Tradition in English Physical Education, 1880–1980.* London: Athlone Press 1984

Foucault, Michel. *Power/Knowledge: Selected Interviews and Other Writings, 1972–77,* ed. Colin Gordon. Brighton: Harvester 1980

– 'The Subject and Power.' Afterword to *Michel Foucault: Beyond Structuralism and Hermeneutics,* ed. Hubert L. Dreyfus and Paul Rabinow. Chicago: University of Chicago Press 1982

Goodale, Thomas L., and Geoffrey C. Godbey. *The Evolution of Leisure: Historical and Philosophical Perspectives.* State College, Pa: Venture Publishing 1988

Gordon, Linda. *Pitied but Not Entitled.* Cambridge: Harvard University Press 1994

Gregory, Susan. 'Women among Others: Another View.' *Leisure Studies* 1, no. 47 (1982), 47–52

Guest, Dennis. *The Emergence of Social Security in Canada.* 2nd rev. ed. Vancouver: University of British Columbia Press 1985

Gurney, Helen. *The CAHPER Story, 1933–1983.* Vanier, Ont.: Canadian Association for Health, Physical Education, and Recreation n.d.

Habermas, Jürgen. *The Structural Transformation of the Public Sphere.* Cambridge, Mass.: MIT Press 1989

Hall, M. Ann. *Sport and Gender: A Feminist Perspective on the Sociology of Sport.* Vanier, Ont.: Canadian Association for Health, Physical Education, and Recreation 1978

Hayek, Friedrich. *The Road to Serfdom.* Chicago: University of Chicago Press 1944

Henderson, Karla A., et al. *A Leisure of One's Own: A Feminist Perspective on Women's Leisure.* State College, Pa: Venture Publishing 1989

Hollands, Robert G. 'Leisure, Work and Working-Class Cultures: The Case of Leisure on the Shop Floor.' In *Leisure, Sport and Working-Class Cultures,* ed. Hart Cantelon and Robert Hollands. Toronto: Garamond Press 1988

Horwitt, Sanford D. *Let Them Call Me Rebel: Saul Alinsky, His Life and Legacy.* New York: Alfred D. Knopf 1989

Howell, Nancy, and Maxwell Howell. *Sports and Games in Canadian Life, 1700 to the Present.* Toronto: Macmillan 1969

Jaspers, Karl. *The Future of Mankind,* trans. E.B. Ashton. Chicago: University of Chicago Press 1961

Keane, John. *Democracy and Civil Society.* London: Verso 1988

Keshen, Jeffrey. 'Wartime Jitters over Juveniles: Canada's Delinquency Scare and

Its Consequences, 1939–1945,' In *Age of Contention*, ed. Jeffrey Keshen. Toronto: Harcourt Brace 1997

Kidd, Bruce. 'Sports and Masculinity.' In *Beyond Patriarchy: Essays by Men on Pleasure, Power and Change*, ed. Michael Kaufman. Toronto: Oxford University Press 1987

Kidd, J.R., ed. *Adult Education in Canada*. Toronto: Canadian Association for Adult Education 1950

Kinnear, Mary. *In Subordination: Professional Women, 1870–1970*. Montreal: McGill-Queen's University Press 1995

Kirschner, Don S. *The Paradox of Professionalism: Reform and Public Service in Urban America, 1900–1940*. New York: Greenwood Press 1986

Konopka, Gisela. *Social Group Work: A Helping Process*. Second ed. Englewood Cliffs, NJ: Prentice-Hall 1972

Laqueur, Thomas. *Making Sex: Body and Gender from the Greeks to Freud*. Cambridge, Mass.: Harvard University Press 1990

Lears, Jackson. 'A Matter of Taste: Corporate Cultural Hegemony in a Mass-Consumption Society.' In *Recasting America: Culture and Politics in the Age of Cold War*, ed. Lary May. Chicago: University of Chicago Press 1989

Lenskyj, Helen. *Out of Bounds: Women, Sport and Sexuality*. Toronto: Women's Press 1986

Little, Margaret. 'The Blurring of Boundaries: Private and Public Welfare for Single Mothers in Ontario.' *Studies in Political Economy* 47 (1995), 95–7

Loney, Martin. 'A Political Economy of Citizen Participation.' *The Canadian State: Political Economy and Political Power*, ed. Leo Panitch. Toronto: University of Toronto Press 1977

Lundberg, George A., Mirra Komarovsky, and Mary Alice McInerny. *Leisure: A Suburban Study*. [Columbia University Press 1934]. New York: Agathon Press 1969

Luxton, Meg. 'Time for Myself: Women's Work and the "Fight for Shorter Hours".' In *Feminism and Political Economy: Women's Work, Women's Struggles*, ed. Heather Jon Maroney and Meg Luxton. Toronto: Methuen 1987

Macintosh, Donald, et al. *Sport and Politics in Canada: Federal Government Involvement since 1961*. Montreal and Kingston: McGill-Queen's University Press 1987

Mackinnon, Catherine A. 'Feminism, Marxism, Method, and the State: An Agenda for Theory.' *Signs* 7, no. 3 (1982), 515–44

– 'Feminism, Marxism, Method, and the State: Toward Feminist Jurisprudence.' *Signs* 8, no. 4 (1983), 635–58

MacPherson, Ian. *Building and Protecting the Co-operative Movement*. Ottawa: Co-operative Union of Canada 1984

Marsh, Leonard. *Report on Social Security in Canada.* [Ottawa 1943]. Toronto: University of Toronto Press 1975

Marshall, Dominique. *Aux origines sociales de l'État-providence.* Montreal: Les presses de l'université de Montréal 1998

Marshall, T.H. *Citizenship and Social Class.* Cambridge: Cambridge University Press 1950

McFarland, Elsie Marie. *The Development of Public Recreation in Canada.* Vanier, Ont.: Canadian Parks/Recreation Association 1970

McIntosh, Mary. 'The State and the Oppression of Women.' In *Feminism and Materialism,* ed. Annette Kuhn and AnnMarie Wolpe. London: Routledge and Kegan Paul 1978

McKnight, John. 'Professionalized Service and Disabling Help.' In *Disabling Professions,* ed. Ivan Illich, et al. London: Marion Boyars 1977

Moscovitch, Allan, and Jim Albert, eds. *The 'Benevolent' State: The Growth of Welfare in Canada.* Toronto: Garamond Press 1987

Mott, Morris, ed. *Sports in Canada: Historical Readings.* Toronto: Copp Clark Pitman 1989

Naylor, James. *The New Democracy: Challenging the Social Order in Industrial Ontario, 1914–1925.* Toronto: University of Toronto Press 1991

Neumeyer, Martin H., and Esther S. Neumeyer. *Leisure and Recreation.* New York: A.S. Barnes and Company 1936

Offe, Claus. 'Democracy against the Welfare State? Structural Foundations of Neoconservative Political Opportunities.' *Political Theory* 15, no. 4 (1987), 501–37

Ontario. Department of Education. *Community Courier.* 1948–63
– Records. Archives of Ontario
– *Report of the Minister of Education.* 1945–65
– Legislature. *Debates.* 1947–9, 1957–8
– Ministry of Tourism and Information. 'Recreation in Ontario: Historical Resources Collection.' Archives of Ontario

Owram, Doug. *Born at the Right Time: A History of the Baby Boom Generation.* Toronto: University of Toronto Press 1996
– *The Government Generation: Canadian Intellectuals and the State, 1900–1945.* Toronto: University of Toronto Press 1986

Pahl, R.E. *On Work: Historical, Comparative, and Theoretical Approaches.* London: Basil Blackwell 1988

Pateman, Carole. 'The Fraternal Social Contract.' In *Civil Society and the State: New European Perspectives,* ed. John Keane. London: Verso 1988
– 'The Patriarchal Welfare State.' In *Democracy and the Welfare State,* ed. Amy Gutmann. Princeton, NJ: Princeton University Press 1988.

Pedersen, Diana L. 'The Young Women's Christian Association in Canada, 1870–1920: A Movement to Meet a Spiritual, Civic and National Need.' PhD thesis, Carleton University 1987

Peiss, Kathy. *Cheap Amusements: Working Women and Leisure in Turn-of-the-Century New York.* Philadelphia: Temple University Press 1986

Pogue, Gail, and Bryce Taylor. *History of Provincial Government Services of the Youth and Recreation Branch (Part I: 1940–1950), Recreation Review.* Supplement Number 1 (November 1972)

– *History of Provincial Government Services of the Youth and Recreation Branch (Part II: 1950–1960), Recreation Review.* Supplement Number 2 (March 1973)

Reid, Kenneth E. *From Character Building to Social Treatment: The History of the Use of Groups in Social Work.* Westport, Conn.: Greenwood Press 1981

Roediger, David R. 'The Limits of Corporate Reform: Fordism, Taylorism, and the Working Week in the United States, 1914–1929.' In *Worktime and Industrialization: An International History,* ed. Gary Cross. Philadelphia: Temple University Press 1988

Rojek, Chris. *Capitalism and Leisure Theory.* London: Tavistock 1985

Romney, G. Ott. *Off the Job Living: A Modern Concept of Recreation and Its Place in the Postwar World.* New York: A.S. Barnes 1945

Ross, Murray G. *Case Histories in Community Organization.* New York: Harper & Row 1958

– *The Y.M.C.A. in Canada: The Chronicle of a Century.* Toronto: Ryerson Press 1951.

Ross, Steven J. 'Living for the Weekend: The Shorter Hours Movement in International Perspective.' *Labour/Le Travail* 27 (1991), 267–82

Rutherford, Paul. *When Television Was Young: Primetime Canada, 1952–1967.* Toronto: University of Toronto Press 1990

Schrodt, Phyllis Barbara. 'A History of Pro-Rec: The British Columbia Provincial Recreation Programme, 1934–1953.' PhD thesis, University of Alberta 1979

Scott, Joan. *Gender and the Politics of History.* New York: Columbia University Press 1988

Shore, Marlene. *The Science of Social Redemption: McGill, the Chicago School, and the Origins of Social Research in Canada.* Toronto: University of Toronto Press 1987

Simcoe County Arts and Crafts Association. Records. Simcoe County Archives

Simcoe County Council. Minutes. Simcoe County Archives

Simcoe County Federation of Agriculture. Records. Simcoe County Archives

Skocpol, Theda. *Protecting Soldiers and Mothers.* Cambridge, Mass.: Belknap Press of Harvard University Press 1992

Smith, David. 'First Person Plural: The Community Life Training Institute – Story of an Idea.' *Interchange* 4, no. 4 (1973), 1–14

Stivers, Camilla. *Gender Images in Public Administration*. Newbury Park, Calif.: Sage 1993

Strange, Carolyn. *Toronto's Girl Problem*. Toronto: University of Toronto Press 1995

Strong-Boag, Veronica. 'Canada's Wage-Earning Wives and the Construction of the Middle Class, 1945–60' *Journal of Canadian Studies* 29, no. 3 (1994), 5–25

– 'Home Dreams: Women and the Suburban Experiment in Canada, 1945–60.' *Canadian Historical Review* 72 (1991), 471–504

– 'Working Women and the State: The Case of Canada, 1889–1945,' *Atlantis* 6, no. 2 (1981), 1–10

Struna, Nancy L. 'Beyond Mapping Experience: The Need for Understanding in the History of American Sporting Women.' *Journal of Sport History* 11, no. 1 (1984), 120–33

Struthers, James. '"Lord Give Us Men": Women and Social Work in English Canada.' In *The 'Benevolent' State? The Growth of Welfare in Canada*, ed. Allan Moscovitch and Jim Albert. Toronto: Garamond Press 1987

Theobald, W.F. *The Female in Public Recreation*. Toronto: Ontario Ministry of Culture and Recreation: Sports and Fitness Division 1976

Trolander, Judith Ann. *Professionalism and Social Change: From the Settlement House Movement to Neighborhood Centers, 1886 to the Present*. New York: Columbia University Press 1987

Valverde, Mariana. *The Age of Light, Soap, and Water: Moral Reform in English Canada, 1885–1925*. Toronto: McClelland and Stewart 1991

– 'Building Anti-Delinquent Communities: Morality, Gender, and Generation in the City.' In *A Diversity of Women: Ontario, 1945–1980*, ed. Joy Parr. Toronto: University of Toronto Press 1995

– 'Mixing Public and Private in the 19th Century.' *Studies in Political Economy* 47 (1995), 44–51

Valverde, Mariana, and Lorna Weir. 'The Struggles of the Immoral: Preliminary Remarks on Moral Regulation.' *Resources for Feminist Research* 17, no. 3 (1988), 31–4

Wethereall, Donald G., with Irene Kmet. *Useful Pleasures: The Shaping of Leisure in Alberta, 1896–1945*. Regina: Canadian Plains Research Center 1990

When All the People Play. Film made for the Department of National Welfare, Physical Fitness Division, ca1948. National Archives of Canada

Whitton, Charlotte. *The Dawn of Ampler Life*. Toronto: Macmillan 1943

Whyte, Jr, William H. *The Organization Man*. New York: Simon and Schuster 1956

Wilding, Paul. *Professional Power and Social Welfare*. London: Routledge and Kegan Paul 1982

Willis, Paul. 'Women and Sport in "Ideology,"' In *Sport, Culture and Ideology*, ed. Jennifer Hargreaves. London: Routledge and Kegan Paul 1982

Women's Institutes of Simcoe County. Records. Simcoe County Archives

Illustration Credits

Index

STUDIES IN GENDER AND HISTORY

General editors: Franca Iacovetta and Karen Dubinsky